Ernst & Young's Retirement Planning Guide

Second Edition

William J. Arnone

Freida Kavouras

Martin Nissenbaum

Glenn M. Pape

Charles L. Ratner

Kenneth R. Rouse

David C. Voss

Patricia A. Wiley

John Wiley & Sons, Inc.

New York • Chichester • Weinheim • Brisbane • Singapore • Toronto

In the preparation of this book, every effort has been made to offer the most current, correct, and clearly expressed information possible. Nonetheless, inadvertent errors can occur, and tax rules and regulations often change.

Further, the information in the text is intended to afford general guidelines on matters of interest to everyone. The application and impact of tax laws and financial matters can vary widely, however, from case to case, based on the specific or unique facts involved. Accordingly, the information in this book is not intended to serve as legal, accounting, or tax advice. Readers are encouraged to consult with professional advisors for advice concerning specific matters before making any decision, and the authors and publishers disclaim any responsibility for positions taken by taxpayers in their individual cases or for any misunderstanding on the part of readers.

This book is printed on acid-free paper. ∞

Copyright © 2001 by Ernst & Young LLP. All rights reserved.

Published by John Wiley & Sons, Inc.
Published simultaneously in Canada.

No part of this publication may be reproduced, stored in a retrieval system or transmitted in any form or by any means, electronic, mechanical, photocopying, recording, scanning or otherwise, except as permitted under Section 107 or 108 of the 1976 United States Copyright Act, without either prior written permission of the Publisher, or authorization through payment of the appropriate per-copy fee to the Copyright Clearance Center, 222 Rosewood Drive, Danvers, MA 01923, (978) 750-8400, fax (978) 750-4744. Requests to the Publisher for permission should be addressed to the Permissions Department, John Wiley & Sons, Inc., 605 Third Avenue, New York, NY 10158-0012, (212) 850-6011, fax (212) 850-6008, E-mail: PERMREQ@WILEY.COM.

This publication is designed to provide accurate and authoritative information in regard to the subject matter covered. It is sold with the understanding that the publisher is not engaged in rendering professional services. If professional advice or other expert assistance is required, the services of a competent professional person should be sought.

Library of Congress Cataloging-in-Publication Data:

Ernst & Young's retirement planning guide / William J. Arnone . . . [et al.].—2nd ed.
    p. cm.
   Includes index.
   ISBN 0-471-39376-2 (cloth : alk. paper)
   1. Finance, Personal. 2. Retirement—Planning. I. Title: Ernst and Young's retirement planning guide. II. Title: Retirement planning guide. III. Arnone, William J. IV. Ernst & Young.
  HG179.E733 2001
  332.024′01—dc21   00-043744

Printed in the United States of America.

10 9 8 7 6 5 4 3 2 1

CONTENTS

ABOUT THE AUTHORS

William J. Arnone is a member of the National Leadership team of Ernst & Young's Employee Financial Education & Counseling practice. He is based in New York. Prior to joining Ernst & Young, he was national director of Financial and Retirement Planning Services for Buck Consultants, Inc. An attorney, Mr. Arnone has published numerous articles about retirement, focusing on the legislative and social implications of Social Security and Medicare. He is an associate editor of the *Columbia Retirement Handbook*. Mr. Arnone was a member of the New York State Delegation to the 1981 and the 1995 White House Conference on Aging. He is a Founding Member of the National Academy of Social Insurance based in Washington, D.C. E-mail address: william.arnone@ey.com

Freida Kavouras is the director of Employee Financial Education Services for Ernst & Young's Lake Michigan Area, located in Chicago, and a member of the practice's National Leadership team. She specializes in employee group education services and has over 15 years of experience in providing communications and financial planning services to all levels of employees in the United States and abroad. She has delivered financial education workshops to over 12,000 employees over the past eight years. As a media representative for financial planning in Ernst & Young's Chicago office, Ms. Kavouras often appears on radio and television to discuss financial planning topics. She is a Certified Public Accountant (CPA) with a Personal Financial Specialist (PFS) designation from the American Institute of Certified Public Accountants. She is a member of the Personal Financial Planning Division of the American Institute of Certified Public Accountants and the Illinois Society of Certified Public Accountants. Ms. Kavouras holds a Bachelor of Science degree in accounting from The Pennsylvania State University. E-mail address: freida.kavouras@ey.com

Glenn M. Pape is Ernst & Young's director for Large Employee Group Services and a member of the National Leadership team of Ernst & Young's Employee Financial Education & Counseling practice. Based in Chicago, he is an attorney, a Certified Public Accountant (CPA), accredited as a Personal Financial Specialist (PFS) by the American Institute of Certified Public Accountants, a Certified Financial Planner (CFP), and through his financial workshops for corporate employees he has earned the Certified Speaking Professional (CSP) designation awarded by the National Speakers Association. Mr. Pape has been quoted in *BusinessWeek*, the *Wall Street Journal*, the *New York Times*, and other financial and benefits publications. He is a member of the American Institute of Certified Public Accountants, the National Speakers Association, and the International Association for Financial Planning. E-mail address: glenn.pape@ey.com

Martin Nissenbaum is Ernst & Young's director of Retirement Planning, specializing in employee benefits and compensation and individual income tax and personal financial planning. He is an attorney and a Certified Public Accountant (CPA) and holds an LL.M. in tax; he is a Certified Financial Planner (CFP) and holds the Personal Financial Specialist (PFS) accreditation from the American Institute of Certified Public Accountants. Based in New York, Mr. Nissenbaum is a speaker on compensation, and personal financial and tax planning to professional organizations, including the New York State Society of CPAs, the National Association of Accountants, the International Association of Financial Planners, the New York University Tax Society, and the Tax Executives Institute. He has been quoted extensively in the media, including the *Wall Street Journal*, the *New York Times*, and *Money* magazine, and has been named by *PR Week* as one of the 10 most quoted people in the business press. E-mail address: martin.nissenbaum@ey.com

Charles L. Ratner is the director of Personal Insurance Counseling for Ernst & Young and a managing director of The Ernst & Young Center for Family Wealth Planning. Mr. Ratner, based in Cleveland, Ohio, devotes his time to providing life insurance consulting services to corporations, financial institutions, and individuals and estate and business succession planning services to closely held companies. Prior to joining Ernst & Young, Mr. Ratner served as director of the Advanced Estate and Business-Planning Group of a major life insurance company. Mr. Ratner is an attorney, a Chartered Financial Consultant (ChFC), and Chartered Life Underwriter (CLU). He is a member of the Association for Advanced Life Underwriting (AALU), the Society of Financial Service Professionals, and the American Bar Association, and is currently the vice-chair of the Committee for Insurance of the Real Property, Probate and Trust Law Section, of the American Bar Association. Mr. Ratner is a frequent author and speaker on financial matters. E-mail address: charles.ratner@ey.com

Kenneth R. Rouse is a member of the National Leadership team of Ernst & Young's Employee Financial Education & Counseling practice. Based in Phoenix, Arizona, his responsibilities include national marketing, design, and implementation of employer-sponsored financial education programs. Prior to joining Ernst & Young, Mr. Rouse was president and founder of the Rouse Companies, Inc., a financial planning education and employee benefits communication firm. Mr. Rouse is a Certified Financial Planner (CFP) and served on the national board of the International Association for Financial Planning for several years. He is the author of the book *Putting Money in Its Place* (Dubuque, IA: Kendall Hunt, 1993). E-mail address: ken.rouse@ey.com

David C. Voss is Ernst & Young's director of Executive Financial Planning Services responsible for marketing, designing, and implementing financial planning programs to executives at major companies. Based in Cincinnati, Ohio, he is a Certified Public Accountant (CPA) and is accredited as a Personal Financial Specialist (PFS) by the American Institute of Certified Public Accountants. Mr. Voss has conducted numerous financial planning education workshops on retirement, investing, and other financial planning topics for corporate employees. He has written articles on personal finance that have appeared in the *Greater Cincinnati Business Record* and the *Cincinnati Enquirer*. He is a member of the American Institute of Certified Public Accountants and the Ohio Society of CPAs and is a former treasurer of the Greater Cincinnati Chapter of the Alzheimer's Association. E-mail address: dave.voss@ey.com

Patricia A. Wiley is a director of Communications and Research for Ernst & Young's Employee Financial Education & Counseling practice and a member of the practice's National Leadership team. In that role, she spends most of her time talking with employees about what will help them learn about managing their money so that they can achieve all of their dreams, including retirement. She works primarily with employers to help them design, communicate, and deliver to their employees through compensation, benefits, and financial planning. E-mail address: patricia.wiley@ey.com

ACKNOWLEDGMENTS

The coauthors gratefully acknowledge the help, care, and insights provided by their colleagues who worked with them to put this book together. Of course, any interpretations of and conclusions drawn from our colleagues input remain the sole responsibility of the coauthors.

First we'd like to thank Jacqueline Hornstein, Ph.D., Mary Lou B. Karp, and Debra Englander for their patience in coordinating and editing this book. And we'd like to thank Deepak Puri and Anne Metzger for their research and contributions to content as well as Patty Carpio and Pauline Scott for assisting in assembling our document.

We'd next like to thank Ernst & Young's National Director of Personal Financial Counseling, Sylvia J. Pozarnsky, and the Area Directors of Personal Financial Counseling, along with the hundreds of professionals who work with them, whose firsthand experience in educating and counseling millions of individuals was distilled into these few hundred pages: Michael F. Bearer, Washington, D.C.; Jeffrey Brodsky, Chicago, Illinois; Robert L. Carson, Boston, Massachusetts; James A. Cox, San Francisco, California; Glenn H. Hascher, New York, New York; A. Mark Harbour, Los Angeles, California; Richard W. Jones, San Antonio, Texas; Richard Joyner, Dallas, Texas; Victor G. Kmetich, Cleveland, Ohio; Charles R. Kowal, Atlanta, Georgia; Richard F. Kraner, St. Louis, Missouri; Carl A. Rhodes, Cincinnati, Ohio.

Their knowledge and dedication have enabled Ernst & Young to become the leading fee-only provider of financial counseling services, including Employee Financial Education and Counseling programs, offering workshops, software, print materials, and face-to-face, telephone, and Web-based counseling, to more than 500,000 individuals over the past three years alone.

We'd also like to thank a group of readers without experience in retirement planning, who took the time to give us their feedback: Jane Canner, Donna Ceravolo, Hans DeWaal, Paul Dismer, Barbara Gray, Dave Hall, John Haworth, Phil Li, Emma Miller, Terry Miller, Mary Myers, David Plum, Annette Ribidoux, and Gary Schell. Thanks also to Arlene Dunn for her insights on retirement health issues.

Finally, we'd like to acknowledge the leadership of:

    Philip A. Laskawy, Chairman and CEO
    James S. Turley, Deputy Chairman
    Richard S. Bobrow, Chief Executive Officer
    William J. Lipton, Vice Chairman, Tax Services

INTRODUCTION

As the 21st century begins, it is becoming abundantly clear that the word "retirement" is being redefined for most Americans. The key terms that describe retirement for people retiring now and in the future are: opportunity, choice, and responsibility.

Because people today are living longer than past generations, and have a greater chance of maintaining good health into later life, American retirees find themselves with opportunities their parents and grandparents never dreamed of. With that multitude of opportunities comes choice:

- They can play or work.
- They can work for pay or volunteer.
- They can start a business, consult, freelance, or work for someone else, part time or full time.
- They can choose a life that involves all of these opportunities: work for pay, volunteer work, or leisure.

Companies that laid off workers in the 1990s today often ask employees who would otherwise retire to stay with the company in a part-time or consulting capacity, to help disseminate their knowledge and experience to the next generation of workers. Some companies specifically seek out older workers, since they often make good employees. The newly "retired" can be seen in huge numbers prowling the corridors of business opportunity fairs.

Colleges and universities offer retirees opportunities for study, either for a degree or for personal growth. Local recreation departments, YMCAs, YWCAs, and Jewish Community Centers often have athletic and fitness programs specially designed for older Americans. Organizations in many communities will assist you in looking for a paying or volunteer opportunity. Your religious group is always seeking people to lend a hand. Schools and day-care centers are always looking for "surrogate grandparents."

The flip side of all this opportunity and choice is responsibility. You are responsible for the happiness you attain in retirement. And increasingly, you are also responsible for your financial condition in retirement. Government programs that were created in the first half of the 20th century and workers' pensions, which began in the late 19th century, can no longer be counted on to provide enough income to sustain working people's lifestyle after they retire.

In the 19th century, most Americans worked until they died, or until they could no longer physically work. In agricultural America, men and women worked their farms until their children took over, at which time the parents eased back. As the country became more urban, and more Americans worked for corporations, older and physically less able workers were pushed out of the workforce to make way for younger and stronger workers.

The pension system started in the late 19th century and gained momentum in the first half of the 20th century as a way to provide a maintenance income for workers who could no longer work. In 1935, as part of the New Deal, the federal government created the Social Security system, so that all workers would have a maintenance income after their working life, regardless of whether their employer had provided a pension.

Social Security has been the greatest antipoverty program in the history of humankind. When it was started, over 50% of the elderly—those over 65—lived in poverty. Today the number is around 11%, lower than the rate for working-age Americans and less than half the rate for American children.

We are currently at the end of the period where the first post–World War II working generation is retiring. These people are the first Americans to create a suburban, middle-class America. And for them, what they have coming from the Social Security system and what they receive in pensions (if they have one), will not be enough to maintain the lifestyles they created for themselves in their working lives.

They have had to save for their retirement. Many have done a good job, but some have not.

The "Baby Boomers"—the generation that will begin retiring shortly after the turn of the 21st century—need to save far more than their parents and grandparents in order to maintain their lifestyles.

This book is designed to help all Americans—those who are retired, those who are retiring now or in the near future, and those who are looking toward retirement 20 or more years from now—to recognize the choices and opportunities and to confront the responsibilities. We have divided our discussion into four parts.

The first few chapters focus on long-term retirement planning. We focus on how you can accumulate savings and investments for retirement; how you can adjust your spending to be able to save and invest more; and how you can structure your lifestyle so it can be maintained and sustained in retirement. Most of all, we stress that the strategies you use today can have a profound influence on the kind of retirement you have in the future.

The next part of the book focuses on the issues you have to confront at the time you retire. These include the tax consequences of the different ways you can take distribution of your tax-deferred savings plans (401(k), 403(b), 457, or Keogh) and your pension as well as issues of Social Security benefits and insurance coverage for those leaving the workforce and entering retirement.

The third section discusses some of the choices and opportunities you have in retirement and how your spending and investing influence those choices.

In the fourth section, we discuss some special situations and how they may affect your retirement planning. This section includes chapters aimed at the self-employed, highly compensated executives, and those who live in "nontraditional" households. And we point you toward some of the sites on the World Wide Web you may want to visit for information regarding retirement. There are literally dozens of Web sites aimed at retirees and those saving for retirement.

Our final chapter covers health-related issues that retirees must face and prepare for.

The book can be used as a reference, or you can read through it or study just the sections that pertain most closely to your circumstances.

WAKE-UP CALL

Retirement. What a fantastic thing! Imagine never having to work again! Or working only by choice!

If you are nearing your 65th birthday now, you will soon join the fastest-growing segment of the American population. In 1900 there were 123,000 Americans age 65 or older. Today there are 34.7 million such Americans. It is estimated that in 2030, there will be 69.4 million Americans over age 65.

The notion of age 65 having some sort of magic is not an American idea. Otto von Bismarck, the 19th-century German chancellor, actually created the first state-funded retirement pension for Germans and set the age at which payments could begin. Half a century later Americans first began to collect Social Security retirement benefits, in 1937.

When Social Security began paying retirement benefits, an American man who reached adulthood had a life expectancy of about 63 years. If a man lived until 65 and began collecting Social Security benefits, he could expect to live another two to three years. When most married men died, they left widows who had not worked outside the home for many years, if at all. Social Security set a policy of allowing surviving spouses with dependent children under 16 and spouses age 60 and over to collect benefits based on what the working spouse had contributed to the Social Security system.

The average life expectancy of Americans increased 50% in the 20th century. A baby boy born in 2000 has a life expectancy of over 72 years, while a baby girl born that year has a life expectancy of over 79 years.

What's interesting is that the older you are, the older you are expected to get. An American turning 65 today and beginning to collect Social Security benefits can expect to receive those benefits for *more than 18 years.* You might think of retirement as *the third full chapter of your life!* What you do today in terms of planning and saving will have a large impact on whether you spend that time in relative financial comfort or worrying about your finances.

Perhaps the most important message in this book is that you are retiring to *something*, and not just retiring from a job. The more you prepare for the potential of those years, the more fulfilling they will be.

It is crucial for you to understand that your retirement will not be like anyone else's. The choices you make about how you will live in retirement, where you will live in retirement, and how you will save and invest for that retirement are among the most important decisions you can make.

OPTIONS AND RESPONSIBILITIES

People retiring today need to do more planning for their retirement than those who retired before them. Why? Because the responsibility for creating a financially secure retirement is yours, not the government's, not your employer's, and not your spouse's.

Retirement is a huge responsibility to shoulder. But it is also a huge opportunity because it gives you many options as to how you want to structure your life today and in the future.

There are some who believe that the Social Security system as constructed today is going to collapse of its own weight, probably some time around 2030, when the entire Baby Boom generation will have reached the traditional retirement age. A number of possibilities have been suggested for extending the life of the Social Security system. We'll discuss them in detail in Chapter 8, but for now let's just say that all of the options assume that a person retiring 25 years from now will not receive as much in benefits in real economic terms as those who have already retired and are currently collecting benefits.

The same is true for the private sector. Today fewer and fewer companies are instituting new defined-benefit pension plans, under which the company puts money aside for retirees and pays them a monthly benefit. In fact, some companies are deemphasizing their current defined-benefit plans and not allowing new employees to enter those plans.

In place of new defined-benefit plans, employers often set up defined-contribution plans. The most common of these is the 401(k) plan, and for not-for-profit institutions 403(b) plans and for state and local governments

457 plans. Under these 401(k)-type defined-contribution plans, each employee *who chooses to participate* has an individual account set up into which the employee puts a portion of his or her pay. This contribution is made from gross pay and before federal, and most state, and city income taxes are withheld (although it is subject to Social Security and Medicare taxes). The money in the account continues to grow with no current tax burden. Taxes are deferred until the money is withdrawn, usually beginning between age 59½ and 70½. Many employers also contribute to their employees' accounts, often matching the contributions up to a certain percentage of pay.

When tax-deferred company savings plans started, they were an add-on to traditional defined-benefit pensions. Today they are the major component, if not the only component, of retirement savings for an increasing number of Americans. In addition, more and more companies are dropping full lifetime medical benefits for their retirees.

It is human nature to seek stability. Unfortunately, today stability in almost anything is rare. Change is here; it is happening throughout our society. The federal government is reexamining "entitlements" and the private sector is moving away from the paternalistic pattern of taking care of its employees from "cradle to grave." There is no more Ma Bell. There is no more Big Blue. AT&T and IBM still exist as companies, but not as the type of paternalistic organizations they used to be.

You can think of this as a sad turn of events, or you can think of it as an exciting time to be working, saving, and investing for your own future.

Companies and the government are telling Americans that there is a "shared responsibility" for retirement security. And ultimately, it is your responsibility to plan for your retirement. The federal government and your employer can help you lay the foundation with Social Security benefits and company matching contributions to a tax-deferred savings plan. But the bulk of the savings has to come from you.

It may not be wise even to depend on your spouse for financial support during retirement. Especially in families with two working adults, each person has to figure out retirement savings for himself or herself. You need to "pack your own parachute."

You Really *Can* Do Your Own Financial Planning

All of this change and all of the responsibility individuals must take for their own retirement planning may sound frightening. Fortunately, though, we live in a time when anyone really can be a saver, an investor, and a planner.

Think about the changes in America's financial institutions in the last 25 years. As late as the 1970s:

- Bank deposit interest rates were regulated.
- Brokerage fees were regulated.
- Money market funds did not exist.
- Mutual funds were "iffy" propositions, and almost all were sold only through brokers.
- Computers meant company mainframes.

Today, banks compete for deposits by offering competitive interest rates on savings, checking, and money market accounts as well as on certificates of deposit (CDs). Mutual fund companies sell directly to the public, and an increasing number of mutual funds are sold without a sales fee, also known as no load. There are more mutual funds in the United States today than there are individual publicly traded stocks on the New York Stock Exchange.

Anyone can track and maintain his or her own portfolio with a personal computer and sophisticated yet simple-to-use software. There are dozens of personal finance software packages available, many of which allow you to do this through a linkage with an on-line information service.

An ever-growing multitude of investment vehicles exists. Individuals can diversify and invest globally more easily than ever before. Doing so can quickly lead to confusion. But where there is ambiguity there is also opportunity for those who can cut through the maze.

The way to turn confusion into opportunity is to understand the process and maybe even learn to enjoy the game of investing.

WHAT ARE THE "NEW RULES" OF THE RETIREMENT GAME?

We've all heard stories about people who seem to do everything right but somehow everything turns out wrong. We all know of folks who went to work every day, paid their taxes, retired at 65, took their gold watch, pension check, and Social Security check, and began going to "senior citizen" events. Now they're 80 and the pension and Social Security checks don't pay the bills. The little bit of savings is gone. Soon the house will have to be sold to put aside a chunk of money to make up the difference between income from the pension and Social Security and the monthly expenses.

What happened?

Some of these people fell into one of the largest American retirement traps. They simply expected their pension and the Social Security system to provide them with enough on which to live. Some didn't expect to live very long after retirement, but did, and outlived their money. But most people simply didn't understand retirement finances.

Social Security benefits, which represent only a portion of many people's retirement income, receive inflation increases each year. Most pension plans have fixed benefits. The monthly pension you receive at age 80 is the same amount you received the first month of retirement. If you don't have enough savings to generate significant income, you can easily end up with a cash shortfall later in life.

There are three basic rules under which those of us new to retirement or who will retire in the future must live. In fact, they are rules under which past generations should have lived as well. But for the not-yet retired these rules are more rigid than for those who have come before. They are as follows:

1. *You are responsible.*

You can't assume anything about the way retirement should be. How each of us wishes to live during retirement is an individual decision, not someone else's. And there's nothing that says you can't change your mind about your particular retirement desires.

2. *You are the expert.*

Only you know what makes you happy. Only you know what you value. Only you know how much risk you are willing to assume with your savings and investments. Only you know how you want to live!

3. *You need to be flexible.*

There is uncertainty in life, in markets, and in the economy. Financial planning for retirement must be as flexible as personal planning. The future probably will not be like the past.

In short, planning for your financial, physical, mental, emotional, and spiritual future is hard work. However, there are many resources available, and one of the purposes of this book is to get you excited about using these tools confidently to put your retirement plan together.

TIME AND MONEY

Time and money are two of the biggest resources in life. Thinking about how you want to spend your time and what you want to do with your money goes right to the heart of how you feel about your life.

Thinking about the time/money trade-off during retirement should ideally begin the moment you start working, not five years before you retire.

There are no pat answers. And there are many "life events" that may occur between the time you begin working and the time you retire:

- A change of homes
- Marriage or a life partner
- Having children
- Education for you, your partner, and/or your children
- Job changes
- Temporary or permanent disability
- First communions
- Bar or bat mitzvahs
- Sweet-16 parties
- Graduations
- Weddings
- Divorce and remarriage
- Helping your parents physically, emotionally, or financially as they age

These all affect both your ability to save for retirement and the way you think about time and money.

Your health also changes as you move through adulthood. After all, quality of life is at least as important as, if not more important than, longevity. A young adult is more likely to suffer a prolonged disability than to die before retirement age. It takes time, and sometimes money, to maintain health.

It's also important to "invest in yourself." In addition to saving capital and spending capital, there is also human capital. That means *you*. Making yourself happier and healthier ultimately makes you more productive.

Investing in your human capital may mean buying a bicycle to ride or a dog to walk, or joining a gym or tennis club. It may mean dropping or reducing overtime work in order to take a course at night. It may be as simple as buying a book to read, a videotape to watch, or an audiotape to listen to while you drive, walk, or jog. It may mean forgoing income opportunities in exchange for a long and well-deserved vacation that helps you recharge your physical and emotional self. In short, there are going to be times when it pays handsomely to invest in yourself rather than in the financial markets.

PLANNING YOUR RETIREMENT JOURNEY

Think about retirement as an adventurous journey. You have some choices you can make along the way. Do you want to drive on highways or take scenic back roads?

There will be excitement and adventure. There will be beautiful scenery. But there will also be risks along the way. When you make a long car trip, you carry clothing, food, water, and flares. Along your retirement journey, there will be *obstacles* and *traps*. To help you around the obstacles and to avoid the traps, you have *tools* and you have *helpers*.

Let's look briefly at the obstacles and the traps, the tools and the helpers. We'll examine these concepts in much greater detail in Chapter 4, which discusses investing your retirement savings in order to create a sizable nest egg.

The major obstacles to a secure retirement are:

- Inflation
- Taxes
- Procrastination
- Inflexibility
- Conventional wisdom
- Catastrophes

The biggest traps into which you might fall are:

- Failing to plan
- Viewing retirement as never having to work again
- Underestimating your life expectancy
- Copying what works for others and not planning for your own life
- Chasing fads
- Looking for a financial wizard to manage your future
- Viewing the future as simply an extension of the past
- Expecting Social Security and pensions to finance your entire retirement
- Failing to involve and communicate with others who are likely to be affected by your retirement plans

Some useful tools you can use are:

- Financial planning software
- Easy-to-use and widely available resources on retirement planning, such as magazines, books, and Web sites
- Health-risk assessment questionnaires that estimate life expectancy

The four key helpers to ensuring a financially secure retirement are:

- Systematic savings
- Diversification
- Tax-deferred savings plans and their natural compounding
- Defining and managing your own expectations

Prior to conducting a retirement seminar for the Los Angeles Police Department a few years ago, one of the authors of this book interviewed retirees to see if they could offer their former colleagues some advice. From these interviews, he boiled the retirement planning process down to six steps.

1. Take responsibility for defining your own retirement needs.
2. Become a real expert at one or two elements of retirement, such as estate planning or relocation, and seek professional assistance for the other areas.
3. Assess your current net worth—your assets minus your liabilities—to create a snapshot of your current financial situation.
4. Determine how you spend your money. Analyze your current living expenses and make conscious spending choices.
5. Make reasonable estimates of your projected living expenses during retirement.
6. Create plans of action in four separate areas:
    - Where you will live
    - Maintaining or improving your health
    - Your estate
    - Communicating with yourself and others

Remember the three rules of retirement—*you are responsible; you are the expert;* and *you have to be flexible.* But remember also that you are not alone. Most of you have at least one important person whose life is affected by your retirement: a spouse, a parent, a child, a sibling, a life partner, or a friend. Look to that person for advice, and understand that person's importance in your life.

Finally, keep in mind that the outcome will be determined by your direct involvement in the process. Crossing your fingers and hoping for the best doesn't work.

ACTION ITEMS		
Item	**Priority***	**Completed**
1. Select a life expectancy for your most reasonable retirement planning scenario. Then project additional scenarios in which you live 5, 10, and 15 years longer.		
2. Make a list of all the activities on which you would like to spend more time if you did not have to work 8 to 10 hours a day. Be as specific as possible when describing what you want to do when you retire. Try to categorize these activities. Possible categories are: time-alone activities and activities with others; self-directed activities and outer-directed activities; active and passive activities; inside-the-home and outside-the-home activities; physical, mental, and spiritual activities; completely new activities; activities you haven't had enough time to do with regularity, and activities you have always wanted to have the time to do.		
3. Identify all of the life events that are expected to occur between now and your retirement, for example, college education for your children. For each, ask what its financial impact might be on your retirement. Then examine what you can do to minimize the potential disruption of each on your retirement.		
4. Select at least one way that you can invest in your own human capital and start on it now.		
5. Pick one subject of retirement in which you will try to become an expert. Lay out a step-by-step plan to achieve expert status in that subject area.		

*A, B, C, or N/A, with A being the highest priority.

2

WILL YOU HAVE ENOUGH TO RETIRE?

This chapter asks the question—Will you have enough to retire?—and we answer emphatically: It depends!

The next logical question is: On what does it depend?

Put simply, it depends on you. It depends on when you want to retire and the lifestyle you wish to have when you retire. Equally important, it depends on how diligently you can save, how well you can invest, and understanding stocks versus so-called safe investments. Most of all, we believe, it depends on how well you understand the implications of the financial choices you make.

Perhaps the biggest mistake people make when planning for retirement is to think that what is "enough" for the first year of retirement will be enough for each successive year. They underestimate their retirement expenses, and, more important, they overestimate how fast their nest egg is growing, forgetting to account for taxes and inflation.

HOW FAST DOES AN INVESTMENT REALLY DOUBLE IN VALUE?

You may have heard about the "miracle of compounding" and the "rule of 72." Briefly this means that by reinvesting your interest and/or dividends continually at the same rate, or by growth in the value of your initial investment, the value of your investment doubles in the number of years equal to 72 divided by your investment return.

EXAMPLE

■ Let's look at an example. Say you have $10,000, invested at a growth rate of 6% annually. In 12 years—72 divided by 6—you will have $20,000; this is due to compounding of investment returns. Many people look at this and say, "Wow!" But there are a few catches.

One *obstacle* is taxes. Let's say your family's total tax rate, combined federal and state, is 30%. That means that your rate of return after taxes is reduced from 6% to 4.2%, because 30% of 6% equals 1.8%, and 6% minus 1.8% equals 4.2%. So to double your money after taxes actually takes 17 years—an increase of five years!

However, taxes are not the biggest obstacle to increasing your savings. A far larger obstacle is inflation. What do you think the average rate of inflation will be over the next 17 years? Want to know what we think it will be?

Answer: We don't know. Your guess is probably as good as ours. When it comes to forecasting the future, there are no true experts.

But we do know that historically, since the 1920s, inflation in the United States has averaged about 3%. That includes the period of the Great Depression, when there was deflation—meaning prices actually went down—as well as the 1970s, when inflation was over 12%. But we're back to a period of about 3% (or lower) annual inflation, so we'll use 3% as our inflation assumption throughout this book.

So, inflation is 3%, and you're earning 6%. That means you're really earning about 3% after inflation. Let's use the rule of 72 again; 72 divided by 3 equals 24. So, with 3% inflation, it will take 24 years to double your money in today's dollars.

Now let's combine inflation and taxes:

Pretax rate of return:	6%
Tax rate:	30% (combined federal and state)
Inflation:	3%
Real rate of return:	1.2% = 6% − (30% × 6%)
	= 4.2% − 3% ■

At that *real after-tax rate of return*, it will take 60 years to double your money. This may make you want to quit right now. If it takes 60 years to double your money, you may never live long enough to enjoy the fruits of your savings. But there is hope, on two fronts.

First, the tax law allows us to save money for retirement in any of a variety of *tax-deferred plans*, either those set up by an employer or an Individual Retirement Account (IRA) you set up. That means that the money you earn on your investments does not get taxed during the time it stays in the tax-deferred plan. The plan can stay in effect throughout your retirement, and you pay taxes only on the money withdrawn from your plan(s). A Roth IRA actually allows you to save money, the earnings on which are never taxed. Even though income in a Roth IRA may be tax-free, we'll call it a tax-deferred plan in this book.

Second, we live in a time when one can invest for higher return without necessarily having to accept an undue amount of investment risk. One way to do this is by using mutual funds, which pool investors' money and buy portfolios of stocks, bonds, or other investment vehicles.

These two *helpers*—tax-deferred retirement savings plans and mutual funds—provide you with the opportunity to accumulate the money you will need for retirement. Tax-deferral allows you to beat the tax bite during the period of accumulation, and since inflation is something none of us can predict, having professional money management through diversified stock mutual funds is the best way for individual "small" investors to stay one step ahead of inflation.

FIVE BIG TRAPS TO AVOID

We've already told you the first big *trap* to watch out for in creating a plan of action to make sure you have enough money for the kind of retirement you need and want. That is:

Not taking into account taxes and inflation, both in the time between now and when you retire—your accumulation period—and during your retirement.

The next big trap is:

Thinking things are going to be okay because they have been okay so far.

There's a joke about a guy falling out of a 15th-floor window, who passes the 12th floor, waves to his friend, and says, "So far, so good." Of course, the problem is the sudden landing. Later in this chapter we'll show you the danger of a sudden landing in retirement if you don't have enough on which to live through retirement.

Other traps include:

Thinking of your home as a retirement windfall.

While your house, cooperative apartment, or condominium may have increased in value, you still need to live somewhere, and the costs of renting a comparable home can eat up your profit. Of course, some people will do very well with a home sale—especially after taking advantage of the $250,000 ($500,000 for married filing jointly) capital gains tax exclusion available to homeowners on the sale of a primary residence. But you shouldn't factor this into your assumptions about the sources of your retirement nest egg. Given the vagaries of the real estate market and the possibility of low inflation, you really have to plan for no profit from a home sale, and use whatever profit you get to add to your retirement fund.

In Chapter 11, which covers spending during retirement, we'll talk about some innovative ways to put your home's value to use without necessarily selling.

Not understanding how to make long-term projections using reasonable assumptions.

Making overly optimistic or overly pessimistic long-term projections can lead to creating investment strategies that are inappropriate to what you will really encounter over the next 5, 10, 20, or more years.

If you suddenly became financially aware in the late 1970s, you might create an investment strategy and lifestyle based on 12% annual inflation. If you are old enough to have lived through the Great Depression of the 1930s, your investment assumptions may be based on the possibility of another worldwide financial collapse.

Neither scenario resembles the beginning of the 21st century, when inflation is averaging less than 3% and the financial system has a number of regulatory checks designed to make sure an economic period like the 1930s cannot occur again.

An awareness and understanding of history, and using it to make reasonable assumptions about what will occur in the future, can help you make projections and create flexible investment strategies to beat inflation over the long term.

Figure 2.1 shows life expectancies for preretirement-age individuals in five-year increments. Figure 2.2 shows the historical inflation rate since World War II.

FIGURE 2.1 DETERMINE YOUR LIFE EXPECTANCY.

ESTIMATING THE LENGTH OF YOUR RETIREMENT

Estimating how long you'll be retired is important in setting realistic goals. That's because your retirement income sources will have to support the lifestyle you seek for all your years of retirement—not just the first year.

To estimate how long you'll be retired, you should know a little about your life expectancy. You can look up the average life expectancy of U.S. citizens of your gender and at an age close to yours in the table below. You should also consider what you know about your health, your own medical history, and your family medical history.

FIND YOUR LIFE EXPECTANCY AND CONSIDER ADDING 5 YEARS*

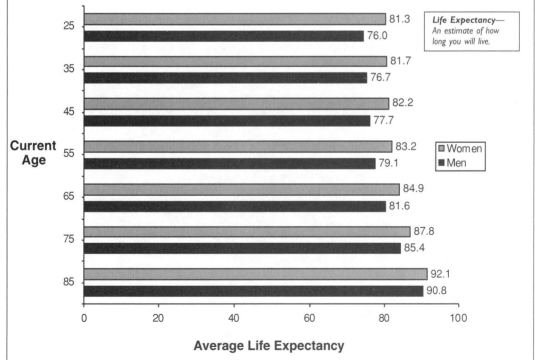

You can live longer or shorter than your life expectancy. Many people choose to add 5 or more years to their life expectancy. Some mortality tables show that there is a 5% chance a 65-year-old man will live to age 91, 94 for a woman.
Source: National Center for Health Statistics, U.S. Department of Health and Human Services (1989).
Data Source: The National Vital Statistics Report, Vol. 47, No. 28, December 13, 1999.

FIGURE 2.2 HISTORICAL CONSUMER PRICE INDEX AND INFLATION RATE.

Year	CPI	Inflation Rate	Year	CPI	Inflation Rate
1945	18.2	2.25	1973	46.2	8.71
1946	21.5	18.13	1974	51.9	12.34
1947	23.4	8.84	1975	55.5	6.94
1948	24.1	2.99	1976	58.2	4.86
1949	23.6	−2.07	1977	62.1	6.70
1950	25.0	5.93	1978	67.7	9.02
1951	26.5	6.00	1979	76.7	13.29
1952	26.7	0.75	1980	86.3	12.52
1953	26.9	0.75	1981	94.0	8.92
1954	26.7	−0.74	1982	97.6	3.83
1955	26.8	0.37	1983	101.3	3.79
1956	27.6	2.99	1984	105.3	3.95
1957	28.4	2.90	1985	109.3	3.80
1958	28.9	1.76	1986	110.5	1.10
1959	29.4	1.73	1987	115.4	4.43
1960	29.8	1.36	1988	120.5	4.42
1961	30.0	0.67	1989	126.1	4.65
1962	30.4	1.33	1990	133.8	6.11
1963	30.9	1.64	1991	137.9	3.06
1964	31.2	0.97	1992	141.9	2.90
1965	31.8	1.92	1993	145.8	2.75
1966	32.9	3.46	1994	149.7	2.67
1967	33.9	3.04	1995	153.5	2.54
1968	35.5	4.72	1996	158.6	3.32
1969	37.7	6.20	1997	161.3	1.70
1970	39.8	5.57	1998	163.9	1.61
1971	41.1	3.27	1999	168.3	2.68
1972	42.5	3.41			

Data Source: Global Financial Data Web site. Copyright 2000.

Thinking that there is "one right answer" to securing your retirement dreams

As we constantly stress throughout this book, your retirement planning strategy should be unique. It is based on your knowledge of how you want to live, how you want to spend your money, what you value in life, and how much investment risk you are willing to assume.

SPENDING, INVESTING, AND LIFESTYLE

To begin securing your retirement, you need to think about three major variables. First is the way you spend. Second is the way you invest. Third is the lifestyle you wish to have now and during your retirement. It's a matter of finding the balance between spending and saving that is right for you.

Each of the next three chapters discusses these issues in detail. Here we touch on the highlights.

Spending

As we've said, many people underestimate what they will spend during their retirement. This happens for two reasons. First, they underestimate what they spend now and then apply a simplistic rule to calculate how much they should spend later. Second, they assume many expenses will be eliminated in the future.

One useful way to determine what you will spend in retirement is to accurately determine what you spend now, then accurately determine what expenses will be reduced or eliminated after retirement as well as which expenses might increase. We'll discuss this in greater detail in the next chapter.

Remember, "rules of thumb" or "replacement ratio" calculations are good only for making rough estimates. The notion that you will need about 75% of your preretirement income on which to live in retirement may be good enough for making broad assumptions and creating broad goals. But it is not accurate for everyone. You need to analyze your situation more closely, especially when fine-tuning both your spending and your investing as you get closer to actually retiring. In later chapters we'll talk in more detail about creating realistic income and expense projections.

Investing

As we'll discuss in detail in Chapter 4, you can create enough wealth on which to retire only if you invest properly. That means creating a diversified portfolio of investments that yields a total rate of return after taxes that beats inflation by a significant enough margin to grow your nest egg over time.

The three most important types of financial investments are cash equivalents, bonds, and stocks (also called equities). These assets are all relatively liquid, meaning they can be converted to money fairly quickly. Other, less liquid investments include real estate, collectibles, precious metals, and investment partnerships. These investments typically provide less diversification and feature higher expenses than widely available financial investments.

Cash includes coins and bills, of course, but for investment purposes it also includes your checking account balance, savings accounts, money market funds at banks or mutual fund companies, certificates of deposit (CDs), and U.S. Treasury bills. Cash investments have historically yielded an average of about 0.5% above the rate of inflation, with savings and checking account balances often yielding less than inflation and money market accounts slightly more.

Bonds, which are essentially loans to corporations or governmental entities, yield on average somewhat more than 2 and 3% above inflation on a historical basis. For our purposes, when we talk about bonds in the context of your retirement funds, we are talking about U.S. Treasury notes and bonds with maturities of 5, 10, or 30 years. Corporate bonds typically offer a higher yield than inflation but carry a risk of default. U.S. Treasuries are fully guaranteed, which means there is no risk of default.

Stocks, which are shares of ownership in companies, have historically generated an average total return before taxes of about 6 to 7% above the inflation rate.

It's important to remember that no matter how you purchase stocks or bonds, either individually or through mutual funds, there are transaction costs—fees for buying and/or selling as well as fund management fees—that reduce your total return. While these costs vary from about 0.25% to more than 2%, we'll use 1% for the typical annual management fee/transaction cost for mutual funds. This means that after transaction costs, bond funds yield about 1 to 2% more than inflation and stocks about 5 to 6% above inflation.

In Chapter 4 we'll talk about structuring different portfolios for people with different risk tolerances and different time horizons.

Lifestyle

What do we mean by your lifestyle, both today and in retirement?

Lifestyle really means what you find important in life. All of financial planning—goal setting, spending, saving, and investing—is a way for individuals, couples, and families to determine what is important in life for them and how they hope to achieve those important things. We like to think of the act of balancing your lifestyle with financial reality as "doing a pleasure calculation."

It is within the realm of thinking of your lifestyle that you ask such questions as:

- At what age do I want to be able to stop working if I choose to?
- Does retirement mean simply leading a life of leisure, or does it mean turning an interest or hobby into a business?
- Do I (we) want to travel after retirement; do I (we) want to relocate; do I (we) want to sell my (our) primary residence and move to the vacation home?

Finally, here's the big question:

- What's more important, retiring at a particular age or retiring with a particular income that I can sustain after inflation?

If it's more important to retire at a particular age, and your calculations show a projected cash-flow shortfall, you may choose either to reduce your living standard in retirement or to change your saving and investment goals.

Retirement age: Determined

Ways to enable you to retire at determined age:

1. Reduce projected retirement living standard
2. Increase earnings from part-time work during retirement
3. Increase savings for retirement
4. Change investment mix of retirement savings

If it's more important to retire with a certain standard of living, you may choose to work longer, or maybe not retire completely but rather semi-retire, continuing to work either in your old occupation or in a new occupation on a part-time basis. Again, you also can get there by increasing your savings or changing your investment mix.

Retirement lifestyle: Determined

Ways to reach determined retirement lifestyle:

1. Work longer
2. Work part time during retirement
3. Save more
4. Change investment mix of retirement savings

Notice that the second through fourth ways are the same for retiring at a determined age or lifestyle. These are important to your financial success regardless of your goals. If you start thinking about retirement early, plan soundly, determine an investment strategy, and consistently follow through on it, you may not have to make any significant compromises on your retirement dreams.

Look at it this way:

Retirement lifestyle = age at retirement + savings + investment strategy + possible part-time work in retirement

What Are the Sources of Retirement Income?

Before you determine how much you must save and how you should invest for retirement, you need to determine how much retirement income you will have from various sources.

We like to think of these sources of retirement income as ingredients in a pie. Everybody's pie has two basic ingredients.

The first ingredient all of us who have worked have is government-mandated retirement savings. For most of us, this will be Social Security benefits (which we assume will continue in one form or another, no matter when you retire). Some federal workers have federal civil service pensions rather than Social Security. Some state and local government workers and workers for quasi-governmental agencies also have alternative systems to Social Security, as do those who have retired from the military.

The second ingredient all of us will add to our personal retirement pie recipe is savings, employer-provided savings and/or personal savings.

An increasing number of people have part of their personal retirement savings in tax-deferred retirement savings accounts—401(k)s, 403(b)s, 457s, Keoghs, SEPs, SIMPLEs, or IRAs. But some people have only taxable personal savings. For purposes of our retirement pie, we'll consider each of these a separate ingredient.

Some people have another ingredient, defined-benefit pensions, while others do not.

Some people have yet another ingredient, tax-deferred savings in universal life or variable life insurance policies, from which cash can be borrowed—typically tax free. In addition, cash values can provide an annuity for retirement income.

Figure 2.3 illustrates all these ingredients.

To determine how much income you expect to receive from Social Security, you need to ask yourself a key question: "Do I believe Social Security will be there to provide benefits for me when I retire?" We'll talk more about Social Security in Chapter 8.

When thinking about your own sources of retirement income it's important to realize that *the higher your income during your working years, the smaller the percentage of your income Social Security benefits will replace*. There are two reasons for this.

First, the system was designed as part of the social safety net to provide long-term low-income workers with a payment in retirement that could, it was hoped, keep them out of poverty. The system is designed to replace about 43% of income for a person with "average" earnings, which for 2000 is about $30,000. As your income goes up from there, Social Security replaces a smaller portion of that income.

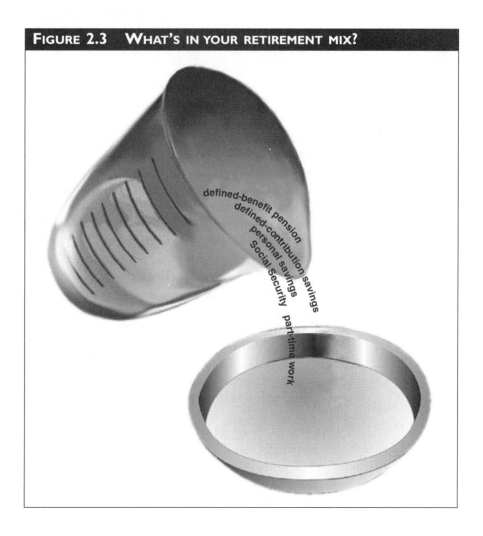

FIGURE 2.3   WHAT'S IN YOUR RETIREMENT MIX?

Once you hit the earnings cap for which Social Security taxes are withheld, you also make yourself eligible to receive the maximum benefit. Whether you earn $76,200 or $650,000 in 2000, your Social Security tax payment (except for the Medicare portion of the tax, which is 1.45%) is capped, as will be your monthly benefit when you retire. While $1,400 per month—the approximate top benefit for a single retiree—is about 22% of the $6,350 per month earned by a $76,200-per-year worker, it is only about 2.6% of the $54,000 per month earned by a $650,000-per-year worker.

Next, look at any income that will be derived from defined-benefit pension plans in which you participate. Many of today's retirees and those who will retire in the next 20 years will receive income from at least one pension plan of a former employer. Those who entered the workforce since the 1990s are less likely to have a substantial portion of their retirement income from any defined-benefit pensions since fewer companies have started new pension plans, and many have stopped funding defined-benefit plans for new employees, instead funding only defined-contribution plans.

THE SUDDEN LANDING

A little earlier we told the story about the man who fell from the 15th-floor window and thought all was well as he passed the 12th floor. We know he did not enjoy the landing.

The same can happen to you if you tap into retirement funds too early, or if you fail to save enough for retirement. And you can end up tapping into funds earlier than you expect if you don't take inflation into account when you determine how much you should save for retirement.

Let's look at an example. A man retires at age 55 with a $100,000 nest egg, which is invested to earn 7% after taxes, or $7,000 annually. He lives off the $7,000 his investments earn. He's living off every penny of current income. He's "okay" in that first year of retirement.

But in year 2, inflation has increased the basic cost of living by 3%. He needs to dip into his principal by a small amount. But already, by reducing his principal by only a few dollars, he has started a trend that will escalate until his savings are gone. This is shown in Figure 2.4.

What's the moral of this story? One might not be able to live 23 years after retirement!

However, many of us will have the good fortune to do so, in good health and with a high level of vibrancy. Today, a person who lives long enough to begin collecting Social Security has a life expectancy of another 18 years. Many will live longer. And those who opt for early retirement at 55 or 60 may have 25, 30, or more years to live in retirement.

FIGURE 2.4 THE IMPACT OF INFLATION.

Year	Beginning Principal	Living Expenses @ 3%	Interest @ 7%	Withdrawal from Principal	Ending Principal
1	$100,000	$7,000	$7,000	$0	$100,000
2	100,000	7,210	7,000	−210	99,790
3	99,790	7,426	6,985	−441	99,349
4	99,349	7,649	6,954	−695	98,654
5	98,654	7,879	6,906	−973	97,681
6	97,681	8,115	6,838	−1,277	96,404
7	96,404	8,358	6,748	−1,610	94,794
8	94,794	8,609	6,636	−1,973	92,821
9	92,821	8,867	6,497	−2,370	90,451
10	90,451	9,133	6,332	−2,861	87,650
11	87,650	9,407	6,136	−3,271	84,379
12	84,379	9,690	5,907	−3,783	80,596
13	80,596	9,980	5,642	−4,338	76,258
14	76,258	10,280	5,338	−4,942	71,316
15	71,316	10,588	4,992	−5,596	65,720
16	65,720	10,906	4,600	−6,306	59,414
17	59,414	11,233	4,159	−7,074	52,340
18	52,340	11,570	3,664	−7,906	44,434
19	44,434	11,917	3,110	−8,807	35,627
20	35,627	12,275	2,494	−9,781	25,846

We suggest a different moral to this story as you ponder the question: "Will I have enough money with which to retire and maintain an acceptable lifestyle?"

If you get to retirement and find that you have not saved enough or invested in a way that provides you with enough to meet all your expenses, you'll need to work to earn more money, change your investment mix, or work diligently to pare your expenses so that you do not have to dip into your savings principal without a plan that assures you will not outlive your money. Regardless of which you choose, unless you plan now you may outlive your money.

It's very tempting in our spending culture simply to "work the income side," and add savings from whatever reserves you have. But if you "work the expense side" early on, you can change your spending habits so that your lifestyle is not damaged, while delaying the time at which you will have to invade your principal. This can help you put off the possibility of a "sudden landing" while you're still healthy and want to continue living a pleasing lifestyle during retirement.

DOING THE CALCULATION

Figure 2.5 shows the results of a 1993 study conducted by Georgia State University that illustrates the percentage of preretirement, pretax income typical workers at various income levels need to replace at retirement: the replacement ratio.

As annual income increases from about $20,000 to $40,000, your replacement ratio decreases. Then, as annual income rises to $50,000 and above, the replacement ratio increases, mostly due to the fact that at particular income levels, a greater portion of your Social Security benefit is subject to federal income tax.

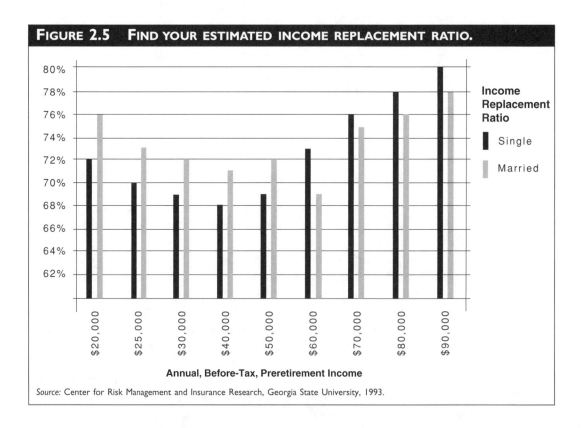

FIGURE 2.5   FIND YOUR ESTIMATED INCOME REPLACEMENT RATIO.

Source: Center for Risk Management and Insurance Research, Georgia State University, 1993.

You can use the table in Figure 2.5 to find the estimated amount of your current pretax income you will need in retirement to maintain your current lifestyle. Then, by completing the table in Figure 2.6, you can add detail to the picture of what your actual postretirement expenses will be.

Now for the big question: What portion of your replacement ratio will each of your retirement sources of income provide?

FIGURE 2.6 PROJECTING THE ANNUAL RETIREMENT INCOME YOU WILL NEED (A CLOSER LOOK).

Description	A. Current Annual Expenses		B. Estimated Annual Expenses During Retirement	
	You	Spouse/Partner	You	Spouse/Partner
1. Housing/mortgage				
2. Other housing expenses (real estate taxes, home owner's insurance, utilities, and maintenance)				
3. Clothing				
4. Food				
5. Car/transportation				
6. Insurance (except medical)				
7. Medical (insurance and other costs)				
8. Education				
9. Travel				
10. Gifts and donations				
11. Entertainment				
12. Savings				
13. Income taxes				
14. Social Security tax				
15. Other				
16. Total				

Take Social Security first. Figure 2.7 shows the approximate replacement ratio Social Security will provide for current incomes ranging from $20,000 to $100,000. While a worker who currently earns $20,000 per year will have about 45% of that income replaced by Social Security at full benefits (benefits are reduced if you begin collecting early), another worker who earns $50,000 per year will have about 28% of his or her income replaced, a worker who makes $70,000 annually will have about 20% of income replaced, and a worker earning $100,000 annually will have about 15% replaced.

Once you have a ballpark idea on your Social Security and living expense figures, you're ready to work through a retirement projection. As you do, it's important to realize that a projection calculated through a worksheet can give you a good ballpark projection, but at some time you may want to use a software projection to incorporate different or more detailed assumptions.

It's also helpful to know that not all worksheets are the same. The worksheets in this book have been carefully designed to take inflation into account, not just until retirement but for the rest of your life. Also, the worksheets calculate whether you have enough income and assets *throughout your retirement*, not just for the first year of retirement.

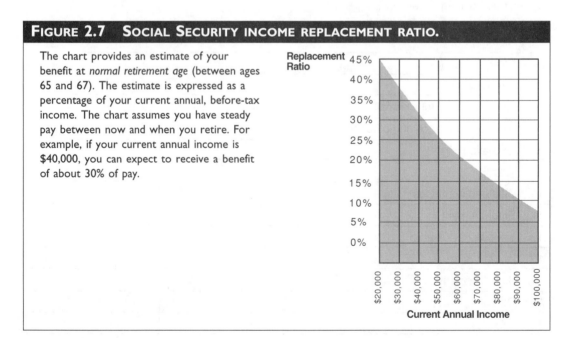

FIGURE 2.7 SOCIAL SECURITY INCOME REPLACEMENT RATIO.

The chart provides an estimate of your benefit at *normal retirement age* (between ages 65 and 67). The estimate is expressed as a percentage of your current annual, before-tax income. The chart assumes you have steady pay between now and when you retire. For example, if your current annual income is $40,000, you can expect to receive a benefit of about 30% of pay.

Replacement Ratio

Current Annual Income

Finally, it's important to realize that any projection depends on the assumptions that underlie it. That's not a point we make to satisfy liability concerns. Instead, it's a real point you need to understand. Even small changes in assumptions can make big changes in the results in long-term projections—and retirement projections are all very long-term projections. So we urge you to do two things. First, play "what if?" to see the effects of different assumptions, especially using some computer software programs. Second, build in a cushion. For example, look to see how you would fare if your living expenses were, say, 20% higher. No one knows how your medical expenses will increase, how your employer's medical program, or retirement plans, or Social Security will change, but we expect that changes will occur. So you want to plan for a "robust" retirement that can weather the surprises and changes that are bound to come.

Figure 2.7 provides an estimate of your benefit at normal retirement age (between ages 65 and 67). The estimate is expressed as a percentage of your current annual, before-tax income. The chart assumes you have steady pay between now and when you retire. For example, if your current annual income is $40,000, you can expect to receive a benefit of about 30% of pay.

The worksheets in Figures 2.8 through 2.15 will help you perform these calculations. As an example, we've filled them in for a fictitious worker named Mark, who earns $40,000 annually and is single.

FIGURE 2.8 WHAT IS YOUR TOTAL INCOME REPLACEMENT RATIO?

		Mark	You	Spouse
1.	Your projected pension income replacement ratio	30%		
2.	Your projected 401(k) income replacement ratio	20%		
3.	Your projected Social Security income replacement ratio	30%		
4.	Sum of lines 1, 2, and 3 = Your projected total income replacement ratio	80%		

FIGURE 2.9 YOUR RETIREMENT PLAN: COMPARING WHAT YOU NEED TO WHAT YOU HAVE.

	Mark	You	Spouse
1. Annual retirement income need in today's dollars	$32,000		
2. Estimated annual, before-tax Social Security Normal Retirement Benefit or Early Retirement Benefit in today's dollars	$12,500		
3. Estimated annual, before-tax pension benefit in today's dollars	$11,500		
4. Projected length (in years) of your retirement	20		
5. If your pension plan does not have an automatic cost-of-living provision, enter adjustment factor from Figure 2.13 that most closely corresponds to the number of years to your projected years of retirement (Line 4) and your assumed investment return in retirement. If your plan does have a cost-of-living provision, enter 1.00.	0.741		
6. Line 3 × Line 5 = Pension benefit adjusted for purchasing power	8,522		
7. Line 1 − Line 2 − Line 6 = Annual retirement income need from 401(k) and other sources in today's dollars	$10,978		
8. Number of years before you retire	25		
9. Based on historical inflation rates, consider an inflation rate of 3% or 4% for the period between now and when you retire.	3%		
10. See Figure 2.10 on page 29. Enter the factor that most closely corresponds to the number of years between now and retirement (Line 8) and your assumed inflation rate (Line 9).	2.16		
11. Line 7 × Line 10 = Annual retirement income need from 401(k) and other sources, in future dollars (adjusted for inflation)	$23,712		
12. See Figure 2.11 on page 29. Enter the factor that most closely corresponds to the number of years closest to the length of your retirement (Line 4) and your assumed investment return in retirement.	14.31		
13. Line 10 × Line 12 = Preliminary lump sum needed to fund retirement income shortfall before Social Security adjustment	$339,319		
14. If you plan to retire before you begin to collect Social Security, multiply Line 2 × Line 9 = Annual Social Security in future dollars. If not, go to Line 17.			

FIGURE 2.9 YOUR RETIREMENT PLAN: COMPARING WHAT YOU NEED TO WHAT YOU HAVE. *(continued)*

	Mark	You	Spouse
15. See Figure 2.12 on page 30. Enter the factor that most closely corresponds to (a) the number of years between the date you will retire and the date your Social Security Normal or Early Retirement Benefit will start (whichever you chose at Line 2), and (b) your assumed investment return in retirement.			
16. Line 14 × Line 15 = Lump sum needed to replace Social Security until it begins			
17. Line 13 + Line 16 = Total lump sum needed at retirement	$339,319		
18. Estimated balance from 401(k) and other personal savings at retirement	$148,000		
19. If Line 18 is greater than Line 17, you have a projected surplus and do not need to complete Figure 2.14. If Line 18 is smaller than Line 17, enter the amount of the shortfall to the right and go to Figure 2.14.	Surplus: $ Shortfall: $191,319	Surplus: $ Shortfall: $	Surplus: $ Shortfall: $

FIGURE 2.10 INFLATION FACTORS.

Years to Retirement	Inflation Rate	
	3%	4%
5	1.16	1.22
8	1.27	1.37
10	1.34	1.48
12	1.43	1.60
14	1.51	1.73
16	1.60	1.87
18	1.70	2.03
20	1.81	2.19
22	1.92	2.37
24	2.03	2.56
26	2.16	2.77
28	2.29	3.00
30	2.43	3.24
32	2.58	3.51

FIGURE 2.11 LUMP SUM NEEDED TO FUND RETIREMENT INCOME SHORTFALL.*

Length of Retirement (in Years)	Investment Return in Retirement		
	6%	8%	10%
5	4.81	4.64	4.48
10	9.19	8.49	7.87
15	13.17	11.67	10.43
20	16.79	14.31	12.36
25	20.08	16.49	13.82
30	23.07	18.30	14.93
35	25.79	19.79	15.76
40	28.26	21.03	16.39

*Assumes 4% annual spending increase.

Figure 2.12 Lump sum needed to fund Social Security from retirement start age.*

Years Until Social Security Starts	Investment Return		
	6%	8%	10%
1	1.00	1.00	1.00
2	1.98	1.96	1.95
3	2.94	2.89	2.84
4	3.89	3.78	3.68
5	4.81	4.64	4.48
6	5.72	5.47	5.24
7	6.62	6.27	5.95
8	7.49	7.04	6.63
9	8.35	7.78	7.27
10	9.19	8.49	7.87

Figure 2.13 Factors to adjust for the purchasing power of your pension.

Length of Retirement (in Years)	Investment Return in Retirement		
	6%	8%	10%
5	.51	.48	.45
10	1.66	1.46	1.30
15	3.21	2.68	2.25
20	5.00	3.96	3.17
25	6.92	5.20	3.99
30	8.87	6.36	4.68
35	10.80	7.41	5.26
40	12.68	8.33	5.72

*Assumes 4% annual spending increase.

Figure 2.14 What additional amount do you need to save annually to reach your retirement goal?

	Mark	You	Spouse
1. Enter the amount of a shortfall, if any, that you wrote on the worksheet in Figure 2.9, Line 19.	Shortfall: **$191,319**	Shortfall:	Shortfall:
2. See Figure 2.15. Enter the factor that most closely corresponds to the number of years between now and your retirement (see Figure 2.9, Line 8) and your assumed investment return before retirement.	.013		
3. Line 1 x Line 2 = Your annual savings goal	$2,487		
4. The annual amount you currently contribute to the 401(k)	$2,000		
5. Annual matching contribution to your 401(k) account	$1,200		
6. Line 4 + Line 5 = Total annual contribution to your 401(k) account	$3,200		
7. Subtract Line 6 from Line 3. If you end with zero or less, write zero at the right. If you end up with an amount greater than zero, enter that amount at the right. This is the additional amount you need to save annually to reach your retirement goal.	$0		

Figure 2.15 Annual savings required at various rates of return.			
Years to Retirement	Investment Return		
	6%	8%	10%
5	.177	.170	.164
8	.101	.094	.087
10	.076	.069	.063
12	.059	.053	.047
14	.048	.041	.036
16	.039	.033	.028
18	.032	.027	.022
20	.027	.022	.017
22	.023	.018	.014
24	.020	.015	.011
26	.017	.013	.009
28	.015	.010	.007
30	.013	.009	.006
32	.011	.007	.005

TRAPS, OBSTACLES, TOOLS, AND HELPERS

We've described in detail a few traps and helpers for this chapter. A more complete list follows:

- The long-term effect of *any* rate of inflation
- Tax rules that penalize the use of tax-favored retirement plans for nonretirement purposes
- Focusing only on the age at which you want to retire, instead of considering the standard of living you want when you retire

- The "Rule of 72" as a way of determining how long it will take for an investment to double in value at a given rate of return
- Tax-deferred retirement plans
- Publications and self-tests on values clarification

- Financial worksheets, tables, calculators, and software to help you make long-term projections
- Public information on cost-of-living statistics for any part of the United States from the Bureau of Labor Statistics of the U.S. Department of Labor
- Job referral services and second-career resources for older workers
- Social Security statements (formerly called "Personal Earnings and Benefit Estimates" or PEBES) from the Social Security Administration
- Employee benefit summary plan descriptions, personal benefit statements, and retirement benefit projections from your employer's human resources, personnel, or benefits office

- Projecting income and expenses only to the first year of your retirement
- Relying exclusively on a "replacement ratio" analysis
- Mixing future dollars and today's dollars instead of being consistent
- Underestimating what you will spend in retirement
- Ignoring taxes and inflation
- Confusing your effective tax rate with your marginal tax rate
- Thinking of the equity in your home as a retirement investment windfall
- Thinking there is "one right answer" to secure your retirement dreams
- Relying heavily on "rules of thumb"

ACTION ITEMS

These action items, which you should try to do as soon as possible, are as applicable to a person in his or her 30s as they are for a person nearing retirement.

Item	Priority*	Completed
1. Take advantage of your company savings plan by contributing in pretax dollars (ideally at least 10% of pay). Consider Roth IRAs too.		
2. Project retirement needs, taking into account both taxes and inflation.		
3. Project retirement resources by not adding in a value for your home (so it's a cushion for conservative analysis) unless you're sure that you'll downsize. If so, add only the amount of equity that you think will be available after buying a new home and paying		

ACTION ITEMS (continued)

Item	Priority*	Completed
all transaction and moving costs (broker, transfer taxes, etc.).		
4. Project your retirement income sources using reasonable and consistent assumptions, with an eye to what the historical figures have been, but understanding that the future will be different. Pretax historical returns after expenses are: Stocks: 5–6% above inflation Bonds: 1–2% above inflation Cash equivalents: 0.5% above inflation		
5. Make the following basic retirement decisions: a. At what age do I want to be able to retire? b. What does "retirement" mean to me? c. Do I want to relocate? d. What is my top priority: maintaining a certain lifestyle or retiring at a certain age?		
6. Choose how you can make up any gap between your income needs and sources: a. Work longer. b. Work part-time in retirement. c. Save more now. d. Spend less in retirement. e. Change investment mix of retirement savings. f. Choose a combination of some or all of the above.		
7. Calculate how much you spend today. Determine which spending categories will not be applicable in retirement. (These might include: mortgage, but not property taxes; education, camp, after-school care for growing children; some recreation fees; and work-related expenses.) Make sure you're getting maximum pleasure from your spending in the categories that will remain applicable throughout your life, such as food, clothing, and transportation (for example, one car vs. two). For each category of expenses, estimate in a "ballpark" way what is likely to happen when you retire. In which categories will expenses increase, and in which will they decrease? Are there any categories of expenses that will dis-		

ACTION ITEMS (continued)

Item	Priority*	Completed
appear altogether? For those categories where you project expenses to increase, try to find ways to slow down the rate of increase.		
8. Tally up your defined benefits in retirement if you are vested in any such plans from any employer. Get from your employer's benefits office both the projection of what your benefit will be if you continue to work there until you retire at the company's "normal" retirement age and receive "typical" (equal to inflation) pay increases and what you will receive at the company's "normal" retirement age if you leave the company tomorrow or choose "early retirement."		
Carefully review your personal Social Security Statement, which you'll receive automatically each year near your birth month from the Social Security Administration. If you do not receive one, call Social Security at 1-800-772-1213 or visit the SSA Web site at www.ssa.gov. You can also request your statement online, or you can download form SSA-7004 from the Social Security Administration (SSA) Website and mail it to them. As an alternative, you can send an e-mail message to webmaster @ssa.gov with your name and address and SSA will mail you a form. You can also access Social Security's on-line retirement planner. It will let you compute estimates of your future Social Security retirement benefits on-line. It also provides important information on factors affecting your retirement benefits, such as military service, household earnings, and federal employment.		
9. Project what you'll need to have accumulated at retirement.		
a. Tally up how much you have in savings and investments dedicated to retirement, both tax deferred and taxable. (Tax-deferred savings include any balances you have in company-sponsored		

ACTION ITEMS (continued)

Item	Priority*	Completed
401(k), 403(b), or 457 plans, what is in any Keogh or SEP plans you maintain for any business or professional practice you run, and any IRAs you have, whether the contributions were taxable or not deductible in the year they were made. Include taxable investments that you have determined are dedicated for retirement.) b. Use a tool, either copies of the worksheet in this book or a computer program, to project the amount of savings and investments you need in both tax-advantaged and taxable savings in order to provide you with enough income to cover the gap between Social Security and pension benefits and living expenses. (Many computer programs allow you to make your own assumption about inflation during your retirement years and to determine how long you want your savings and investments to provide you with income —in other words, how long you plan to live after retirement maintaining your desired standard of living. If you use a worksheet or computer program provided by others, make sure it factors in inflation and does not give you the false notion that if you're okay for year one of retirement you're okay forever.) 10. Calculate both your effective (i.e., average) and marginal tax rates, including state income taxes. (Use your effective average tax rate to monitor your overall tax burden and as an element of financial projections. Use the marginal rate to determine the after-tax gains from receiving an additional taxable income, the net savings from income-tax deductions, and the point at which tax-exempt investments are more valuable than taxable investments.) Your *effective tax rate* is the average rate of tax you pay on your taxable income. You can calculate it by simply dividing the total amount of income		

ACTION ITEMS (continued)		
Item	**Priority***	**Completed**
taxes you pay by your total taxable income. Your *marginal tax rate* is the rate that applies to your last dollar of taxable income. It is also often referred to as your "tax bracket." You can determine it by looking at federal and state income tax tables. Your marginal tax rate is often higher than your effective tax rate.		

*A, B, C, or N/A, with A being the highest priority.

3

SPENDING

There is a simple truth about money. Every dollar you come to possess will be spent. Certainly something to think about.

Either you will spend it, or you will authorize someone else to spend it for you: your loved ones, charitable institutions to which you donate it, or the governments to which you pay taxes. It will be spent either in your lifetime or after.

Spending will occur. The questions are:

- Who will spend the money?
- When will the money be spent?
- How will the money be spent?
- Will you feel good about the way in which it was spent?

Too often financial planners say the only way to have enough money for retirement is to reduce your level of spending now. They tell you to ask of every purchase you make: "Do I really need this, or would the money be better used as savings for retirement?"

Unfortunately, this approach leads people to feel guilty about the way they spend their money. Feeling guilty about the way you spend your money is one of the big mistakes Americans make. Another is underestimating how much you actually spend. If you can learn to understand how you spend your money, and what value you get for the money you spend—emotional value as well as product value—you can develop a healthier balance between spending and saving.

First, you have to explode the greatest myth of spending: *I don't have choices.* One of the main objectives of this book is to demonstrate clearly that all of us have decisions to make every day—choices that shape what happens today and what is likely to happen in the future.

THE PLEASURE PRINCIPLE

In reality, your spending plan *is* your financial plan. Notice that we use the words "spending plan." The key to creating a spending plan is to understand your answers to the following four questions:

1. Who is spending the money?
2. When is the money being spent?
3. How is the money being spent? For what?
4. Am I happy about the way in which the money was spent?

The major financial activity each of us undertakes in our lives is spending.

Think about it: Someone who starts working at age 22 and earns $10,000 per year, increasing at, say, 3% inflation each year until retirement at age 60, will earn $722,000 over his or her lifetime. (We used these round numbers so you can easily translate these for your own situation—for example, if you earn $30,000, you'll earn in the ballpark of $2,166,000 [$722,000 × 3] over your lifetime.)

What will happen to all that money? You guessed it—you'll *spend* it. We spend money in each transaction we make for the purchase of a product or service. We buy groceries and pay the plumber, the baby-sitter, the home health aide, insurance, taxes, and so on.

While we're making all these necessary payments, we also want to make some transactions that are fun; we want to buy things we *desire*, even if we don't really need them.

Remembering that, at some point, all the money you come to possess will be spent, the issue becomes not one of spending less (remember, you can't spend less—you, or someone else, will spend it all) but of spending *better*. Your goal should be to redirect your spending toward things that give you the most pleasure.

ACCUMULATION OF SMALL ADVANTAGES

Chess grandmaster and teacher Aaron Nimzewich wrote in his book, *My System*, of the principle he calls "the accumulation of small advantages." Nimzewich argues that to win a chess match you don't need a bold, decisive move that severs the opponent's entire game. Rather, you need to gain advantage every time you can, in small and incremental ways.

How can this principle be applied to spending? Note that this is just one principle that you may choose to accept or reject in redirecting your spending to give you the most pleasure over the long term.

■ Jack used to go out to lunch every day. Lately he has found that by brown-bagging his lunch once a week, he can save $5 each week. In 48 work weeks, that is $240 a year. After a year, he put in a little extra money and opened a mutual fund account for his two-year-old daughter as a college fund. Now he has arranged with the fund to have $60 per quarter taken automatically from his bank account and invested in the mutual fund. He has not only redirected his spending, he has put his savings plan on automatic pilot. ■

■ Barry came to the conclusion that the smoking cessation class he took last year has not only helped his blood pressure, it has helped his savings account as well. Cigarettes are $5.50 a pack. At a pack a day, that is $24.50 a week, or $1,274 a year. Barry has saved over $1,400 in just 15 months since the course ended. Quitting wasn't easy, but he loves the results. Barry has added $1,200 to his 401(k) this year by increasing his weekly salary reduction. Again, Barry's savings are now automated through weekly payroll deduction. ■

■ Glenn used to spend $2 a day at the vending machine for soda and other snacks. That's $10 each work week, or $480 a year. He now buys soda by the case and brings cans from home. He buys candy in bulk and has a tin on his desk with candy bars. Glenn probably doesn't save much on the candy—his colleagues are always taking some. But overall he still reduces his cost for soda and candy by about $200 a year. Glenn could add his savings to his 401(k) plan or a Roth IRA, through payroll deduction or automatic bank transfers, so he has more to spend later. ■

■ Sylvia has become an avid golfer in the last few years. She loves the game and plays at every opportunity. She used to spend at least $10 a week at the driving range. Sylvia lives in Illinois, and has about 35 good golf weeks each year. That is $350 a year in range fees. One day she saw someone hitting golf balls in the field behind the high school. So she went out, bought a "shag bag" for $20, three dozen reconditioned balls for another $20, and now has unlimited range time at the schoolyard. Every two or three months she has to buy another package of balls, but she also throws the ones she finds on the golf course into her shag bag. She reduced her spending on golf by over $300 the first year. Sylvia too is using her savings to add to her retirement fund, by increasing the amount she sets aside in her Keogh plan. ■

If you can find a way to chop $1,000 off your spending this year by accumulating small advantages, and for 20 years you save the same amount, adjusted for inflation—at 3%—in the last year you will save $2,107. If you invest each year's savings and earn 6% on that investment, in 20 years you will have a pot of money worth $50,800.

You don't have to save it all. You can substitute a larger purchase for a number of small purchases, get more pleasure out of your spending, and gain some overall savings as well. Sylvia could very easily have used her no-more-driving-range savings to pay for part of a golf week at one of the country's golf resorts. The others could have saved their small advantages for large purchases as well, or could have directed the money to one of their other goals—setting aside money for potential long-term care or retiree medical expenses, disability or life insurance, getting a will updated.

Just as economists talk about the "time value" of money—getting a dollar today is worth more than getting a dollar a year from now because of what you can earn on that dollar if invested—you can think of the "pleasure value" of money. Sometimes we get less pleasure by spending today than we would get by spending more in the future; in other situations, we truly do derive more satisfaction by spending today rather than later. The choices you make in spending now or later truly define your goals and priorities.

Even if you save the windfall in the short run, in the long run you will spend it, because saving is actually deferred spending. Think about that: A decision to save a dollar today is a decision to spend that dollar, plus earnings on it, some time in the future. A decision to save today is really just a decision to spend more later.

THE EVAPORATION OF CASH

One of the big traps of spending is overuse of your bank's cash machine. Remember the old days? You used to take your paycheck to the bank, deposit a portion of it into your checking account, take a portion back as cash, and, if you were lucky, put a little away into savings. How many of us still make that once-a-week cash last the whole week?

If you find yourself going to the cash machine every day or two and withdrawing small amounts each time, you may find that you are spending more cash than you used to when you knew how much you had for the entire week and had to make it last.

Cash simply seems to evaporate!

■ Chris decided to force herself to justify all of these small cash purchases. She got herself a tiny spiral-bound notebook and recorded her cash expenditures just as she did the petty cash at the office. She also recorded each time she went to the cash machine.

For a few weeks she jotted down every 56 cents for a newspaper—Chris lives in Connecticut, where newspapers are subject to sales tax—every 75 cents for a can of soda, and trips to the dry cleaner, the candy counter, the post office, and the drugstore for a tiny bottle of another perfume she wanted to try.

Keeping this cash withdrawal and expense log became such a hassle, she actually found herself avoiding certain purchases just because she didn't want to write them down. Finally, she asked herself, "How important is this purchase if I will not make it just so I don't have to record it? Am I really getting pleasure out of it, or is it just spending as habit?" Keeping track of how she spent her money was a kind of wake-up call for Chris. When she looked at how she was spending her money, she realized that she was not spending on her top priorities.

Chris took her little experiment one step further. She listed all the things she bought during her two weeks of record keeping, then determined if there were less expensive and more efficient ways of purchasing them. By bulk buying the things she really enjoys, she now can get cash once a week again and still have a few dollars in her wallet the next week when she takes her next cash withdrawal. ■

Two huge obstacles we all face in our spending patterns are:

1. *Artificial enticements to spend.* Think of it: Most of the messages we receive on television, in the newspaper, on billboards, or through junk mail are to spend money now. You may field numerous calls each week from people trying to sell you something.
2. *Easy access to credit.* Worse than the phone calls from salespeople are the ones from people offering you yet another credit card so you can buy more.

In December 1996 the *Washington Post* featured a lengthy article about the increase in personal bankruptcy filings due to huge mountains of unpaid credit card debt. One man told the *Post* reporter that even after his bankruptcy, he continues to get mail and phone offers from credit card companies offering lines of credit of up to $10,000. "Somebody must be playing a joke on me," he said. "Me and my wife, we just sit and laugh."

It is not just credit cards. Car manufacturers will finance a car in minutes. Banks solicit your business for home equity loans. Even your retirement plan at work might offer loans.

Many Americans are drawn into these bad spending habits by salespeople asking not "What do you want?" or "What do you need?" but rather "What's the most you can afford?" or "How much can you finance each month?"

E X A M P L E

■ Courtney and Matt went looking to buy their first home. Every real estate agent they encountered wanted to prequalify them by going through the paperwork that a mortgage lender would to find out how big a monthly payment they could afford. This seemed like a good idea at the time. But after they computed how much they could afford, they found that agents showed them only houses at the high end of their price range, even if the houses weren't of the type they told the agent they wanted, or in their preferred location.

Time after time, their conversations with real estate agents went something like this:

MATT: We don't need an attached garage and a screened-in porch.

AGENT: They're so convenient and the difference in your monthly payment is pennies.

COURTNEY: But we only need three bedrooms.

AGENT: It's in your budget; the bank will lend you enough to buy it; and let's face it, you can't have too much room.

COURTNEY: How much would a three-bedroom house close to the train station cost?

AGENT: Believe me, just buy the most expensive house you can afford now. One day you'll thank me. ■

The bottom line is that some agents want to sell the most expensive house, for the biggest commission. If you can afford more, they want to sell you more.

The situation is much the same in new-car showrooms. Who hasn't had a car salesman say, "How much do you want to pay a month?" They don't ask, "Are you looking for a small car, a family car, a wagon? Do you *need* power windows and power locks?" The question is, in effect, "How much can I get you to sign up for as a monthly payment?"

If you want to be an effective spender, you need to create a strategy that allows you to fight that human habit to spend to the limit of your resources. You need to go into buying situations—especially for big-ticket items—with a strategy that comes from asking yourself:

- What do I need or want?
    Example: A television set.
- What features would be nice to have?
    Example: Stereo sound, 25-inch screen, built-in VCR.
- Would I be willing to go into debt, or extend debt, in order to obtain each of those features?
    Example: Stereo, no; 25-inch, yes; built-in VCR, no.
- If I spend more on this, what will I spend less on? If I spend less on this, how can I redirect that savings to something else?

Most of us are vulnerable to the techniques of salespeople and ads today because we do not have clear, written financial goals. We have not taken the time to think through and define what we really would like or what really makes the best sense. When salespeople suggest that it would be nicer to have that something extra, they're often right—it *would* be nice. We know we don't need it, but what else are we going to do with the money? It's not easy for us to make the calculation that a few dollars here and a few dollars there really do add up, and compound over the years, to make the difference between retiring at age 55 or 65, or to have the kind of retirement that can withstand high retiree medical expenses or long-term care expenses.

Traps, Obstacles, Tools, and Helpers

Watch out for the following traps and obstacles, and take advantage of the tools and helpers.

- Believing you don't have choices
- Acting out of habits and routines
- Ignoring your cash transactions
- Carrying credit card balances
- Buying unneeded items because they are on sale as saving money
- Spending, instead of saving, boosts in income received during the year

- Automatic teller machines (ATMs), which allow instant easy access to cash
- Lack of goals, of knowing what you really want
- Easy access to credit, tempting you to borrow more than you should

- Ledgers and record keepers to track and illustrate your spending
- Low-fee credit cards with low interest rates
- Financial planning software with net worth and cash-flow modeling tools

- Personal, documented spending plan
- The "rule of 72" as a way of determining how long it will take for money to lose half its value at a given rate of inflation (divide 72 by the rate of inflation): At 3% inflation what costs $10,000 today will cost $20,000 in 24 years (72/3 = 24)
- Accumulating small advantages
- Increasing the amount you save each year by at least the rate of inflation
- Before shopping, asking yourself: What is the most I choose to spend?
- Using payroll deduction and automatic investments into mutual funds from your bank account to put your savings plan on automatic pilot

ACTION ITEMS

Item	Priority*	Completed
1. Look at your checkbook register at the end of the month. Ask: Did the product, service, event, or other item give me pleasure? Did I have fun? Could I have had more fun spending it in a different way, or saving it to be spent later?		
2. Keep a ledger of cash purchases for a week or a month. Ask: Did each purchase give me pleasure? Did I have fun? Could I have had more fun spending it in a different way, or saving it to be spent later?		
3. List three products, services, or other items you want to obtain in the next five years that you are *willing to go into debt for*, and the reasons why. Rank order the choice, and limit them to three.		

ACTION ITEMS

Item	Priority*	Completed
Examples: car, boat, vacation, membership in private club, home computer. **Item** **Amount** **Rank** **When?** _____ _____ _____ _____ _____ _____ _____ _____ _____ _____ _____ _____ 4. Think of ways to reduce spending on small items so you can accumulate small advantages and pay for one of the items you listed above, preferably the first choice, without going into debt, or by carrying much less debt than otherwise. Ask: "Does this directly relate to my retirement planning?" The answer is, *absolutely*! If you don't enjoy *getting there*, you probably won't enjoy *being there*. And, if you don't have the funds to support what you enjoy, it won't be possible to continue having fun in those exciting retirement years.		

*A, B, C, or N/A, with A being the highest priority.

4

INVESTING

The step from saving to *investing* is the largest step you can take on the road to long-term financial success and making your retirement dreams a reality. Saving means putting money away, typically earning just interest. Investing means being an owner, typically of stocks, bonds, real estate, or other assets.

But, to many if not most Americans, investing seems a daunting task. After all, don't investment professionals get paid hundreds of thousands of dollars a year for picking the right investments? Yes, they do. Fortunately, in today's financial marketplace, you can get the benefit of their expertise and their experience without having to be a millionaire. The ability of "small" investors to tap into the expertise of investment professionals is the most important feature of the current investment climate in the United States, where over 40% of households own stocks in publicly traded companies, either through an individual brokerage account or through mutual funds. The Investment Company Institute, a research organization, estimates that from 1993 to 1995, investors poured at least $378 billion into stock mutual funds.

When a newcomer to the world of investing looks at the investment options available, the choices seem infinite. But if you take it step by step, the decisions can be made smaller and less intimidating. This is because the real decision you need to make is whether to invest as an owner or a lender, then whether you want to invest in highly liquid investments, such as stocks or bonds, or in nonfinancial and less liquid investments, such as real estate, collectibles, and precious metals.

The three keys to investing for retirement are as follows:

1. *Consider your goals.*

Saving and investing to purchase a home in three years calls for a different strategy than does saving and investing for retirement. The goal of a financially secure retirement is not a onetime event; rather it involves creating the financial ability to maintain your desired lifestyle over a period of time.

2. *Consider your time frame.*

Regardless of your age, at least a portion of your retirement investment portfolio should be invested for the long term. Assuming you are investing for the long term, you can live with the short-term swings in investment markets. Over any period of time greater than 10 years, stock owners can expect to receive a higher average annual rate of return than do lenders, who invest in cash or bonds.

3. *Consider your personal tolerance for risk.*

Remember, money is supposed to add fun to your life. If you're constantly worrying about how risky your investments are, you won't have much fun. Just the same, the old adage "no risk, no return" is quite true.

INVESTMENT RETURN: THE KEY TO GROWTH

In previous chapters, we suggested that you analyze your spending to determine how much income you actually need to pay your expenses today. Later, in Chapter 11, we'll talk about spending in retirement and detail why you might need more or less during retirement than you do today.

One way to increase your income in retirement is to spend less today, so you'll have more to spend tomorrow. The other piece to the puzzle of making the most of your retirement savings is the investment return you earn on those savings.

When determining your overall investment strategy, you want to look at what is called "total return," which is the combination of interest or dividends paid, plus the increase or decrease in the underlying value of the investment itself, minus any transaction costs or fund management fees.

Some investments—cash and bonds, for example—have no assumed increase in the principal (the original amount invested). If you buy a $1,000 U.S. Treasury bond, you will get back $1,000 when it matures. Along the way, you will receive fixed interest payments of, say, 6.75%. You make investments in these vehicles because of their safety in repaying principal if held to maturity and their defined return.

When you invest in stocks, on the other hand, you are investing in the hopes of an increase in the value of the stock. Many stocks pay no stated return at all, while others pay a modest dividend, usually no more than 3 or 4%.

Figure 4.1 is a table of compound interest for $1.00 invested. The vertical axis (the numbers on the side) shows the time you hold an investment. The horizontal axis (the numbers across the top) shows the annual percentage yield from the investment or portfolio returns.

You can estimate how much your portfolio will be worth by multiplying the dollar amount invested by the factor from the chart that corresponds with the annual rate of return and number of years the investment is held.

For instance, let's say you are 40 years old and wish to contribute to your company's 401(k) tax-deferred retirement savings plan. Let's say you can safely have $2,000 withheld from your pay during the year and still meet your current financial obligations. Let's further assume that you plan to begin withdrawing from this tax-deferred plan by April 1 of the year following the year in which you turn age 70½, when you normally must by law begin taking withdrawals if you've retired.

If your $2,000 earns an average of 6% a year in total return—interest and dividends plus any growth in the value of the investments—in 30 years it will be worth $11,480 in future dollars ($2,000 × 5.74).

What if you were able to double your contribution? A $4,000 contribution, earning the same 6% total return for 30 years, would be worth $22,960 in future dollars.

But what if you were able to get 9% total return on the same $2,000? How much would it be worth after 30 years? The answer: $26,540 ($2,000 × 13.27). If you could double your contribution to $4,000 and earn 9%, 30 years from now you would have $53,080.

That's just for this single year of contributions.

Another thing to keep in mind is that *increasing your investment return* has a much greater impact on the total value of your investments over a long time than does *increasing the contribution*.

Read that sentence again.

Now let's look at the three variables that impact the value of your investments over the long term:

1. Contribution Amount
2. Total Investment Return
3. Time Horizon

Let's rework the previous example to show the time variable more closely.

FIGURE 4.1 COMPOUND INTEREST OF $1.00 PRINCIPAL.

The Amount to Which One Dollar Will Accumulate at the End of the Specified Number of Years

Years	5%	6%	7%	8%	9%	10%	12%	14%	15%	16%	18%	20%	36%
1	1.05	1.06	1.07	1.08	1.09	1.10	1.12	1.14	1.15	1.16	1.18	1.20	1.36
2	1.10	1.12	1.14	1.17	1.19	1.21	1.25	1.30	1.32	1.35	1.39	1.44	1.85
3	1.16	1.19	1.23	1.26	1.30	1.33	1.40	1.48	1.52	1.56	1.64	1.73	2.52
4	1.22	1.26	1.31	1.36	1.41	1.46	1.57	1.69	1.75	1.81	1.94	2.07	3.42
5	1.28	1.34	1.40	1.47	1.54	1.61	1.76	1.93	2.01	2.10	2.29	2.49	4.65
6	1.34	1.42	1.50	1.59	1.68	1.77	1.97	2.20	2.31	2.44	2.70	2.99	6.33
7	1.40	1.50	1.61	1.71	1.83	1.95	2.21	2.50	2.66	2.83	3.19	3.58	8.61
8	1.48	1.59	1.72	1.85	1.99	2.14	2.48	2.85	3.06	3.28	3.76	4.30	11.70
9	1.55	1.69	1.84	2.00	2.17	2.36	2.77	3.25	3.52	3.80	4.44	5.16	15.92
10	1.63	1.79	1.97	2.16	2.37	2.60	3.11	3.71	4.05	4.41	5.23	6.19	21.65
11	1.71	1.90	2.10	2.33	2.58	2.85	3.48	4.23	4.65	5.12	6.18	7.43	29.44
12	1.80	2.01	2.25	2.52	2.81	3.14	3.90	4.82	5.35	5.94	7.29	8.92	40.04
13	1.89	2.13	2.41	2.72	3.07	3.45	4.36	5.49	6.15	6.89	8.60	10.70	54.45
14	1.98	2.26	2.58	2.94	3.34	3.80	4.89	6.26	7.08	7.99	10.15	12.84	74.05
15	2.08	2.40	2.76	3.17	3.64	4.18	5.47	7.14	8.14	9.27	11.97	15.41	100.71
16	2.18	2.54	2.95	3.43	3.97	4.60	6.13	8.14	9.36	10.75	14.13	18.49	136.96
17	2.29	2.69	3.16	3.70	4.33	5.05	6.87	9.28	10.76	12.47	16.67	22.19	186.27
18	2.41	2.85	3.38	4.00	4.72	5.56	7.69	10.58	12.38	14.46	19.67	26.62	253.33
19	2.53	3.03	3.62	4.32	5.14	6.12	8.61	12.06	14.23	16.78	23.21	31.95	344.53
20	2.65	3.21	3.87	4.66	5.60	6.73	9.65	13.74	16.37	19.46	27.39	38.34	468.57
21	2.79	3.40	4.14	5.03	6.11	7.40	10.80	15.67	18.82	22.57	32.32	46.01	637.26
22	2.93	3.60	4.43	5.44	6.66	8.14	12.10	17.86	21.64	26.19	38.14	55.21	866.67
23	3.07	3.82	4.74	5.87	7.26	8.95	13.55	20.36	24.89	30.38	45.01	66.25	1178.60
24	3.23	4.05	5.07	6.34	7.91	9.85	15.18	23.21	28.63	35.24	53.11	79.50	1602.90
25	3.39	4.29	5.43	6.85	8.62	10.83	17.00	26.46	32.92	40.87	62.67	95.40	1280.00
26	3.56	4.55	5.81	7.40	9.40	11.92	19.04	30.17	37.86	47.41	73.95	114.47	2964.90
27	3.73	4.82	6.21	7.99	10.25	13.11	21.32	34.39	43.54	55.00	87.26	137.37	4032.20
28	3.92	5.11	6.65	8.63	11.17	14.42	23.88	39.20	50.07	63.80	102.96	164.84	5483.80
29	4.12	5.42	7.11	9.32	12.17	15.86	26.75	44.69	57.58	74.01	121.50	197.81	7458.00
30	4.32	5.74	7.61	10.06	13.27	17.45	29.96	50.95	66.21	85.85	143.37	237.37	10143.00

Remember, if you are able to earn a 6% average rate of return for 30 years, your $2,000 investment increases to $11,480. And if you are able to get 9% average total return for 30 years, the same $2,000 increases to $26,540.

But what if you only have 15 years for your investment to grow? What if your $2,000 contribution is being made at age 55?

Look at Figure 4.1, the compound interest chart. If you can earn 6% annually for 15 years, your $2,000 increases to $4,800. If you get 9%, your $2,000 increases to $7,280.

Far more of the increase in the value of your portfolio occurs in the 16th through 30th years than in the 1st through 15th years, as shown in Figure 4.2. The reason for this is fairly simple. Each year the pot of money that is growing is bigger than it was the previous year. Or, in other words, you are able to see the impact over time of investment earnings growing on investment earnings.

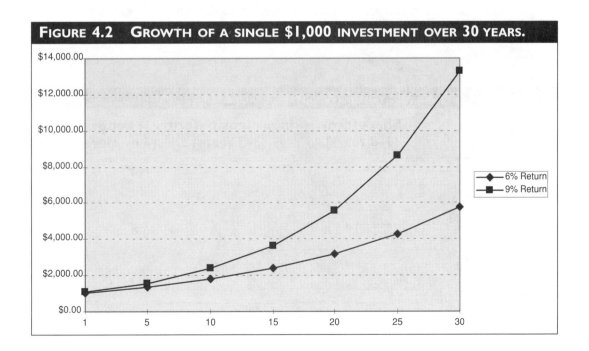

FIGURE 4.2   GROWTH OF A SINGLE $1,000 INVESTMENT OVER 30 YEARS.

THE STEP-BY-STEP INVESTMENT PORTFOLIO DESIGN PROCESS

When you have money to invest, you go through a five-step process of designing an investment portfolio, using the following steps.

1. Determine your investment goals.
2. Understand your investor profile.
3. Understand your investment choices.
4. Determine your investment mix.
5. Monitor your portfolio.

STEP 1 | DETERMINE YOUR INVESTMENT GOALS

The first step in the investment planning process is determining your goals (see Figure 4.3). In order to determine your strategy, you need to consider the time horizon of those goals. In the case we are discussing in this book, it's easy. You are investing for retirement. Retirement is almost always considered a long-term goal because you may spend 20 to 30 years in retirement, and you are not going to need all of the money on one day.

FIGURE 4.3 WHAT ARE YOUR INVESTMENT GOALS?			
Goals	**Short Term (1–3 Years)**	**Intermediate Term (3–7 Years)**	**Long Term (7 or More Years)**
Car Purchase	⟶		
Vacation	⟶		
Home Purchase	⟶		
College	⟶		
Retirement	⟶		

But you may have other goals—perhaps a home, a college education, a new car, a special vacation. For each one of these goals, you will ideally create a separate investment portfolio.

STEP 2 UNDERSTAND YOUR INVESTOR PROFILE

Typically, there are three factors that you should consider in determining your personal investor profile:

1. When do you need the money (time horizon)?
2. How comfortable are you with change in value (risk tolerance)?
3. What rate of return do you need (investment objective)?

These are the "golden rules" of investment planning, We have broken down investor profiles into three main categories: conservative, moderate, and aggressive. Target rate of return, risk tolerance, and time horizon help define each category. You may be a very different type of investor for each of your different investment goals due to different time horizons and risk tolerance. For example, if your investment goal is to save money for the purchase of a new car in the next two years, you may be a very conservative investor with these savings since you have a need for high liquidity, low risk tolerance, and a low need for a high target rate of return. Ideally, you would like to always find investments that are low risk and give a high return. But, unfortunately, the relationship between risk and return tends to work in the same direction. In addition, as your time horizon gets longer, typically your risk tolerance and target rate of return may also get higher.

Figure 4.4 helps identify the key criteria for each of these different types of investors.

The second key point in determining your investor profile is determining your risk tolerance. How much fluctuation in the value of your investment can you handle? The ideal investment would provide a high rate of return with very little risk. Unfortunately, there is no such investment.

In the investment world, there is a direct correlation between risk and return: The higher the potential return, the greater the risk. Risk cannot be avoided, it can only be managed.

When you think of risk, you are most likely thinking of the possibility of losing all or a portion of the value of your investment. It's important to understand and manage that view of risk, but there is another model of risk that is just as dangerous. That is the risk that your investments will not maintain their purchasing power. In other words, your money is still there in the years ahead but it doesn't buy you very much.

FIGURE 4.4 INVESTOR PROFILES.			
	Short Term	**Intermediate Term**	**Long Term**
Target Rate of Return	Low (2–6%)	Medium (7–9%)	High (10%+)
Objective	Liquidity, Stable Value	Income, Some Growth	Growth
Risk Tolerance	Conservative (little to no price fluctuation)	Moderate (some price fluctuation)	Aggressive (greater price fluctuation)
Years to Goal	1–3 years	3–7 years	More than 7 years
Liquidity Need	High	Moderate	Low

The key to successful investing is learning to balance both views of risk. To do so, you need to manage different types of risk as you create your ideal investment portfolio.

Risk 1: Inflation Risk

This is the risk of inflation eroding the purchasing power of your investments. Let's look at a very simple example of inflation risk. Say you have $5,000 you want to invest in a certificate of deposit (CD). Suppose inflation is currently running at about 3%. If you purchase a CD with a one-year maturity, you might earn 3.5%—0.5% above inflation. If you are willing to take a two-year CD, you might earn 4%, and if you are willing to take a five-year CD, you might earn 5%.

Taking a look at current economic conditions, suppose you feel pretty confident that inflation will continue to run somewhere between 3% and maybe 3.5% for the next year, so there's little inflation risk in a one-year CD.

But how much confidence do you have that inflation will remain relatively tame for five years? Many of us remember how rapidly inflation rose in the late 1970s. Is 5% interest—2% above the current rate of inflation—enough to entice you to take that risk? Thought of the other way, if you are willing to accept more inflation risk—by extending the term you are willing to hold the CD—you can get a higher interest rate for the entire length of time you invest and beat inflation with a federally insured bank deposit.

Risk 2: Credit Risk

This is the risk that an individual creditor will not be able to pay its debts. This is important if you are thinking of investing in corporate bonds. What's the likelihood the company you choose to lend money to by purchasing a bond will be able to pay you back? How do you find out?

In this country, there are bond-rating services—Moody's and Standard & Poor's—that grade corporations on their historic ability to repay as well as their current business fundamentals. You should look for bonds carrying the highest ratings, such as AAA or A$^+$.

The greater the possibility of the company having a problem repaying bonds, the more the company has to offer bondholders in the form of interest to entice people to buy. If you are willing to assume more risk of non-payment, you can earn a higher interest rate.

One way to accept some but not all of this risk is to invest in a mutual fund that in turn invests in more risky corporate bonds. In this way, if one bond issuer has difficulty repaying, you still own bits and pieces of investments in dozens if not hundreds of companies that are repaying.

Risk 3: Interest Rate Risk

Interest rate risk is another risk you accept when you buy bonds. Let's say that you buy a 10-year U.S. Treasury bond, which pays interest of 6% a year. Treasury bonds pay their interest twice a year, so for a $10,000 bond, you receive a check for $300 and another check for $300 six months later.

Remember, you don't have to hold bonds until they mature. There is a market for bonds at any point in their lifetime.

Interest rate risk can be illustrated in two ways.

First, let's say interest rates are rising. One year after you buy your bond, the interest rate offered on 10-year Treasury bonds is 6.5%. Your bond is now worth less on the open market than its face value. That's because if someone bought your bond, he or she would be accepting a smaller interest payment than if he or she bought a new bond. In order to accept less interest, a buyer would want you to "discount" the price of the bond so that over the remaining life, he or she will have earned 6.5% of the amount paid.

The flip side of interest-rate risk is falling rates. This may not seem to be a problem, given the fact that you would then have an interest rate locked in that is *higher than* the prevailing rate. But in the case of falling rates, it will be harder to find ways to invest your $300 interest payments and generate acceptable returns. This is also known as reinvestment risk.

To get around the falling-interest-rate risk, some investors purchase what are known as zero-coupon bonds. These bonds do not generate periodic interest payments. Instead they are sold at a discount so that at maturity they return the full face amount.

For instance, the State of Israel sold bonds in the United States in the summer of 1996 to pay for infrastructure roads, bridges, airports, housing, and so on. The bonds had a face value of $6,000, payable in 10 years, in 2006, and offered an *effective yield* of 7.5%. The cost of each bond was $2,840. The $2,840 purchase price, with a constantly compounding 7.5% annual interest rate, brings the bondholder a payment of $6,000 at maturity 10 years later.

The downside of taxable zero-coupon bonds is that you are taxed on the interest the bond earns each year even though the interest is not paid to you but rather added to the value of the bond.

Risk 4: Market/Business Risk

This is the risk you accept when you purchase stocks. Business risk is the risk that the value of an individual business—and hence the stock it issues—will decline. Market risk is the risk that the entire stock market or the segment of the market in which you have invested will lose value.

The best way to mitigate business risk is to invest in a broad portfolio of stocks, most easily through purchasing shares in mutual funds. The best way to decrease your market risk is to invest for a long period of time. You will find that the amount of risk, or "bounce," your money experiences will decrease substantially the longer you hold onto the investment. Thinking long term (i.e., more than 20 years) helps reduce risk.

Risk 5: Risk of Outliving Your Money

This is probably the biggest risk retirees face. In order to mitigate this risk, you may need to accept more of the other risks than you have previously thought.

This may sound frightening. It may even seem to be illogical. You may think of yourself as a person who doesn't like risk, and shies away from it, especially with regard to your investments. But stay with us here as we explain why risk is necessary and very tolerable.

First, you have to change your basic concept of risk. Stop thinking of risk as linear, as shown here:

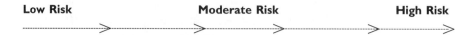

Instead, think of risk more as a pentagon, with each type of risk stationed at one of the five points on the pentagon, as seen in Figure 4.5. By looking at

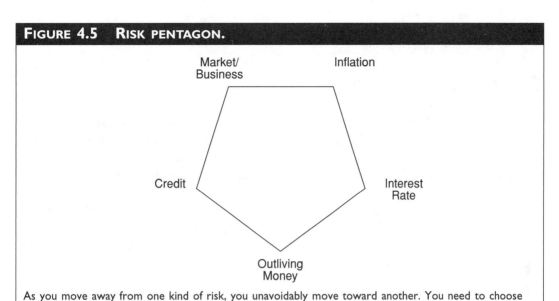

FIGURE 4.5   RISK PENTAGON.

Market/
Business

Inflation

Credit

Interest
Rate

Outliving
Money

As you move away from one kind of risk, you unavoidably move toward another. You need to choose the trade-off that you feel is right.

risk this way, you can see that you can never really avoid risk; you can only trade off one risk for another, or find a place where the risks balance out.

The marketplace for various kinds of investments has created a rank order of these risks. This ranking can be determined by looking at the potential rewards involved. The market tells us that it is willing to reward investors who accept the greatest amount of market/business risk by investing in stock and those who are willing to accept the greatest amount of credit risk by investing in bonds of companies that are not considered to be good credit risks.

Remember our discussion of total return. In order to achieve more return, you will need to accept more market and credit risk. Investing in mutual funds can minimize that risk for investors with smaller portfolios.

Now that you have an idea of what kind of investor you are, we need to review your investment choices and how they fit into your profile matrix. That is the third step in the investment process.

STEP 3   UNDERSTAND YOUR INVESTMENT CHOICES

There are four primary categories of investment choices, also known as asset classes. Each asset class or investment choice has a different risk and return level:

1. Cash and cash equivalents
2. Fixed income securities

3. Equities (stocks)
4. Hard assets

Cash and Equivalents

Cash and equivalents are the most conservative type of investment asset class. They tend to pay interest income, have less than two years to maturity, and have little or no fluctuation in value. Examples of cash and equivalents include Treasury bills, savings accounts, money market funds, and certificates of deposit.

Historically, investments in cash and equivalents have yielded just a little above inflation before taxes, meaning that your retirement fund will only grow at close to the same rate at which inflation is growing if you maintain your retirement savings in bank deposits or money market funds.

Fixed-Income Securities

Fixed-income securities tend to pay a higher rate of interest income, have a maturity of greater than or equal to two years, and have some fluctuation in value. Examples of fixed-income securities are corporate and municipal bonds, certificates of deposits, and fixed-income mutual funds.

Basically, if you want to be a lender, you can deposit your money in a bank, where others will borrow it, or you can lend your money by buying bond mutual funds or individual bonds, such as U.S. savings bonds. You will earn a rate of interest, which will be less if you need to have your money available at all times and more if you are willing to leave your money in a CD for a longer time.

Another way to be a lender is to invest in bonds, either by purchasing individual bonds or by investing in a bond mutual fund. The bond issuer (borrower) promises to pay the bond buyer (lender) a rate of interest over the life of the bond and return the bond's full face value at maturity. You also can buy or sell bonds before they mature, creating opportunity for capital gain or loss because of the relationship between the bond's interest rate and the rate being offered on new bonds of a similar maturity issued by the same issuer. (This is explained in detail below.)

Historically, investments in intermediate-term (10 years) and long-term (30 years) U.S. Treasury bonds have yielded 2 to 3% above the rate of inflation, before taxes, meaning that you can expect some growth in real terms by having your retirement savings in Treasury bonds. Corporate bonds have a higher yield, but you sacrifice the safety of knowing that your principal will be paid back at maturity, as with Treasury bonds.

EQUITIES (STOCKS)

By investing in stocks you are basically owning a portion of a company. Equities may or may not pay dividends, have potential for growth in value, and have a greater fluctuation in value. There are three primary categories of equities, including large company stocks, small company stocks, and foreign stocks.

Ownership in private enterprise, through the purchase of stocks, has historically been the way to increase retirement savings. The average rate of return on a balanced, diversified portfolio of U.S. stocks since World War II has been about 6% above inflation. That's twice the rate of bonds.

Increasingly, working Americans saving for their retirement who wish to become stock owners are turning to mutual funds. Mutual funds are pools of money, managed by professional investment managers, created by regulated investment companies that exist under strict guidelines of the Securities and Exchange Commission (SEC).

A mutual fund, or other pooled-investment fund such as a unit trust, gives a small investor the opportunity to own shares in a portfolio, which in turn owns shares in many companies. This gives each individual the ability to invest a relatively small amount of money in a well-diversified portfolio and to have that money managed professionally.

Many mutual funds offer the ability to make an initial investment of as small as $500 for a tax-deferred retirement savings account and will accept additional investments of as little as $100 after that.

Some mutual funds invest in both stocks and bonds. These are sometimes called balanced funds because they allow you to diversify your portfolio by including these two types of financial assets in one mutual fund.

HARD ASSETS

Hard assets are tangible assets—something you can see or touch; they provide little liquidity, have the potential for growth in value, and may have a greater fluctuation in value. Typically, hard assets are used as a hedge against inflation over the long term. Examples of hard assets include real estate, natural resources, precious metals, and collectibles.

For purposes of this discussion, we are going to focus on the first three investment choices—cash, fixed income, and equities—since they are the more common investment choices. Let's look at the historical performance of these three investment choices and compare them to inflation. (See Figure 4.6.)

You can see the last 73 years of investment performance by asset class. We have illustrated the historical long-term growth and average annualized returns of each asset class by putting it in dollar terms—showing you the growth of $1 by asset class from 1926 through 1999.

As you can see, Treasury bills tend to track inflation and are relatively stable; thus they do not offer much growth over the long term. Long-term bonds have some fluctuation in value but still do not have nearly as much growth as stocks. Stocks have generated the highest rate of return over the long term but also have the greatest amount of volatility. Does this mean that you should invest all your retirement assets in stocks? Of course not, because past performance is no guarantee of future performance, and you need to think about your investment objective, risk tolerance, and time horizon as you select your investment choices.

At this point, we've reviewed the general characteristics of each asset class, but now we should focus on the risk/return characteristics of each class. Based on our prior discussion of the different types of risk, it is important to emphasize that risk cannot be avoided, only managed. As you recall, some of the primary risks we focused on were:

• *Market risk:* the chance that an investment will go up or down in value, particularly in the short term

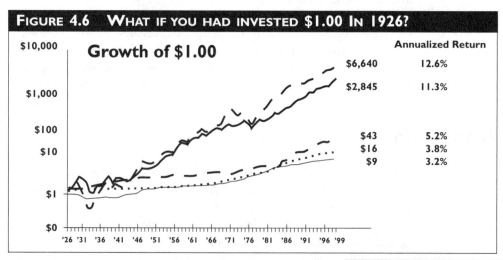

FIGURE 4.6 WHAT IF YOU HAD INVESTED $1.00 IN 1926?

	Annualized Return
$6,640	12.6%
$2,845	11.3%
$43	5.2%
$16	3.8%
$9	3.2%

Legend:
— — Small Stocks
——— Large Stocks
- - - Government Bonds
...... T-Bills
——— Inflation

Past performance is no guarantee of future results.

- *Business risk:* the uncertainty surrounding a company's earnings and ability to meet obligations or pay dividends
- *Inflation risk:* the possibility that you will not earn enough money to offset the increases in cost of living; if your investment return over a given period is lower than the inflation rate, you lose buying power

The following are ways to manage these risks.

Holding period or long-term time horizon is a way to manage *market risk*. If you look at a one-year, five-year, or twenty-year holding period for stocks, you see the average return is almost the same, but the fluctuation in value for a one-year holding period is so much more significant than for a five-year or twenty-year period. Bonds also fluctuate in value, more so in a one-year holding period compared to a five- or twenty-year holding period, but the returns for bonds is half of what the returns for stocks have been. Treasury bills are stable in value regardless of the holding period, but as you can see, have earned a return that is about what inflation was. Therefore, an investment mix of stocks, bonds, and cash is a way to meet both long-term and short-term goals and manage market risk, as shown in Figure 4.7.

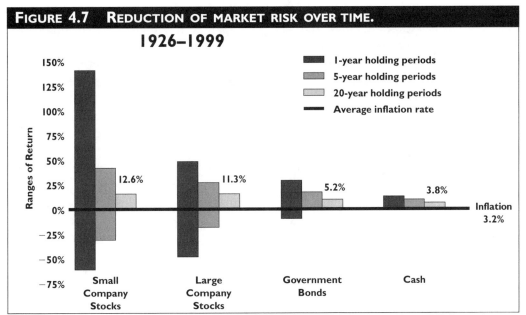

FIGURE 4.7 REDUCTION OF MARKET RISK OVER TIME.

Each bar shows the range of compound annual returns for each asset class over the period 1926 to 1999. Past performance is no guarantee of future results.
Source: Stocks, Bonds, Bills and Inflation 2000 Yearbook, © 2000 Ibbotson Associates, Inc. Based on copyrighted works by Ibbotson and Sinquefield. All rights reserved. Used with permission.

Diversification of asset classes and investments is a way to manage *business risk.* "Diversification" means that you invest in different types of investments within an asset class (e.g., small-company stocks, large-company stocks, different industries, etc.) to help offset the potential risk of loss on any one investment. You want to make sure that you're investing in a sufficient number of securities, different size companies, and a variety of industries. The concept applies to all asset classes.

Asset allocation or a mix of asset classes is a way to manage *inflation risk.* By holding assets classes in a portion of your portfolio that historically have outpaced inflation, you are able to manage inflation risk.

To summarize, you can manage risks through a long-term strategy of investment mix and diversification. Your investment mix or asset allocation is one way to balance your risk and return over the long term.

STEP 4   DETERMINE YOUR INVESTMENT

We've all heard the adage "Don't put all your eggs in one basket."

An individual with $30,000 in a retirement savings account could realistically own blocks of shares in, at most, probably only 10 individual companies. But by investing that $30,000 in one, two, or three mutual funds with different investing philosophies, you can own shares in a pool that owns shares in literally hundreds of companies. If some companies suffer losses in stock price, others may be increasing.

Of course, you pay for the privilege of sharing market risk with your fellow investors in the mutual fund—a 1 to 2% annual service charge that is factored into the share value of the mutual fund at any time.

The same is true for any investment you want to have in corporate bonds. By investing through mutual funds, you get diversification and minimization of credit risk.

Now let's look at what is called portfolio risk—the amount of risk you are willing to accept in all five areas across your investment holdings. Again, the concept of not putting all your eggs in one basket is a good one. You can reduce portfolio risk by investing in assets and even asset classes that behave differently from one another. This is what is meant by diversifying your portfolio.

You can use your knowledge of investments and your understanding of risk and return to structure an investment portfolio.

Diversification theory is based on the premise that the market values of some assets tend to rise and fall together, whereas the market values of other assets move in opposite directions. Factors independent of the financial characteristics of a particular investment, such as economic, political, and social events, also can affect their values. While portfolio risk cannot be totally eliminated, it can be reduced by constructing a diversified portfolio that contains a mix of asset types whose values have historically moved in opposite directions or in the same direction but to a greater or lesser magnitude.

If you're searching for a particular rate of return, you could combine various assets together to generate this expected return. Many portfolios might provide the same expected return (based on the assets' historical average returns), but these portfolios would have different risks.

If you're shrewd, you would select the portfolio that meets your return goal but has the lowest possible risk. This is the objective of what is often called *asset allocation*. Asset allocation simply means investing in different types of assets so as to have a diversified portfolio with the highest expected return at a given level of risk. Computer software asset allocation models can help you identify the asset allocation with the highest expected return for a given level of risk.

Figure 4.8 shows three possible investment allocations for retirement investments for each of three different stages in life. Of course, these asset allocation models only go to the first level of complexity, whether the assets are stocks, bonds, or cash. Within each of these broad categories, there are a number of options, each of which presents a different historical return as well as a different level of risk.

For instance, within the broad category of stocks, you can buy "blue chip" stocks, which are companies that have large market capitalization and are household names; there are also growth stocks, mid-size company stocks, and small-company stocks. There are also foreign stocks. The total value of a company's outstanding stock is called the company's market capitalization. Stocks in small-capitalization companies are called small-cap stocks and stocks in middle-size companies are called mid-cap stocks. Guess what stocks of large-capitalization companies are called?

For stock mutual fund investors, funds often categorize themselves as small-cap funds; mid-cap funds; growth-stock funds, which invest in stocks of rapidly growing companies; growth and income funds, which invest in some growth companies and some companies that pay dividends; foreign funds; or sector funds, which invest in narrow market areas such as healthcare or technology or banks.

There are also funds that invest in all the companies that are listed on a certain stock index. A number of mutual fund companies run S&P 500 index funds, which invest in all of the companies in the Standard and Poor's index of 500 stocks. Some investment advisors argue that over a 20-year or longer time horizon, an investment in an S&P 500 index fund is possibly the best one for a small investor. Historically, the S&P 500 index has grown faster than 90% of all managed mutual funds over any 20-year period.

FIGURE 4.8   SAMPLE INVESTMENT MIXES.

These are just sample mixes of investment funds. You may be able to mix and match the funds in different ways and still achieve a similar long-term return and risk profile.

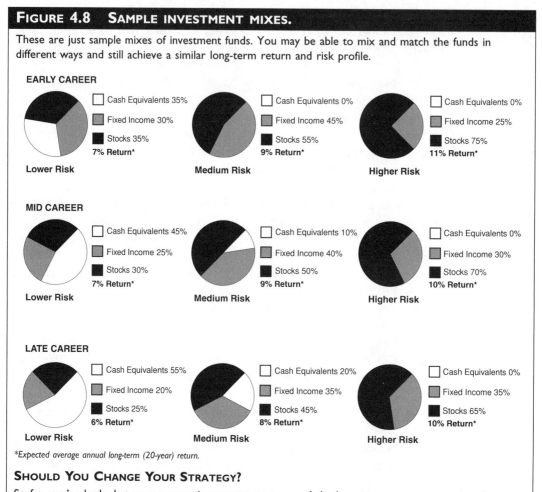

EARLY CAREER

Cash Equivalents 35%
Fixed Income 30%
Stocks 35%
7% Return*
Lower Risk

Cash Equivalents 0%
Fixed Income 45%
Stocks 55%
9% Return*
Medium Risk

Cash Equivalents 0%
Fixed Income 25%
Stocks 75%
11% Return*
Higher Risk

MID CAREER

Cash Equivalents 45%
Fixed Income 25%
Stocks 30%
7% Return*
Lower Risk

Cash Equivalents 10%
Fixed Income 40%
Stocks 50%
9% Return*
Medium Risk

Cash Equivalents 0%
Fixed Income 30%
Stocks 70%
10% Return*
Higher Risk

LATE CAREER

Cash Equivalents 55%
Fixed Income 20%
Stocks 25%
6% Return*
Lower Risk

Cash Equivalents 20%
Fixed Income 35%
Stocks 45%
8% Return*
Medium Risk

Cash Equivalents 0%
Fixed Income 35%
Stocks 65%
10% Return*
Higher Risk

*Expected average annual long-term (20-year) return.

SHOULD YOU CHANGE YOUR STRATEGY?

So far, you've looked at your current investment strategy and the long-term return you project from that strategy. You've also explored a number of investment options available to you. Does adjusting your investment strategy help you eliminate any of your shortfall?

You should not try to achieve your planned asset allocation overnight. For reallocating your investments, consider a strategy that will help you to be less affected by the market at any point in time.

You can implement your new allocation for your total investment strategy over time. For example, for your retirement savings in your 401(k) plan, you can change how your future contributions to it are invested or by reallocating existing balances gradually. Move some money now and then make monthly or quarterly changes over the next 6 to 18 months.

■ To see an example of the power of diversification and the acceptance of risk, let's look at two small investment portfolios and how they are invested.

Frank and Laurie are married and both are 45. Frank is conservative with his money. He invests his $10,000 of retirement savings in Treasury bonds that carry a yield of 7%. He earns that 7% year in and year out for 25 years.

Laurie believes in taking risks with her money. She splits her $10,000 retirement savings fund into five investments of $2,000 each.

After 25 years, one investment has not earned anything; it has remained worth $2,000. A second investment has earned 4% annually. Her third investment earned a 7% average annual total return, the same as her husband earned on his entire investment. Her fourth investment earned an average annual total return of 10%. And her final investment earned an average annual total return of 15%.

At age 70, they both begin taking withdrawals from their retirement accounts. Frank's fund is worth $54,272. Laurie's is worth $105,695. ■

Figure 4.9 shows some steps you can take in order to manage the various forms of risk.

Once you have determined your target asset allocation, you need to implement your strategy. The first step in implementing your strategy is to determine your current asset allocation. We have provided in Figure 4.10 a worksheet to help you identify your current asset allocation. You then need to compare where you are currently relative to your target asset allocation. At that point, you can determine which asset classes need to be increased or decreased in value so that you can achieve your target asset allocation.

FIGURE 4.9 YOU CANNOT AVOID ALL RISKS: YOU CAN ONLY ACCEPT AND MANAGE RISKS.

Risk	How to Manage
Inflation risk	Be an owner as well as a lender
Credit risk	Diversify and buy higher quality
Interest rate risk	Stagger maturities
Market/business risk	Set investment mix, diversify, and hold onto for long periods of time
Outliving your money	Plan

FIGURE 4.10 OVERALL ASSET ALLOCATION WORKSHEET.

Asset Class	A Current Allocation	B Current Allocation	C Planned Allocation	D Planned Allocation	A–C Change $	B–D Change %
Cash Equivalents:						
Checking/Savings Accounts	$ _____		$ _____		$ _____	
Short-Term CDs	$ _____		$ _____		$ _____	
Money Market	$ _____		$ _____		$ _____	
Other	$ _____		$ _____		$ _____	
Subtotal	$ _____	_____ %	$ _____	_____ %	$ _____	_____ %
Fixed Income:						
401(k)	$ _____		$ _____		$ _____	
Bonds	$ _____		$ _____		$ _____	
Other	$ _____		$ _____		$ _____	
Subtotal	$ _____	_____ %	$ _____	_____ %	$ _____	_____ %
Equities:						
Stock Options	$ _____		$ _____		$ _____	
401(k)	$ _____		$ _____		$ _____	
Other	$ _____		$ _____		$ _____	
Other	$ _____		$ _____		$ _____	
Other	$ _____		$ _____		$ _____	
Subtotal	$ _____	_____ %	$ _____	_____ %	$ _____	_____ %
Hard Assets:						
Real Estate	$ _____		$ _____		$ _____	
Collectibles	$ _____		$ _____		$ _____	
Other	$ _____		$ _____		$ _____	
Subtotal	$ _____	_____ %	$ _____	_____ %	$ _____	_____ %
TOTAL	$ _____	_____ %	$ _____	_____ %	$ _____	_____ %

Some of the easiest ways to increase or decrease allocations to certain asset classes include the following:

- Move existing balances gradually: Liquidate from certain asset classes (be careful of any adverse tax consequences in doing this) and increase exposure in another asset class.
- Redirect new savings into asset classes that need to be increased.
- A combination of both strategies.

When reallocating existing balances, it is often preferable to first reallocate within tax-deferred plans, such as your IRAs or company 401(k) plans, since there is no tax cost (i.e., capital gains) associated with liquidating investments and reallocating to other investment choices.

STEP 5 ■ MONITOR YOUR PORTFOLIO

It's important to monitor your portfolio, not so much in terms of individual investments as to see what changes in your own or your company's circumstances might cause you to change your portfolio structure.

Remember, because you are investing for the long term, for retirement, you can live with dips in the market or in individual investments. In addition, if you are investing in a tax-deferred retirement account, there is no reason to sell investments at a loss, since they are not deductible.

At least on an annual basis, you should be monitoring your investment plan. Most importantly, you should be reevaluating your goals and objectives in investing, reviewing the investment return you need to meet your goals as well as considering whether your investor profile still remains the same.

Four other things that you may be looking for in assessing whether you should adjust your portfolio include:

1. *Changes in the plan.* If your employer switches the investment options in your plan, and you are suddenly offered investment options you have not had before, you may want to adjust your portfolio accordingly. If the company changes its policy on how much it matches your contributions, this may change the total going into your plan, which in turn could change the return you need to generate in order to fund your retirement.
2. *Changes in your health,* or in the health of a family member, spouse, parent, or child could impact your goals and objectives in investing.
3. *A major change to the Social Security system*—such as raising the normal age for full retirement benefits again or changing the benefit formula— that has an effect on what you can expect from the system could also change the return you need to generate in order to fund your retirement.

4. *Dramatic changes in the economy* that fundamentally alter the assumptions about how you must fund your retirement.

A WORD ABOUT REBALANCING

One technique that you can use to keep your investments on track is called rebalancing. Rebalancing periodically helps to bring your portfolio back into the *balance* you designated at some earlier time (that is, back to your target asset allocation).

Using Figure 4.11, let's say that you are in mid-career and can tolerate a high level of risk. A hypothetical asset allocation for that situation is 70% stocks and 30% bonds.

If you had set up a portfolio with this allocation on the first day of the year, by the end of the year your portfolio would have been drastically out of balance. That is because during the year the stock market went way up and the bond market didn't do as well.

At the beginning of the new year, in order to rebalance your portfolio, you would have had to sell some of your stock holdings and buy more bonds.

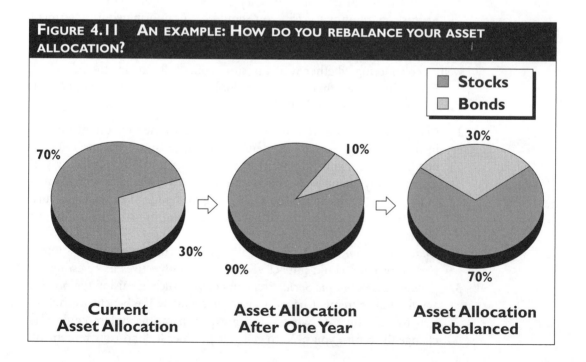

FIGURE 4.11   AN EXAMPLE: HOW DO YOU REBALANCE YOUR ASSET ALLOCATION?

Stocks
Bonds

70%   30%   **Current Asset Allocation**

10%   90%   **Asset Allocation After One Year**

30%   70%   **Asset Allocation Rebalanced**

Some people don't wait for the end of the year; they rebalance their portfolio every time one asset class or another drifts, say, 10% away from its desired place. Money managers who manage large portfolios for private investors, and mutual fund managers who manage large portfolios for fundholders, often rebalance their portfolios as frequently as every week.

When you rebalance, you will want to remember and take into account that you may owe income taxes when you sell some of your investments. Some investors will rebalance more gradually by redirecting more of their ongoing investments (e.g., monthly) to the kind of asset they are trying to accumulate more of.

Portfolio rebalancing is based on the notion that you don't want a static portfolio but rather one that is both dynamic—moving with the market—yet fixed in how the asset classes relate to each other.

A WORD ABOUT INDEXING

You may be like many people who are confused by the multitude of mutual funds in the marketplace today. You see a lot of advertising from mutual funds about their one-, five-, and ten-year average total return (assuming reinvested dividends and capital gains). You read about "hot" managers leaving one mutual fund to go to another, or to start their own company.

If chasing fads, looking for hot managers, and keeping track of the top actively managed stock mutual funds is simply too much for you or not what you want to do, you should consider putting the portion of your portfolio that is in stock mutual funds into an index fund or a few index funds.

Index funds buy shares of most or all the companies that make up an index, in effect mirroring the index itself. As the index moves, the fund moves.

The most popular index for mutual funds to mirror is the Standard and Poor's 500 index. The S&P 500 has been designed by the Standard and Poor's company as an index that has a representative sampling of large U.S. companies from all of the major segments in the economy.

It is estimated that, in any given year, the S&P 500 outperforms at least 50% of all actively managed stock mutual funds and in some years it outperforms more than 75% of the actively managed funds.

You can become a millionaire in retirement if:

1. You can put away $5,000 each year into a tax-deferred savings plan beginning at age 35.
2. You can wait until the mandatory withdrawal age of 70½ before beginning withdrawals from this pool of money.

3. You can earn a steady 10% total return for that 36-year period.

If you had put that entire investment into the stocks of the S&P 500 for any 36-year period beginning at the end of World War II, you would have been successful.

Since the end of World War II, the S&P 500 has returned an average of 11.8% a year including reinvested dividends. There have been 16 calendar years when the index has returned over 20%, 10 years when it has returned over 30%, and one year when it returned over 50%. The worst decade for the S&P 500 since World War II was the 1970s when the index returned an average of 5.8% annually.

Many stock mutual funds invest in other indexes, such as the Russell 2000® or Wilshire 4500 (two indexes of smaller American companies) or in indexes of international companies.

TRAPS, OBSTACLES, TOOLS, AND HELPERS

Watch out for the following traps and obstacles, and try to use the following tools and helpers.

- Investing in anything you don't understand
- Investing in anything that seems too good to be true
- Not linking each investment to a specific goal
- Losing sight of the real after-tax rate of return on your investments
- Investing in anything that causes you to lose sleep at night
- Thinking of risk as linear
- Hoping to avoid all investment risk
- Chasing last year's highest-performing mutual funds
- Market timing
- Reacting to daily swings in the Dow Jones Industrial Average
- Not taking full advantage of employer-sponsored tax-deferred retirement plans and employer matching contributions
- Having tax-exempt bonds or tax-exempt bond funds in IRAs
- Overinvesting in the stock of one company
- Focusing only on the risk of losing money and overlooking the risk that your money will not be worth much when you need it
- Risk tolerance quizzes that attempt to associate financial risk with personal adventuresome activities

- Holding only bonds or only equities
- Risk in all of its forms
- Constantly changing and confusing investment product marketplace
- Investment expenses

- Compound interest tables
- Credit risk rating services
- Risk tolerance worksheets
- Ibbotson Associates data on historical investment performance since 1926
- Morningstar® Inc. data on U.S. equity (large, medium, and small value, blend, and growth), international, and fixed-income mutual funds
- Indices like the S&P 500 (broad U.S. stock market), Russell 2000, or Wilshire 4500 (small-company stocks), Morgan Stanley Capital International's Europe, Australia, and Far East (EAFE) index (international securities), and International Finance Corp.'s emerging market index

- Time horizon
- Asset allocation among different asset classes
- Diversification within each asset class
- Rebalancing
- Total return
- Compounding
- Reinvested dividends
- Dollar-cost averaging
- Pretax and tax-deferred plans
- Mutual funds
- Securities and Exchange Commission efforts to simplify mutual fund prospectus standards
- Lower tax rate on long-term capital gains

ACTION ITEMS		
Item	**Priority***	**Completed**
1. Invest, ideally with pretax dollars, a set percentage of pay in a tax-deferred retirement savings plan. Invest at least the amount into your company plan (if you have one) that will get the maximum company match. (We'll discuss this in greater detail in Chapter 6.)		
2. Increase your investment each year, not just in dollar terms but as a percentage of pay, until you reach the maximum allowable pretax investment by law or by the terms of the company plan. (If you have reached the maximum and still have money you don't need for immediate or shorter-term goals, open a Roth IRA.)		
3. Diversify. The best way to do this for most of us is through investing in mutual funds. Many people wonder how much of their money they should put in their employer's stock. Ultimately, this is a personal decision that depends on the particular company and your personal circumstances. But, you should consider three things: • First, typically you have several "baskets" of retirement assets, including the value of Social Security and defined benefit pensions that are really like interest-bearing investments. Even if your 401(k) plan is heavily invested in your company's stock, your entire retirement savings may be well balanced. • Second, the "bounce" of investing in stocks is smoothed out the longer you hold them. • Third, you need to judge the prospects for the company.		
4. Become an owner rather than a lender, at least with a part of your portfolio. This means investing in stocks rather than bonds, money market accounts, CDs, and guaranteed investment contracts (GICs) also called stable value investments.		

ACTION ITEMS (continued)

Item	Priority*	Completed
5. Take the five-step approach to investing: • Step 1: Determine your goals 　a. How much? 　b. When do I need it? • Step 2: Understand your investor profile 　a. Understand risks: inflation risk, credit risk, interest rate risk, market/business risk, risk of outliving your money • Step 3: Understand your investment choices 　a. Cash and equivalents 　b. Fixed Income securities 　c. Equities 　d. Hard Assets • Step 4: Set your investment mix • Step 5: Monitor your portfolio		
6. Reevaluate your risk tolerance annually. Many students of investing note that individuals' tolerance for risk seems to *increase* as a factor of their getting older, as a factor of an increased amount of investable cash, and as a factor of their familiarity with investing.		
7. Monitor your portfolio and rebalance it to return it to your desired asset allocation. Determine the criteria under which you will rebalance. This may be once a year, or it may be when the market moves in such a way that asset classes become out of balance by, say, 10%.		

*A, B, C, or N/A, with A being the highest priority.

5

LIFESTYLE

The amount of retirement income you need depends on the lifestyle you wish to maintain. This sounds like a simple statement. But think about it carefully.

Many retirement planning advisors say that the amount of retirement income you need is whatever it takes to finance the lifestyle you have in the year before you retire. But who says that's the lifestyle you desire in retirement? Let's think for a moment about the lifestyle changes most of us go through during the course of our lives.

Most of us start out after finishing our schooling—be it high school, college, postgraduate schooling, or training—and getting our first job by either continuing to live at home with our folks or renting an apartment and furnishing it in what might be called "early Goodwill" style. A sofa from Grandma, a secondhand dining-room set, the television from home, you get the picture. We drive a used car, eat out a lot, go to the movies often, sit in the bleachers when we go to see the home team, buy soda by the case, and generally celebrate our adulthood. But we don't save a nickel!

Of course, this is a generalization. There are homebodies, entrepreneurs, and investors in the 20-something crowd, but let's face it, almost all of us went through a period of life something like the one just described for anywhere from one to 10 years.

By the time we're 30 or so we've had a couple of raises, maybe moved up to a more responsible position, possibly changed jobs once or twice. Many of us are married; some have families. Perhaps it's the time to look for a house—the federal government says that in the third quarter of 1996,

65.7% of American households owned their own home, the highest percentage since 1980. How about a washer and dryer so we don't have to go to the laundromat, and a 25-inch television with VCR? We should really buy that first new car.

What do we have in the way of savings? Not much.

Some of us have started taking advantage of that big helper, putting a few dollars into the 401(k) at work, if one is offered. But others have fallen into one of the big traps—pulling out the credit card and charging anything we want, figuring we'll pay it back with the next raise.

Our lifestyle is getting more "middle class." It's not grand, but we're finding ways to spend all or almost all of our income.

By 45, despite the fact that the two kids are getting toward their teens and we've got to start thinking about college, we really need to buy a bigger house or build an addition. Even if Mom and Dad aren't both working outside the home, we need two cars. And they cannot be unreliable; aren't there jobs to get to and kids to shuttle around?

We can afford it, since in the past 15 years there have been annual increases in pay, more responsibility, another job change, a couple of years with bonuses.

Have we saved? A little. The 401(k) is helpful. Each kid has a bank account, and we put a little in there each year, along with the birthday and holiday money from the grandparents. There's $2,000 in the checking account at all times in case of an emergency. But it is amazing that as we earn more, we keep creating a "wealthier" lifestyle.

The kids go to camp and take music and tennis lessons. We've joined a health club. We've taken the advice of friends and started leasing new cars for four-year periods. After all, who wants to drive a car for eight years?

The behavior described above is a common problem for many Americans. We call it *Lifestyle Creep*.

LIFESTYLE CREEP

Lifestyle creep occurs when increases in income cause a similar increase in the things you acquire. Think about it—if you make $80,000, why should you live like you make $40,000?

We've all read stories about elderly people who die in rundown homes after years of eating canned soup and crackers every day. When their estates are sorted out, it turns out they were worth $2 million. But who really wants to live like that?

After all, remember what we said in Chapter 3. Every dollar that comes into your possession will be spent—by you, your heirs, or the government. Why not spend it yourself?

Our philosophy is not "don't spend it." Our philosophy is "spend it in ways you find personally fulfilling." You need to be conscious about your spending and not just spend in ways you feel obliged to in order to maintain some arbitrary level of lifestyle.

And remember if you stay healthy, you will need to have some money to spend when you're 80, maybe even 90, or older.

So as you consider your lifestyle today, you need to be considering your lifestyle in retirement. Are you comfortable trading off things for the future for things today? Or would you rather cut back now to have more in the future? For example, perhaps you've given in to some lifestyle creeps but are planning for—looking forward to—a much simpler lifestyle once you retire from full-time employment. Maybe you feel that while you are working you need more comforts. Perhaps you need to buy more clothes. Perhaps you "treat" yourself to compensate for long hours spent in the office or on the road. And you envision that one day you will be content to wear old blue jeans and T-shirts. Perhaps not. Some people envision their retirement years as filled with certain luxuries they did not have during their working years, when their free time was limited and they had many responsibilities, such as the time and cost of raising a family. The point is, you need to examine your current lifestyle and plan for your retirement lifestyle by defining goals and making financial choices.

STOP! LISTEN TO YOUR HEART

Socrates said, "The unexamined life is not worth living."

How many of us are really asking ourselves if we "need" this increasingly wealthy lifestyle? How many of us ask ourselves at the end of each year: "For all the money I've spent, for the level of lifestyle I've created, am I better, worse, or the same as last year?"

Many people will say they are better. And that's terrific. We're certainly not going to tell you not to spend money on what makes you happy and what makes your life more fulfilling. That's not our job. Remember, we're not the experts about how you should live your life; you are.

But if you ask yourself if you're better off and the answer is "No, I'm completely stressed out," and you're worrying that if your business has a dip or if the business your husband works for lays him off, or if he can't continue to get 10 hours a week of overtime, your whole lifestyle will come crumbling down around you, maybe it's time to rethink your priorities.

Sometimes the employment level you achieve drives you into lifestyle creep. At a certain corporate or professional level, you might be expected to entertain clients and other executives, either in your home or at outside dinners.

When you reach a certain level of work, you may also have to pay for services you no longer have time to perform yourself. You may still enjoy cutting the lawn, but your travel schedule might not make it possible. You may enjoy having friends over for a cookout, but you may be forced to entertain clients in more formal settings.

But you can get used to this way of living and decide that you "must" maintain that lifestyle in retirement. Is that really true? And is that what you really will enjoy?

UNFUNDED LIABILITIES

We need to take off our philosophers' hats now and put on our financial planners' hats again.

If you get caught in lifestyle creep, you're going to need huge amounts of money at retirement in order to maintain that lifestyle.

Let's look again at our retirement needs from Chapter 2. If inflation averages 3% a year, it will take $2 in 24 years to buy what it costs $1 to buy today. (Hint: Remember the rule of 72.)

Think about it another way. If at age 21 you have a lifestyle that costs $25,000 a year to maintain—not including payments of taxes or your savings for the future—it will cost $50,000 to maintain that lifestyle at age 45 and $100,000 a year to maintain that lifestyle at age 70, in the early years of retirement.

If by age 45 you've created a lifestyle that costs $80,000 a year to maintain—not including taxes or savings—now you will need $160,000 a year to maintain that lifestyle in retirement.

But you will be funding this lifestyle with income from accumulated assets. How much do you need to accumulate? Roughly speaking, it takes $20 in retirement assets to provide $1 of income for a 20-year period, taking inflation into account during your retirement years.

■ Dale and Kim just learned that $20 of accumulated assets would fund $1 of living expenses at a retirement seminar sponsored by Kim's employer. They are each about 45, and realized after the seminar that they have not saved nearly enough for retirement. They also learned at the seminar that they can reach their retirement goals by doing any one of or a combination of four things:

1. Retiring later or working part-time in retirement
2. Saving more
3. Investing what they save more wisely
4. Changing their lifestyle

On their way home that night, they decided to look at each of the issues separately for each of the next four nights. They decided to think of the lifestyle change issue first, deciding as many people do that looking at the spending side of the equation is probably the most clear-cut. Also, if they could reduce spending they could increase savings.

After dinner the next night, they started categorizing their living expenses in order to determine if there were places to save now and also if there were expenses that would be reduced or eliminated in retirement. They categorized in their own way, lumping items into house, transportation, work, children, vacations, and so on. In each category they determined which items were needs and which were desires.

Let's look at how they thought through one item: cars.

Dale is an insurance claims adjuster. He earns about $50,000 a year. He deals with claims having to do with property damage to homes, businesses, and boats by fire, theft, storms, and so on. His territory extends approximately from Baltimore to Philadelphia, west to Harrisburg, and south to West Virginia. Needless to say, he drives a lot.

Kim is a manager at a company that provides data entry services for credit-card companies and other businesses. She also earns about $50,000 annually. Her commute is about 12 miles each way.

Dale drives about 30,000 miles a year, while Kim drives about 8,000 miles each year. Dale customarily buys a new car every four years. When he gets a new car, Kim drives the old car—which by then has about 120,000 miles—for four more years, adding about another 32,000 miles.

Dale likes nice cars. Kim likes to drive a car that she feels is big and safe.

As their income has increased, so has the amount they spend on cars, relative to the average cost of a new car. At this point, Dale is three years into a $30,000 Ford Explorer. Kim is driving a seven-year-old V8 Ford Thunderbird that cost about $21,000.

Dale and Kim are pretty proud of themselves and the way they have purchased cars. They have always justified buying expensive, well-built cars because of all the driving Dale does and because Kim wants to drive a safe car. They have always purchased a car with a loan they pay off in three years, then tried to put the equivalent of a year's loan payments into the bank to add to the down payment for the next car.

In this way, they have been using one of the tools the seminar instructor discussed, known as *paying yourself first*. But their car expenses still nag them. They discuss options, both for now and for their retirement.

First, they discuss the possibility of buying less expensive cars. Dale loves his Ford Explorer and has thought about buying another. The equivalent of the model he now drives is about $35,000. If the car they buy next year for Dale can be purchased for $25,000 instead of $35,000, they can save about $12,000—the difference between the sticker prices, in addition to the interest savings on the smaller loan they would need to finance the purchase.

However, Dale has difficulty with this idea. First, he truly believes that with cars you get what you pay for. By spending some extra money, you get a car that is more reliable, especially since they keep them for eight years. Second, his current car is the most comfortable he has ever owned. He drives a lot, and he's not getting any younger. Third, it's a very safe car, important for him and especially for Kim.

They move on to the second option, buying a new car every five years instead of every four. This seems to work better. Giving themselves an extra year between purchases to save would allow Dale to buy the car he wants and take out a loan more in line with the lower-priced car, by having two years of savings for a down payment instead of one year. Or they could use the second year of savings to fund their retirement, and keep their car purchases using the same relative amount of current income. This also supports Dale's argument about reliability, since now they will be asking a car to give them 10 years and about 190,000 miles instead of eight years and about 152,000.

It's getting late. Kim wants to make a decision about what to do with the extra year of savings—she would like to put more away for retirement. Dale needs to be up early to drive 100 miles for his first appointment. Kim knows that her husband has made a major concession regarding the one discretionary item about which he feels very strongly. She agrees to put aside the issue of how best to use the savings until the next night.

She tells her husband she will do some calculations during her lunch break the following day to determine whether it would be better to reduce their borrowing costs by paying more up front for the car or to add the savings to Jim's 401(k). They need to know which strategy would produce larger investment accumulations after 20 years. She also adds another item to the next night's agenda—car or cars in retirement. ■

TRAPS, OBSTACLES, TOOLS, AND HELPERS

Watch out for the following traps and obstacles, and try to use the following tools and helpers.

- Equating your retirement lifestyle with your standard of living in your last year of work
- Borrowing now and justifying it on the basis of future payback from raises
- Falling victim to lifestyle creep

- Being house-rich and income-poor
- High-interest, minimum-payment credit cards
- "Conspicuous consumption"
- Conflicting objectives
- Inflation
- Discretionary spending

- Employer-sponsored retirement plans
- Employee Assistance Programs (EAPs)
- Stress-reduction programs

- Automatic savings through payroll deduction to pay yourself first
- Making carefully considered lifestyle choices

ACTION ITEMS

Item	Priority*	Completed
1. Make well-reasoned lifestyle choices.		
2. Understand and accept or reject the short-term financial consequences of each lifestyle "upgrade" you make—that is, a bigger house means a bigger mortgage, higher property taxes, higher costs for heating and/or air-conditioning. Accept or reject lifestyle creep. Develop a plan to eliminate that upgrade when you retire.		
3. Understand and accept or reject the long-term consequences of each lifestyle upgrade you make, making sure you are able to fund your retirement plan to meet that upgrade if you want to maintain it during retirement.		
4. Consider using a software program to track living expenses so you can be more aware of your spending choices.		

*A, B, C, or N/A, with A being the highest priority.

6

TAX-DEFERRED SAVINGS PLANS FOR RETIREMENT

You can get there by inheriting a fortune or by winning the lottery. But, if you are going to be financially independent in retirement, it will probably be because you took full advantage of the tax-deferred savings plans available to you.

Pension plans and tax-deferred savings plans have been around for decades. Today, however, the choices available are greater, and the decisions each of us must make require a much greater understanding of what is involved—in saving, investing, and, finally, taking money out of the tax-deferred savings plans in which you invest for retirement. The opportunities may be the same for everyone, but the results will, predictably, be a different story.

The plans we will discuss in this chapter are as follows:

- Individual Retirement Accounts (IRAs)
- 401(k)-type plans (Those who work for nonprofit organizations may have the opportunity to contribute into a 403(b) or 457 plan, which works in a similar way to a 401(k).)
- Keoghs and Simplified Employee Pensions (SEPs)
- SIMPLE plans
- Defined benefit pension plans

We will also touch on a number of other retirement-asset accumulation vehicles:

- Stock purchase plans
- Stock option plans
- Employee Stock Ownership Plans (ESOPs) and stock bonus plans
- Military retirement plans
- Civil service pensions

INDIVIDUAL RETIREMENT ACCOUNTS

Although most people are familiar with the term "Individual Retirement Account (IRA)," there is still confusion over how they work and who is eligible to use the tax-sheltering benefits they provide.

First, it's important that you understand two key concepts:

1. Anyone can set up an IRA, provided they have earned income. You may set aside up to $2,000 each year in an IRA, provided you earned at least $2,000. Earned income means salary, wages, self-employment income, alimony, and farming income. This limit applies to your total contributions to both regular IRAs and Roth IRAs.
2. A married couple can contribute up to $4,000 to IRAs, $2,000 for each spouse, even if only one spouse works, as long that spouse earned at least $4,000.

All of the accumulated interest, dividends, and capital gains within an IRA are tax-deferred until the money is withdrawn (tax-free if the money is in a Roth IRA and you meet certain requirements). Since you don't pay annual taxes on the interest, dividends, or capital gains in this account, it will grow much faster, as we discussed in Chapter 4. There are two different kinds of IRAs—regular IRAs and Roth IRAs.

Regular IRAs

The income that's generated in a regular IRA is tax-deferred until withdrawal, but your original contribution may or may not be deductible, depending on your specific circumstances. Whether your IRA contribution is deductible from current-year taxes is an important issue, but not necessarily the deciding factor as to whether you should set up an IRA. To enjoy deductibility, you need to meet one of three conditions.

First, *if neither you nor your spouse participate* in any of the other qualified retirement plans we discuss in this chapter, you may make a tax-deductible contribution to an IRA no matter what your income.

Second, *even if you or your spouse participate* in another qualified plan, you may make a deductible IRA contribution if your earned income is below a threshold amount. In 2000, any single taxpayer who participates in a qualified plan with adjusted gross income below $32,000 can make a fully deductible IRA contribution. Between $32,000 and $42,000 of adjusted gross income, your contribution is partially deductible, according to a pro-rating scale. If your adjusted gross income is above $42,000, your contribution is not deductible against current-year income. After 2000, this threshold range increases each year until 2005, when the deductible range will be $50,000 to $60,000.

For married taxpayers who file jointly, the threshold amount in 2000 to make fully deductible contributions is $52,000 of household adjusted gross income. Between $52,000 and $62,000 the contribution is partially deductible. Above $62,000, no deduction is allowed. After 2000, this threshold range increases each year until 2007, when it will be $80,000 to $100,000.

Third, *even if your spouse participates* in another qualified plan, you can make a deductible contribution to an IRA if your adjusted gross income is below $150,000. The availability of this deduction phases out between $150,000 and $160,000 of adjusted gross income.

If you make a contribution to a nondeductible regular IRA, your withdrawals from that IRA will be nontaxable to the extent that you get back a pro-rata part of your original contributions. If you're only able to make a nondeductible regular IRA contribution, a Roth IRA contribution will usually make more sense, if you're eligible to make one.

Roth IRAs

An alternative to contributing to a regular IRA is to make a nondeductible contribution to a Roth IRA, which allows *tax-free* buildup of income. You are eligible to make a contribution if your adjusted gross income is below $95,000 ($150,000 for joint filers) and phases out between $95,000 and $110,000 ($150,000 to $160,000 for joint filers). The income earned on a Roth IRA is tax-free if you leave the money there for five years after your first contribution and distributions take place after age 59½, death, disability, or for up to $10,000 to a first-time home buyer. You also can elect to convert your regular IRA into a Roth IRA by paying income tax on the value of your regular IRA at the time you convert. The advantage of the conversion is that any future income may be tax-free. You're eligible to convert only if your adjusted gross income is not more than $100,000.

Here are some important features of IRAs:

• Investment choices are fairly broad. You can invest in stocks, bonds, bank deposits, and other financial instruments. Precious metals and collectibles, except for certain U.S. and state coins and certain types of bullion, may not be held within an IRA, however.

- There are no loan privileges with an IRA, as there are with many other retirement planning vehicles.
- You can't contribute to an IRA, and you must begin taking minimum distributions, after you turn 70½. (Neither of these rules applies for a Roth IRA.)
- Not more than $2,000 per individual can be contributed to a combination of nondeductible, deductible, and Roth IRAs in a year.

Some special features of Roth IRAs:

- You can continue making contributions to a Roth IRA after age 70½.
- You don't have to take any minimum distributions during your lifetime.
- All distributions from Roth IRAs are considered to have come from after-tax contributions.
- If your adjusted gross income is $100,000 or less, you can convert a regular IRA into a Roth IRA with no 10% premature distribution penalty, although you pay income tax on the conversion. A calculator to help you decide whether to convert is available at www.ey.com/pfc, or visit www.rothira.com for more information.

401(k) Plans

Probably the most popular and widely used retirement accumulation vehicle today is the 401(k) plan. In religious, charitable, educational, and other nonprofit organizations, the similar plan is called a 403(b) or 457, although nonprofit organizations can establish 401(k) plans as well.

Large and medium-size companies have installed 401(k) plans to encourage employees to save and invest. Increasingly, even smaller companies are setting up 401(k) plans. Many companies match a portion of the money employees put into the plan. This match typically ranges from 25 cents to $1 from the company for every $1 the employee puts in, up to a certain percentage of employee income, usually somewhere between 3 and 6%.

Most companies limit the amount of pretax income employees can put into the plan, up to the government-regulated maximum, which in 2000 was $10,500. This maximum dollar amount is periodically increased for inflation in $500 increments. Another limit that applies is that the combined employee and employer contributions cannot be more than 25% of pay.

So, let's say your salary is $40,000, and your company matches dollar-for-dollar up to 5% of your salary. If you put 5%—$2,000—into the 401(k), the company will also contribute $2,000. You automatically double your money!

If you contribute $6,000 your company would still put in its maximum match, 5%—$2,000. You would then have $8,000, which would earn interest, dividends, and capital gains tax-deferred until you began withdrawals.

The maximum you could put in and still receive your full company match would be $8,000. That amount plus the company match is 25% of your pay, calculated as follows:

$$\$8,000 + \$2,000 = \$10,000$$
$$\$10,000 = 25\% \times \$40,000$$

Most 401(k) plans offer a broad array of investment options, although a few require 401(k) participants to make some or all of their investment in company stock. Many employers make their matching contributions in company stock, regardless of how you invest your contribution.

Many 401(k) plans also include loan features. Generally, the tax law limits the amount you can borrow from your 401(k) plan to 50% of the vested account balance up to a maximum of $50,000. The loan usually must be repaid within 5 years, although some loans for the purpose of buying a home qualify for a longer payback period. The repayment is done through payroll deduction. Interest rates on the borrowing are usually tied to the prime lending rate. Usually interest payments are not deductible.

Borrowing from a 401(k) plan may look at first like a good option. But you must do a complete calculation. If you have sources of borrowing that are tax-advantaged, such as equity in your home, you need to see if the rate for the loan from your 401(k) plan is better than your after-tax rate from a home-equity loan.

And remember that the low rate on a 401(k) loan means that your 401(k) is earning a low rate of return on the money you borrow.

By borrowing from your 401(k) plan, you lose the benefit of the tax-deferred compounding growth you would earn on the money you have borrowed to the extent that you could have earned more than the interest you paid to the plan. Equally important, these loans are usually due when you separate from your employer. If you can't pay off the entire balance at that time, the loan balance is considered taxable income, as if you had taken a lump-sum payout. In addition, if you are not 55 or older, the balance is subject to another 10% federal tax for early withdrawal as well as state income taxes.

KEOGHS AND SIMPLIFIED EMPLOYEE PENSIONS— PLANS FOR THE SELF-EMPLOYED

For the self-employed, a number of tax-deferred savings vehicles are available. Some of the most widely used are in the family of plans called Keoghs. There are defined-benefit Keoghs and different versions of defined-contribution

Keoghs. For those who do not want to go through the paperwork of setting up and administering an individual Keogh plan, there are plans called *Simplified Employee Pension* (SEP) plans offered by brokerages, banks, and other financial institutions. These basically allow you to have your own plan under their umbrella qualification. Paperwork for these SEPs is usually only a one- or two-page form for starting such a plan.

Your contributions to self-employed pension plans are always fully deductible, regardless of whether you or your spouse participate in other plans, and regardless of your total household income. For instance, a marketing-materials writer with a salary of $50,000, who participates in a retirement plan at a university, then earns another $50,000 writing textbooks on the side, can still set up a Keogh or SEP, into which she can put the maximum contribution allowed by law.

SEPs were designed to give small businesses and sole proprietors the ability to accumulate retirement funds for themselves and their employees without the complexity and expense of administering a large, individually qualified plan. Any company can use the SEP.

A *profit-sharing* Keogh plan or a SEP allows you to contribute an amount up to 15% of your net self-employment earnings, up to a maximum of $25,500 in 2000, and you can contribute a different amount each year. (This maximum is based on the maximum earnings that can be taken into account—$170,000 in 2000, and adjusted for inflation thereafter—$170,000 $\times$ 15% = $25,500.) Your allowable contribution may actually be less than 15% of your income because your contribution is limited to 15% of total net earnings (earnings after expenses) minus your 15% contribution.

Sticking with our previous example, the marketing writer who writes textbooks on the side, let's say that after expenses (including half of her self-employment tax), her self-employment income is $40,000. She can put into her SEP 15% $\times$ $40,000 minus the SEP contribution. That amount works out to $5,217, so she can contribute 15% of $34,783, or 13.043% of $40,000.

A *money-purchase* Keogh plan allows you to contribute up to 25% of your net self-employment earnings, up to a limit of $30,000. While you can put away more in the money-purchase plan, you have to state the percentage of net earnings you will contribute, and do so each year. You trade the ability to shelter more income from current taxes and create a larger tax-deferred retirement account for reduced flexibility.

Of course, you can have it both ways by having one of each plan. You can commit to a fixed 10% contribution to your money-purchase plan, then make flexible contributions up to the 15% maximum each year into your profit-sharing plan, up to a maximum contribution of $30,000 in both plans combined.

If you're over 40, you might want to consider a *defined-benefit* Keogh. This is a plan where the amount you put in is based on a projected benefit at your retirement, as calculated by an actuary. (See the discussion later in this chapter about defined-benefit plans.) The deductible amount you can contribute is limited by the amount of your earnings. This means that you could contribute and deduct an amount equal to your entire earnings for the year.

This type of plan provides you with the least amount of flexibility, however, and has the highest administration cost. You might actually have to make a contribution even if you had *no income* during the year. But it may allow you to put away more tax-deductible contributions than any other type of plan. To maximize your contributions, you might want to consider establishing both a profit-sharing/money-purchase plan and a defined-benefit plan. Because of a change in law that became effective in 2000, you can now get the maximum benefit under each type of plan simultaneously.

Here's one important thing to remember: If you have employees, generally you must make the same proportionate payments into your Keogh/SEP plan for them as well, unless you create an integrated, age-weighted plan or comparability plan, which takes some time and paperwork—and probably some professional assistance.

Another important thing is that unless you allow your employees to do so, you manage all of the assets in the plan, so you have *fiduciary* responsibility for the money you are putting in the plan for your employees. What this means is that if you don't handle this responsibility well, your employees may have a legal basis to recover any losses they have incurred.

MAKING IT SIMPLE

An employer with 100 or fewer workers who each earn at least $5,000, and which has no other retirement plan, may establish a Savings Incentive Match Plan for Employees (SIMPLE). The SIMPLE, which is not subject to some of the complicated rules that apply to other types of retirement plans, can be set up using an IRA for each employee or a 401(k) model. The maximum annual pretax contribution an employee may make under a SIMPLE is $6,000. You would consider a SIMPLE if you want a plan that allows your employees to contribute on a pretax basis.

With certain exceptions, employees who make at least $5,000 must be eligible to participate. Generally, the plan requires the employer to make a dollar-for-dollar matching contribution for every employee who elects to participate in the plan, to a maximum of 3% of each employee's pay. Alternatively, the employer can contribute a flat 2% for every employee, regardless of whether the employee elects to participate.

All contributions under a SIMPLE IRA must be 100% vested. Employer contributions under a SIMPLE 401(k) can be subject to a vesting schedule.

However, you as a business owner would be required to satisfy certain nondiscrimination tests with respect to contributions, should you set up a vesting schedule.

If you have no employees, you probably would be better off with a Keogh than a SIMPLE plan, since the deductible contribution limits are substantially higher for a Keogh. A SIMPLE plan might be better if you have a low level of income, since the contribution is not limited to a percentage of income.

Defined-Benefit Plans

If you work for a company that provides a defined-benefit pension plan, this can be a significant part of your retirement planning picture. Although you have little or no choice as to how the plan is operated, it's important to understand how it works.

First, rather than the contribution being defined, as is the case with IRAs, 401(k)s, SEPs, or most Keoghs, the *benefit* you will receive when you begin collecting is defined.

To make sure you receive that benefit when you retire, your company must fund its pension plan at a sufficient level. The formula for determining your particular benefit is outlined in a plan document and describes the ways in which the benefit is calculated.

The typical formula includes your years of service with the company, your final average salary, and a percentage multiplier.

- Years of service (usually is the total years with the company, but could be less).
- Final average salary could be the average for your entire years of service, or an average of your highest-earning years (say the highest five in the last ten years of service).
- The multiplier typically ranges somewhere between 1 and 2%.

Unless you plan carefully, accepting yearly retirement can be a real trap. For instance, Jack contemplated whether to retire at 55 or keep working until 65. He had worked for his company for 15 years and figured that by staying an extra 10 years, he would probably add about 60% to his pension. When he looked more closely at the numbers, however, he found that if he worked another 10 years, he would get 300% more. Here's why.

First, if Jack worked an extra 10 years, and received 4% pay increases each year, his pension would be based on a final salary that is more than 50% higher than his current salary.

Second, he would have 10 more years of cumulative service.

Third, he would not suffer from the "age reduction" provision built into his and many other pension plans. This type of provision generally reduces pension payments by 3 to 4% or more for every year you retire and start receiving payments before normal retirement age.

This is not to say that you should never consider taking an early retirement offer. It is only to say that by doing so you may be sacrificing much more pension benefit than you think. For many people, working only two extra years—from age 60 to age 62, for example—can mean the difference between a financially secure retirement and one that is insecure. Delaying drawing your pension and spending from your personal retirement savings by only those two years, while increasing your pension, can make an enormous difference.

Our point here is that you should find out by getting projections from your employer. Reviewing these projections can help you make an informed decision.

Some plans are integrated with Social Security benefits. Since the company puts money into the Social Security system on the employee's behalf, the law allows companies to reduce the pension benefit by up to 50% of the individual's projected Social Security benefit. Let's say your pension is calculated at $20,000 annually, and your Social Security projected benefit is $10,000. The company could reduce your pension benefit by $5,000 (50% of $10,000) and give you a net pension benefit of $15,000.

Most defined-benefit plans have provisions for early retirement, and some have additional supplemental benefits that will be paid until you are eligible for Social Security.

One of the most important elements of a defined-benefit plan to check is when you are *vested* in the plan. Being vested means that you are eligible to receive the money put into the plan on your behalf. Some vesting schedules give you immediate ownership of the benefits accruing on your behalf; others gradually vest you in the plan; and still others have full or "cliff" vesting at some point in the future, for example, five or ten years from your date of hire. (The concept of vesting also applies to employer contributions in defined-contribution plans.)

If you change jobs frequently and never stay with one employer long enough to become vested in a pension plan, you will have no defined-benefit pension when you retire.

If you change jobs frequently and stay with some or all employers long enough to become vested, you still will not collect in defined-benefit pensions as much as you would have if you had stayed with one employer for your entire career. Pension formulas almost always average the highest salary for some period late in your career with the company. If you jump from job to job, the pension formula will hurt you. This action item is not to avoid switching jobs, but to be aware of the consequences and increase your investing for retirement to compensate.

We'll discuss distribution of pension benefits if you go from one company to another in Chapter 7.

Cash-Balance Plans

A type of defined-benefit plan that has gotten much publicity is the "cash-balance" plan. Under this type of plan you would have an account balance but your employer would guarantee the rate of return received on the balance. Your account would also grow based on pay credits that your employer contributes. This differs from a profit-sharing or money purchase plan, where the ultimate value of your account depends on investment performance. In other words, with a cash-balance plan, the employer still has the responsibility for providing the final benefit based on the plan's interest rate and pay credit formulas. Cash-balance plans offer more portability than traditional pension plans because you can take your vested account as a lump sum whenever you terminate employment and it will not be reduced because of your age.

OTHER TYPES OF TAX-DEFERRED RETIREMENT PLANS

Other plans that might be available to you as part of your retirement benefits or compensation include the following:

Profit-Sharing and Money Purchase Plans. These are defined-contribution plans that are similar to those discussed above for self-employed individuals. Your employer makes contributions to an account and your balance is based on the investment performance of those contributions.

Stock Purchase Plans. Under these plans, employees can have amounts withheld from their salary and used to buy employer stock (sometimes at a discount). The employee pays no tax until he or she sells that stock. These plans are a wonderful way to accumulate large amounts of stock over a period of time at a relatively low cost.

Stock Option Plans. There are two types of stock option plans—nonqualified stock option plans (NQSOs) and incentive stock option plans (ISOs). These plans give employees the right to buy a given amount of company stock, for a certain period of time, generally at the price at which the stock was selling when they received the option. For example, if your employer's stock is worth $10 a share today, and you receive a nonqualified stock option to buy 100 shares for a period of 10 years, you would be able to "exercise" your option and buy up to 100 shares for $10 a share at any time in the next 10 years. If during this time the stock price doubles to $20 per share, and you exercise your options, you are taxed at your ordinary tax rate on the difference between the value of the stock at the time of exercise and the price you paid for the stock. In this case, the difference is $10 per share.

If the option in the above example had been an ISO, you would not pay ordinary tax at the time the option was exercised (although you may be subject to the alternative minimum tax). You will pay tax at capital gain rates when the stock is sold at a gain provided the stock has been held at least two years from the date the option was granted and one year from the date of exercise.

ESOPs and Stock Bonus Plans. These plans are similar to qualified profit-sharing plans but are invested mainly in company stock.

Military Retirement Plan. The military has a defined-benefit pension system for service members who may receive an immediate annuity after 20 years of service. (Many state and municipal police and many municipal firefighter pensions work the same way.)

Civil Service Pension. The U.S. government has a pension system for its employees. In order to be eligible for a Civil Service Retirement System and Federal Employee Retirement System retirement annuity, you must complete at least five years of civil service.

TRAPS, OBSTACLES, TOOLS, AND HELPERS

Do your best to avoid the following traps and obstacles, and take advantage of the tools and helpers.

- Not keeping up to date on tax-law changes
- Failing to "snatch the match" by not taking full advantage of employer matching contributions
- Contributing no more to your tax-deferred savings plan than the amount your employer matches

- Not contributing to an IRA because your contribution is not deductible
- Borrowing against your retirement plans
- Using retirement funds for nonretirement purposes
- Failing to understand your employer's defined-benefit pension plan formula
- Taking early retirement without calculating all of the financial consequences
- Not understanding how your pension might be coordinated with Social Security benefits
- Assuming that your defined-benefit pension payments will automatically be increased each year in retirement to protect you against inflation
- Having many different IRAs, resulting in extra expenses and uncoordinated retirement funding

- Complexity of federal and state tax laws and regulations
- Complexity of defined-benefit and defined-contribution plan features
- Record keeping for nondeductible IRAs using IRS Form 8606
- Lack of portability in traditional defined-benefit pension plans

- Employer-sponsored financial education and planning programs
- Personalized pension projections
- Written descriptions of plan investment options
- U.S. Department of Labor's Pension and Welfare Benefits Administration, which oversees ERISA and includes the Pension Benefit Guarantee Corporation (PBGC)

- Defined-benefit pension plans, traditional and "hybrid," like cash-balance plans
- Section 401(k) plans
- Section 403(b) plans
- Section 457 plans

- IRAs
- Keoghs
- SEPs
- SIMPLEs
- Employee stock ownership, bonus, and purchase plans
- Stock option plans
- Civil service and military retirement plans

ACTION ITEMS

Item	Priority*	Completed
1. Contribute the maximum to pretax, tax-deferred retirement plans.		
2. Calculate the percentage of before-tax pay that you are saving for retirement. (If it is less than 10%, begin increasing your retirement savings now. Make every effort to increase it over time to 15 to 20%, especially as you reach your peak earning years.)		
3. Determine the true cost of any loans you have from your employer's 401(k) or similar plan, including the loss of investment returns on the borrowed funds and the double taxation of interest paid on the loan. (Be sure to consider the tax consequences if you leave your job with an outstanding plan loan that you are unable to repay immediately. Explore alternative sources of loans, such as home-equity lines of credit, life insurance cash value, credit card advances, or family members. Set these up before you need them.)		
4. Look for ways to take advantage of tax-favored retirement plans for the self-employed.		
5. Understand the formula used to calculate your pension under your employer's defined-benefit pension plan. (Pay particular attention to: vesting, the multiplier, the definition of pay used, the normal retirement age and early-retirement reduction factors, and how the plan coordinates with Social Security.)		

ACTION ITEMS *(continued)*		
Item	**Priority***	**Completed**
6. Look at all of your IRAs and determine their costs in fees and expenses. Explore consolidation to reduce costs, simplify record keeping, and simplify your retirement funding.		
7. Consider converting your current IRAs into Roth IRAs.		

*A, B, C, or N/A, with A being the highest priority.

TAX AND PLAN DISTRIBUTION ISSUES

A very important consideration when you retire, or when you leave one employer for another, is how the money you save for retirement is taxed.

For many Americans, the primary source of retirement income comes from employer-sponsored retirement plans. These plans, and others like them, are absolutely key to a successful retirement savings strategy because taxes on the money saved within them will be *deferred* until the funds are disbursed. That way, contributions and earnings have the chance to grow tax-free as long as the money stays in the plan.

The rules governing the taxation of distributions from retirement savings plans such as 401(k)s, 403(b)s, and IRAs are very complex. Not only can the tax rules for ordinary retirement plan withdrawals be confusing, but the tax law also provides for complicated penalty taxes if distributions are received *too early* (generally before age 59½), if distributions begin *too late* (generally after April 1 of the year following the later of either the year you turn 70½ or the year you retire), or if you *fail to take at least the minimum required distribution*. And, of course, tax rules are constantly changing, so you need to keep up with them to avoid any penalties.

LUMP SUMS AND ROLLOVERS

So, you are retiring today. You have worked long enough for the same employer to have become vested in the defined-benefit pension plan and can begin receiving a monthly pension. A few defined-benefit pension plans (and most defined-contribution plans) allow you to take a lump-sum distribution instead of traditional monthly pension payments. If yours is one of these, you have an important decision to make.

A pension is essentially a series of payments in the form of an *annuity*, payable to you by the company and based on your life expectancy at retirement. It can also be based on the combined life expectancy of you and your spouse or another person you designate as beneficiary if you so desire (and your spouse consents). If you have also participated in a company-sponsored defined-contribution plan such as a 401(k) or 403(b) plan, you can either begin taking distributions from that plan at retirement or wait, but not later than April 1 of the year following the year in which you turn 70½, unless you are still working for the company that sponsors the plan. If you continue to work, you must begin distributions by April 1 of the year after you stop working.

For IRAs (other than Roth IRAs), you must begin taking your distributions by April 1 of the year following the year in which you turn 70½, *even if* you are still working. This rule generally applies to people who own 5% or more of a business as well, with respect to a qualified plan.

Then again, you could take a *lump-sum* distribution of your defined-contribution plan and *roll it over* into an IRA, in which you would manage all of these investments the way you desire.

If your lump-sum distribution includes employer stock, special considerations apply. You should consult a financial and tax advisor before making your election if your plan includes employer stock.

For those who retire early—in their 50s—and for job changers who have been taking advantage of defined-contribution plans, these decisions become more critical. Young retirees may have cash needs that must be met immediately, for example, to start a business or to pay for a child's education or wedding. But there are a number of tax traps designed to encourage you to maintain these funds for retirement and keep you from simply pocketing them.

A rollover is a tax-free transfer of cash or other assets from a qualified retirement plan to an "eligible retirement plan." An eligible retirement plan is an IRA, a qualified retirement plan, or a qualified annuity plan. A rollover may also include a distribution from one IRA followed by a contribution to another.

The rollover must be completed not later than the 60th day following the day on which you receive the distribution. Generally, only one rollover per IRA is allowed per year. If you transfer funds directly between trustees of your IRAs and you never actually control or use the account assets, however, this is not considered a rollover and you may transfer your accounts as often as you like.

When you leave your employer, you have three options regarding your tax-deferred defined-contribution account for it to retain its tax-deferred status:

1. Leave it in the company's plan. Most companies allow you to do this, and they are obligated to by law if your account balance is more than $5,000. It's safe to say that most companies would rather you take the funds out of the plan, since it often costs the company a management fee for the trustee to maintain your account.

2. You may transfer your account balance to a new employer's qualified plan if that plan allows you to. If it does not, or if you don't want to, you can transfer the balance to an IRA.

3. You may take the distribution as cash. If you put the entire distribution back into an IRA or into your new employer's plan within 60 days, you owe no taxes. If, however, you don't put it into an IRA or your new employer's plan, the distribution is treated as taxable income. Furthermore, if you are not yet 55, you may incur an additional 10% tax for an early distribution. (For these purposes, you are considered to be 55 if your 55th birthday is within the year you leave your employer.)

    You can use this final option to give yourself a short-term (60-day) tax-free loan. But be careful; if you don't have all the money available to go into your new account in two months, whatever you don't roll over is taxable income and subject to the extra tax if you are not yet 55.

There's another complication. A mandatory withholding tax of 20% is imposed on distributions eligible for rollover unless the distribution is made directly to the trustee of a new plan. For instance, on a $20,000 distribution made directly to you, your former company would be required to withhold $4,000. You would therefore get a check for $16,000. If you wanted to roll over the entire amount of your distribution within the 60-day window, you would need to find $4,000 to replace the $4,000 your former employer withheld and sent to the Internal Revenue Service.

If you are able to make a full rollover of $20,000, the $4,000 withheld is refundable, but without interest, when you file your tax return for the year. If you are only able to roll over the $16,000, the $4,000 is taxable at your regular tax rate and subject to the additional 10% tax if you are under 55. Simply put, unless you really need the money, have distributions from tax-deferred employer-sponsored plans made directly to the trustee of a new plan, either your new employer's or an IRA.

There is an important exception to the mandatory withholding rules—distributions from an IRA are *not subject to the 20% mandatory withholding requirement*.

Now, let's try to attack the two biggest potential traps surrounding lump sums and rollovers.

Trap No. 1:

Taking a retirement distribution in the form of a lump sum without doing the calculations.

For many, especially those who are not comfortable managing their own investments or who don't want to be bothered with managing their retirement portfolio, taking lifetime payments from a defined-benefit pension plan and level payments in the form of an annuity from a defined-contribution plan is the way to go. In addition to being relieved of the investment burden, you are guaranteed a fixed monthly amount no matter how long you live. If you choose to base the benefit on your life expectancy and the life expectancy of a beneficiary, he or she can continue to receive a monthly benefit after your death for as long as he or she lives.

However, there are some downside risks in taking lifetime pension payments, regardless of whether you take the payout based on one life expectancy or two:

- Inflation will erode the purchasing power of the monthly benefit. Very few companies provide cost-of-living increases or index pension benefits to keep pace with inflation. As a consequence, pension payments will lose some of their purchasing power as time goes by.
- Your family could lose out on a significant inheritance if you die soon after retirement. Even if you took the surviving spouse option, if both you and your spouse die soon after retirement, your family would not receive any more benefits.
- Access to your assets is limited to the monthly payment.

There are some advantages to taking out the balance in your plans all at once, especially if you roll it over into a qualified tax-deferred retirement vehicle such as an IRA.

- You can invest the proceeds according to your own desires, not those of your employer's pension plan administrator or the company's investment manager.
- You have access to your entire asset balance in case of an emergency, or if you want to start a business or make a large gift for a special occasion.

Of course, the downside is that you may not invest your fund well, or you may be tempted to overspend, making it difficult to create a comfortable long-term budget and opening up the frightening possibility that you or your spouse will outlive your retirement benefits.

A few plans allow you to take a one-from-column-A-and-one-from-column-B approach. You can leave some of your accumulated assets in the plan and receive monthly benefits based on that reduced amount. At the same time, you can take a distribution of the rest. And with that distribution, you can roll some or all of the money into an IRA to maintain its tax-deferred status. Any funds taken out and not rolled over will be taxable today but can be used as you wish.

Remember, most pension plans do not offer a partial or complete lump-sum settlement option.

If you have been contributing to your organization's 401(k) or 403(b) or 457 plan, you have been managing that money already, although within the limits of the allowable investments under the plan. There may be no reason to move this money from the plan after retirement, especially if it offers attractive investment choices and pays plan administration costs. Most companies would prefer that you did move it, to relieve them of the expense of having the plan trustee administer your account. If your plan allows you to defer your decision, you may want to do so, at least for a short while. You don't need to be in a hurry and certainly shouldn't make a decision to take your money out of the plan based on pressure from investment salespeople to let them invest your money. This should be a well-thought-through decision about how you can best finance your retirement.

Trap No. 2:

When you change jobs, having your 401(k) lump-sum distribution check made out to you, with the notion that you will roll it over later into an IRA and, in the meantime, get a short-term, interest-free loan.

There's a hitch here—the 20% withholding tax on lump-sum distributions. Taking the distribution as cash when you change jobs is one of the biggest mistakes you can make. A staggering number of Americans do this, and very few actually make up the difference and roll the entire amount into an IRA within the 60-day window. Not only are they paying a hefty tax—such a onetime distribution can bump middle-income taxpayers into a much higher tax bracket than they normally pay as well as trigger the 10% early distribution tax—but they are losing forever all the remaining years of tax-deferred compounding on the money they take.

10-YEAR AVERAGING

If you were born before 1936, you can elect to use 10-year averaging to tax any lump-sum distribution you receive. Some people born after 1935 may also use the 5-year tax option. In brief, this option allows you to take your distribution from a qualified employer pension plan, stock bonus plan, profit-sharing plan, or another retirement plan in a lump sum and have it taxed for federal income tax purposes as if you took the payout in 10 equal annual installments. This does not apply to IRAs, or 403(b) or 457 accounts. The entire tax is due in the year of the distribution.

The computation is complex, and you should speak with your tax specialist as well as your financial planning specialist before you make an election. You may make only one such election in your lifetime.

For more detail on all of these special tax treatments, see Appendix I.

DISTRIBUTION PENALTIES: EARLY, LATE, OR MINIMUM

Timing your retirement benefits requires careful planning and calculation. It's important that you determine both the right amount of money for your needs and when to take the distribution.

Early Distributions

In order to discourage use of the money for reasons other than retirement, a 10% additional income tax is imposed on distributions taken before age 59½ from any qualified retirement plan, including 403(b) plans and IRAs. This additional tax does not apply to distributions from 457 plans. The tax applies to any early distribution, including lump-sum distributions even if they were involuntary. The tax is not imposed on lump-sum distributions that are rolled over into an IRA or another qualified plan. There are many exceptions to the rule, most notably the following six:

1. If you leave your job in or after the year in which you reach age 55. Figure 7.1 shows this schematically. This exception does not apply to IRAs.
2. If you take *substantially equal periodic payments* over your life expectancy. This is a complex formula, and you should consult a tax professional if you are thinking of doing this. This exception applies to a qualified plan only if payments begin *after* you leave employment. (A fuller discussion of "substantially equal periodic payments" and how to calculate distributions can be found in Appendix I.)
3. Disability of the plan participant.
4. Death of the plan participant.
5. Distribution to offset the participant's deductible medical expenses.
6. Distributions to another person designated in a qualified domestic relations order (QDRO).

Other exceptions, which apply only to IRAs, is for distributions that are used to pay health insurance premiums when you are unemployed, distributions used to pay for higher education expenses, and distributions of up to $10,000 to pay for first-time home-buyer expenses.

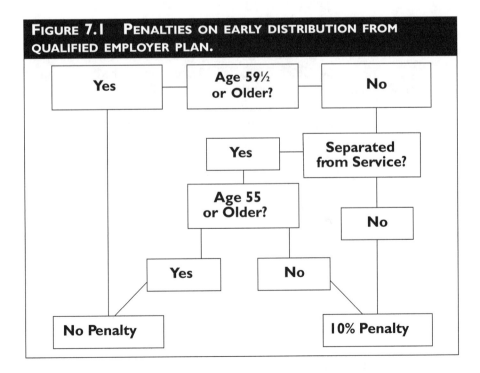

FIGURE 7.1   PENALTIES ON EARLY DISTRIBUTION FROM QUALIFIED EMPLOYER PLAN.

Late Distributions

Generally, you must begin taking distributions from all IRAs (except Roth IRAs) by April 1 of the year following the year in which you turn 70½, or, in the case of a qualified defined-contribution or defined-benefit plan, the year you retire if that is later. If you are a 5% or more owner of the business that is the pension plan's sponsor, you must begin receiving distributions by April 1 of the year after you turn age 70½, even if you have not yet retired. You are not required to take any distributions from a Roth IRA during your lifetime.

The "minimum" distribution requirement is designed to encourage employees to withdraw all of their retirement savings over one of the following four periods:

1. The employee's life
2. The lives of the employee and his or her designated beneficiary
3. A period of time not extending beyond the life of the employee
4. A period of time not extending beyond the joint life expectancy of the employee and his or her designated beneficiary

Failure to take a timely distribution of all or part of your minimum required distribution opens you up to a nondeductible excise tax of 50%—that's right, 50%—of the amount required to be, but not actually, distributed. This is one of the stiffest "penalty" taxes in the IRS arsenal.

Let's look at a couple of examples.

Nick's birthday is in May, so he turns 70½ in November. He must take his first distribution by April 1 of the next year, just before his 71st birthday.

Mary Jo's birthday is in September, so she doesn't turn 70½ until March. She does not have to take her first distribution until April 1 *of the following year*, after she has turned 71½. She gets an extra year for her retirement fund to grow tax-deferred.

Both Nick and Mary Jo need to calculate whether they should take their first distribution in the calendar year in which they turn 70½, or whether they should wait until the next calendar year and take two distributions. For both, it is a decision between allowing the fund to grow another year tax-deferred and whether two distributions in one year as opposed to one will bump their income into a higher tax bracket and force them over the threshold to where 85% of their Social Security benefits are taxable as opposed to 50% or more.

Calculating the Minimum Distribution Amount

Your minimum distribution depends on your life expectancy at the time you begin taking distributions. The formula that is used to determine your minimum distribution is designed to "bleed the pot dry" by the time you reach the end of your actuarially determined life expectancy.

If you want to reduce the amount you must take, you can calculate your distribution based on your life expectancy plus that of a beneficiary. For instance, if your spouse is five years younger, you can take distributions over the joint life expectancy of both you and your spouse. If your beneficiary is not your spouse, in calculating your joint life expectancy, you must treat your beneficiary as if he or she is not more than 10 years younger than you.

If you elect to take the distribution based on your life expectancy alone, or you and your spouse's, you can recalculate your life expectancy annually. If you choose to take the distribution based on your joint life expectancy with a nonspouse beneficiary, you may not recalculate your beneficiary's life expectancy. Or you may choose not to recalculate your and/or your spouse's life expectancy so that your balance is paid over a fixed period of time.

Recalculation is complex, and you must perform this calculation to determine if you would benefit from it or not. You may wish to get IRS Publication 590, which discusses recalculation.

The next example illustrates the difference between electing to determine the minimum distribution amount with recalculating and without recalculating.

E
X
A
M
P
L
E

■ Dale Schiltz, an unmarried participant in his company's 401(k) plan, was born on April 1, 1930. He turned 70 on April 1, 2000, and 70½ on October 1, 2000.

His first distribution calendar year was 2000 and his minimum required distribution (MRD) for that year had to be taken by April 2, 2001 (April 1, 2001 is a Sunday). The fair market value of his account under the plan was $100,000 on December 31, 1999.

Assume that his account's investment rate of return is 10% each year.

Dale completed his benefit election form, on which he elected to have his account distributed to him over his single life expectancy. He further elected *not to recalculate* his life expectancy. His life expectancy, using the expected return multiples in the Treasury Regulations, was 16.0 years.

Based on this set of assumptions, Dale's MRDs for each year are shown in Figure 7.2.

Assume all the same facts as above except that Dale elected to recalculate his life expectancy each year. Based on this set of assumptions, Dale's MRDs for the distribution calendar years are shown in Figure 7.3.

If Dale dies before age 86, the entire balance would have to be paid to his heirs by the end of the year following his death if he was recalculating. If he was not recalculating, the balance could be paid over the remainder of his life expectancy. ■

FIGURE 7.2 MINIMUM REQUIRED DISTRIBUTION BASED ON NOT RECALCULATING LIFE EXPECTANCY.

Age	Year	Account Balance*	Multiple	Minimum Required Distribution
69	1999	$100,000	0	$ 0
70	2000	103,750	16	6,250
71	2001	107,208	15	6,917
72	2002	110,271	14	7,658
73	2003	112,816	13	8,482
74	2004	114,696	12	9,401
75	2005	115,739	11	10,427
76	2006	115,739	10	11,574
77	2007	114,453	9	12,860
78	2008	111,592	8	14,307
79	2009	106,809	7	15,942
80	2010	99,689	6	17,802
81	2011	89,720	5	19,938
82	2012	76,262	4	22,430
83	2013	58,467	3	25,421
84	2014	35,080	2	29,234
85	2015	0	1	38,588
86	2016	0	0	0
87	2017	0	0	0
88	2018	0	0	0
89	2019	0	0	0
90	2020	0	0	0

*Assumes that the distribution is made at the end of the year, and Dale dies at age 90.

FIGURE 7.3 MINIMUM REQUIRED DISTRIBUTION BASED ON RECALCULATING LIFE EXPECTANCY.

Age	Year	Account Balance*	Multiple	Minimum Required Distribution
69	1999	$100,000	0	$ 0
70	2000	103,750	16.0	6,250
71	2001	107,344	15.3	6,781
72	2002	110,726	14.6	7,352
73	2003	113,833	13.9	7,966
74	2004	116,592	13.2	8,624
75	2005	118,924	12.5	9,327
76	2006	120,823	11.9	9,994
77	2007	122,117	11.2	10,788
78	2008	122,809	10.6	11,521
79	2009	122,809	10.0	12,281
80	2010	122,162	9.5	12,927

FIGURE 7.3 MINIMUM REQUIRED DISTRIBUTION BASED ON RECALCULATING LIFE EXPECTANCY. *(continued)*

Age	Year	Account Balance*	Multiple	Minimum Required Distribution
81	2011	$120,652	8.9	$13,726
82	2012	118,354	8.4	14,363
83	2013	115,208	7.9	14,982
84	2014	111,160	7.4	15,569
85	2015	106,166	6.9	16,110
86	2016	100,450	6.5	16,333
87	2017	94,027	6.1	16,467
88	2018	86,934	5.7	16,496
89	2019	79,225	5.3	16,403
90	2020	71,302	5.0	15,845

*Assumes that the distribution is made at the end of the year, and Dale dies at age 90.

Excess Distributions and Excess Accumulations

The tax law used to impose penalty taxes on excess distributions from, and excess accumulations in, qualified plans and IRAs. These taxes were repealed by the Taxpayer Relief Act of 1997 retroactive to January 1, 1997.

PENSION PLAN PAYMENT OPTIONS

Company pension plans as well as most government retirement plans usually offer retiring employees a range of choices on how to receive payments in retirement. These choices are almost always irrevocable: Once you retire and begin receiving a form of payment, you typically cannot request a change in the form of payment.

The monthly benefit from defined-benefit pension plans will differ dramatically depending on whether you retire early, late, or at the normal retirement age. The amount of your benefit will also be affected by whether you elect to provide a survivor benefit to your spouse (or another beneficiary) or not.

A few pension plans provide benefits that are indexed to inflation, and, on occasion, some companies voluntarily increase the pension payments they make to retired employees. But most pension plans provide monthly benefits that are calculated on a set formula of average pay and years of service and remain *level* until the retired employee (and his or her beneficiary, if covered) dies.

If you choose to have your pension payments based solely on your life expectancy ("life-only" or "straight-life" option), the payments during your life will be larger, but your survivors will be left with nothing. If you choose to have your pension based on the joint life expectancy of you and your beneficiary, you will typically have to decide whether your beneficiary will receive the same benefit as you received before death, in which case you would choose the 100% joint-and-survivor (J&S) option. You can also elect to have your beneficiary receive a smaller payment than the one you are receiving while you are alive; usually you can elect either a 75% J&S option or a 50% J&S option. Some plans permit you to elect any percentage up to 100%.

Of course, the more your beneficiary is to receive after your death, the lower your benefit will be during your lifetime, in recognition of the actuarial likelihood that some benefit will be paid to your beneficiary after your death.

Let's look at the pension options in a little more detail.

Single-Life Annuity

This may also be referred to as a "life-only" or "straight-life annuity." This form of payment provides a monthly amount to the retiree for the rest of his or her life. When the retiree dies, payments stop.

Since this option provides no income to a survivor, it will be the highest possible level of monthly payment. If the pension plan accepted or required employee contributions, however, then the remaining amount of employee contributions will be paid out to the retiree's estate in the event the retiree dies before having received back all of his or her contributions.

This option may make sense for an individual who has no others likely to be dependent on his or her pension after death. Individuals in good health who can expect to live a long time in retirement also may find that this option makes the most sense.

Pension plans governed by ERISA require that a married individual who wants this option must obtain a waiver from his or her spouse, who by law has survivor rights. The waiver must be notarized or witnessed by a plan representative.

Joint-and-Survivor (J&S) Annuity

This may also be referred to as a "survivor income annuity" or a "spousal income annuity." This form of payment provides a monthly income to the retiree. At the retiree's death, a percentage of what the retiree was receiving will be paid to a designated beneficiary for the rest of that person's life.

Because this option provides the potential for retirement income for two lifetimes—the retiree's and his or her surviving beneficiary—the monthly amount received by the retiree will be reduced from the single-life annuity amount. The reduction in the retiree's monthly payment will usually be based on two factors: the percentage to go to the beneficiary and the age difference between the retiree and the beneficiary.

Everything else being equal, the higher the percentage going to the beneficiary, the less will be the monthly amount received by the retiree. Some plans may provide more choices; some may let the retiree specify any percentage desired. Generally, the younger the designated beneficiary, the less will be the monthly payment to the retiree.

Some plans offer what is called a "pop-up option." This lets the retiree who elects a survivor annuity, but whose designated beneficiary dies before the retiree, get back some of the reduction in his or her pension. Usually, the longer the designated beneficiary lives after the employee retires, the less will be restored to the retiree's monthly pension after the death of the intended beneficiary. Often, if the intended beneficiary dies after a certain period of time following the employee's retirement, there will be no restoration to the retiree.

If a married retiree wishes to elect a survivor option of less than 50%, or if the retiree wishes to designate someone other than his or her spouse as beneficiary (if there is a spouse), ERISA again requires a waiver by the spouse.

Retirees with a spouse or other dependent who is likely to outlive the retiree and who needs additional income at the retiree's death may find that this option makes the most sense.

E
X
A
M
P
L
E

■ Beth is 65 years old and decided to retire at the normal retirement age. Her base annual retirement benefit is $30,000, and, under her company's pension plan, she can elect a life-only option or a joint-and-survivor option with her 65-year-old husband of 50%, 75% or 100%. The payments payable under each of these options would be:

Annual Benefit

Life Only	50% J&S	75% J&S	100% J&S
$30,000	$28,800	$27,500	$26,700 ■

Life Annuity with a Term Certain

This is also referred to as a "period certain annuity" or a "guaranteed payment annuity." If a retiree dies within a designated period of time, full payments are made to one or more beneficiaries for a limited amount of time. The number of payments to the beneficiary will depend on the length of time elected by the retiree and the number of payments already received by the retiree before dying.

For example, if the retiree elects a 10-year term certain plan and dies 12 years after retirement, no payments will be made to the beneficiary, since the retiree outlived the term. On the other hand, if the retiree dies after three years, then seven years of payments will be made to the beneficiary.

The longer the guaranteed term, the less the retiree will receive each month. With this option, however, the age of the beneficiary usually has no effect on the amount of the retiree's monthly reduction. This form of payment also usually permits the naming of multiple beneficiaries or an estate or an organization.

Retirees who want to provide income to a beneficiary for a limited time in the event that the retiree dies early in retirement may find that this option has some value. For example, a retiree who wants to provide some income to a child who may be attending college early in the retiree's retirement may elect this option.

This option would be preferable to a joint-and-survivor option, since the retiree is not interested in providing lifetime income to the child. Also, under a J&S option, the age difference between the retiree and the child would result in a major reduction in the retiree's monthly pension. Under a term certain plan, the beneficiary's age is usually irrelevant.

Once again, if the retiree is married, his or her spouse must consent to this option, since it requires a waiver of lifetime survivorship rights.

Lump Sum

Although most defined-benefit plans do not offer this option, some do, and in certain industries (i.e., energy) it is commonly offered. In effect, by electing a lump sum a retiree relieves the pension plan of the promise to pay lifetime benefits. Instead, the retiree receives one check and is on his or her own to manage the amount so that it takes the place of the missing monthly pension benefit.

The amount of the lump sum depends on three factors: the amount of the single-life annuity based on the pension plan's formula, the age of the retiree, and the interest rate used by the plan to convert a future stream of payments into a current dollar amount.

Everything else being equal, the younger the retiree, the larger will be the lump sum. This is because the younger individual will have a longer life expectancy. The longer life expectancy of a younger retiree may be offset, however, by early retirement reduction factors used in the single-life annuity formula.

Generally, the lower the interest rate used by the plan, the higher the lump-sum amount. This is because at a lower assumed rate of interest, you will need more money now to be invested and take the place of the lifetime pension represented by the lump sum. The higher the interest rate, the lower the lump sum.

Lump sums make sense for retirees who believe that by investing the money they can produce a higher monthly income for their lives and the lives of others dependent on the missing monthly pension benefit. Lump sums also make sense for retirees in poor health who wish to leave behind some of their pension as an estate to heirs. Finally, lump sums may offer the opportunity for favorable tax treatment.

Once again, if the retiree is married, his or her spouse must consent to this option, since it requires a waiver of lifetime survivorship rights.

TRAPS, OBSTACLES, TOOLS, AND HELPERS

Try to avoid the following traps and obstacles, and use the following tools and helpers.

- Using retirement plans to accumulate funds for nonretirement purposes
- Electing a distribution option from employer plans without analyzing your personal needs and the long-range financial consequences of each option
- Having a plan distribution check made out to you or taking it as cash instead of directly transferring it to an IRA or another employer's qualified plan
- Rolling over employer stock into an IRA
- Commingling IRA rollovers with regular IRAs
- Waiting until the last possible time to begin taking distributions from your retirement plans
- Making irrevocable decisions and then looking back and second-guessing yourself during retirement

- Complex and changing federal and state tax rules
- Mandatory withholding on distributions that are not directly transferred to an IRA
- Ordinary income tax treatment of all IRA distributions, even to beneficiaries upon the death of the IRA owner
- 10% additional tax on "early" distributions
- 50% penalty tax for failure to make the "minimum required distribution"

- Employer communications describing plan distribution options and their consequences
- Employer-sponsored preretirement planning and retirement counseling programs
- Financial planning software that projects retirement income streams under different distribution scenarios

- IRA rollovers
- 10-year averaging
- Pre-1974 capital gains
- Net unrealized appreciation on employer securities
- Substantially equal periodic payments and age 55 exceptions to the additional 10% tax on early distributions from qualified plans
- Exceptions to additional early distribution tax on withdrawals from IRAs

ACTION ITEMS

Item	Priority*	Completed
1. Identify all lump-sum opportunities from employer plans and perform all necessary federal and state tax projections before making your decision about how to take the distribution.		
2. Inquire about your employer's procedures for keeping your defined-contribution retirement plan with your employer even after you retire. (Specifically, determine the investment options that remain available to you, administrative expenses that will be passed on to you, and the limits on postretirement withdrawals.)		
3. Obtain IRS Publication 590 (1-800-Tax-Form or www.irs.gov) on IRAs and discuss life expectancy options with your financial advisor (especially applicable for those nearing age 70).		

*A, B, C, or N/A, with A being the highest priority.

8

SOCIAL SECURITY ISSUES

The assets of the combined OASI (Old Age and Survivor Insurance) and DI (Disability Insurance) Trust Funds are expected to continue growing over the next 25 years, based on the intermediate assumptions. By the end of 2024, the assets are estimated to reach $6.05 trillion, in nominal dollars. The assets are then estimated to decline until the funds are exhausted in 2037, 3 years later than estimated in last year's report. With the retirement of the "baby-boom" generation starting in about 2010, OASDI costs will increase rapidly relative to the taxable earnings of workers. By the end of the 75-year projection period . . . annual tax revenue would be sufficient to cover only about ⅔ of annual expenditures at the end of the 75-year period.

—Annual Report of the Social Security Trustees, March 2000

Right now, America is passing through a wonderfully benign demographic period in which a huge crop of [76,000,000] Baby Boom workers are swelling our tax receipts while a relatively small generation retires. But before we know it, these demographic forces will be thrown abruptly into reverse.

—Peter G. Peterson, *Will America Grow Up Before It Grows Old?*
(Random House, 1996)

Social Security is a subject that generates extraordinary anxiety for many Americans. For 63% of Americans age 65 and older, Social Security is the primary source of income. It contributes 90% of the income received by about one-quarter of that age group. Without Social Security, the poverty rate among older Americans today would be over 50%.

On the other hand, younger Americans, especially younger Baby Boomers and Generation Xers, believe that Social Security benefits will be cut or eliminated by the time they are eligible to receive them. Figure 8.1 dramatizes the changing dimensions of retirement.

Remember our description of the retirement pie in Chapter 2? We said that there are several common ingredients that go into everyone's pie. The first is some sort of federally mandated retirement benefit. For most of us, that is Social Security. The second common ingredient is personal savings. Other ingredients for this pie include a defined-benefit pension plan, income from a part-time job, and, for a fortunate few, an inheritance.

Remember that everybody's pie will have a different proportion of ingredients. The Social Security system is designed in such a way that for a worker who earns "average earnings" throughout his or her career, full Social Security benefits at normal retirement age will replace about 43% of that income. In today's dollars, average U.S. earnings are about $30,000. For those who continually earn right around the maximum income from which Social Security taxes are paid, which in 2000 is $76,200, Social Security is designed to replace about 24% of those earnings. Obviously, for those who earn more, Social Security will replace a proportionately smaller percentage of their before-retirement pay.

Figure 8.2 shows roughly what portion of your retirement income pie you can expect to be filled by Social Security benefits, and what portion you will have to fill yourself.

In this way, the Social Security system has built into it a degree of social progressivism in its benefit payout. This will be an important issue when it comes time to make the kind of modifications to the system that will enable it to continue to provide benefits for the Baby Boom generation and those who retire after they do.

Today, the Social Security system pays benefits of over $1 billion per day. The average Social Security monthly benefit for a retired worker is $804 and the maximum benefit for a 65-year-old retiring in 2000 is $1,433 a month.

FIGURE 8.1   THE CHANGING DIMENSIONS OF RETIREMENT.

PRIMARY RETIREMENT VEHICLES (or, using our new analogy, biggest slice of the retirement income pie)

GROUP	VEHICLE	Age Started Working*	Years	Retire	Years	Die	Ratio*
Great-Grandparents	Their children	15	55	70	5	75	11:1
Grandparents	Social Security	20	45	65	15	80	3:1
Parents	Pensions	20	40	60	20	80	2:1
Us (Boom)	401(k)	25	30	55	30	85	1:1
Children (Xers)	Themselves	30	20	50	40	90	1:2

*Ratio is years of work to years in retirement.

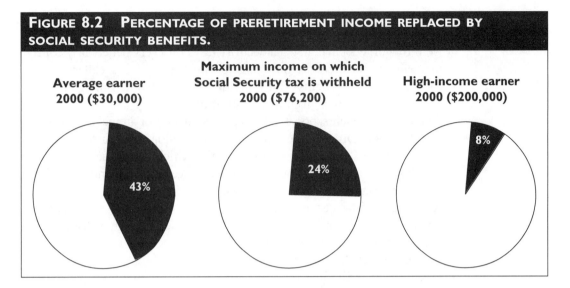

FIGURE 8.2 PERCENTAGE OF PRERETIREMENT INCOME REPLACED BY SOCIAL SECURITY BENEFITS.

Clearly the most confounding aspect to each individual's assessment of how much he or she should depend on Social Security benefits are reports that the Social Security system will eventually "go bankrupt." The most recent *Report of the Trustees of the Social Security Program* says that the system will be able to pay full benefits only to the year 2037, just as Generation Xers are staring retirement in the face.

Despite this, the increasingly popular myth that "Social Security benefits won't be there when I retire" needs to be debunked. Even though you should not assume that Social Security benefits will be all that you will need in retirement, neither should you assume that they won't be available at all.

SOME CHANGES WILL BE MADE

While it is possible that those of us under 50 today will receive lower monthly benefits than today's retirees, it is most probable that we will get something. And with constantly increasing longevity, those of us retiring today may collect more in cumulative benefits than did our parents or grandparents.

When Social Security was enacted in 1935 and the normal retirement age was established at 65, the life expectancy for an American man—most workers were men—was 63, and the life expectancy for a man who reached age 65 was about another two years. Today, the life expectancy for a worker retiring at 65 is 16.6 years for men and 19.9 years for women.

Clearly, some time before the Baby Boom generation begins to retire in about 2010, some changes will need to be made. Those changes could include any combination of the following options:

- An increase in Social Security withholding taxes—known as Federal Insurance Contribution Act (FICA)—on current workers. In 1950, there were 16 workers paying Social Security taxes for every beneficiary collecting, while today there are only three paying for every one collecting.
- Means testing of benefits—meaning that benefits would only go to those with income below a given threshold of need.
- Reduction of benefits, possibly through a reduction of annual cost-of-living adjustments (COLAs), either across the board or for higher-income retirees.
- Increasing the "normal" retirement age at which people can collect full benefits. This is already scheduled to rise to age 67 by the end of the Baby Boom generation's entering the system. (See Figure 8.3.)
- Allowing the Social Security trustees to invest a portion of Social Security taxes collected in the stock and bond markets, rather than using Social Security trust funds to fund other government programs in exchange for specially issued Treasury bonds.
- Establishing individual accounts for every individual who pays Social Security taxes, into which all or a portion of the withholding would be invested by individuals (essentially a government-sponsored 401(k) plan).

While all of us who are writing this book believe that Social Security benefits will be there for most, if not all, Americans, it's increasingly important that individuals plan to depend less on Social Security than previous generations have. This means building a stronger personal savings component.

When you add all of your ingredients together and do your "Will I have enough to retire?" calculations, try doing the calculation three or four times, each time adjusting for less and less in Social Security benefits. Do it with full benefits if there are no changes in the system; then assume that changes will net out to a 25% reduction in benefits; then compute at a 50% reduction in benefits. If you want to be ultraconservative, do an absolute worst-case calculation with no Social Security benefits at all.

When Should You Start Taking Social Security Benefits?

That depends. If you were born before 1938, you are eligible to receive full Social Security benefits at age 65. That age will increase slowly over the next 30 years, until an individual born in 1960 or later must be 67 to receive full benefits, shown in Figure 8.3.

You can begin collecting benefits at age 62. If you choose today to collect benefits at age 62, you will receive 80% of the benefit you would have

---

FIGURE 8.3 NORMAL RETIREMENT AGE.

Your Normal Retirement Benefit is the unreduced benefit payable at your Social Security Normal Retirement Age. You can start receiving a reduced benefit—called an Early Retirement Benefit—as early as age 62. In this worksheet, you can estimate:

- your Normal Retirement Benefit, or
- your Early Retirement Benefit payable at age 62.

WHEN IS YOUR SOCIAL SECURITY NORMAL RETIREMENT AGE?

	Mark	You	Spouse
1. See the table below to determine your Social Security Normal Retirement Age—the age at which you're entitled to collect a full Social Security benefit. Enter your Normal Retirement Age at the right.	66 and 4 months		

Year of Birth	Normal Retirement Age
Before 1938	65
1938	65 and 2 months
1939	65 and 4 months
1940	65 and 6 months
1941	65 and 8 months
1942	65 and 10 months
1943 to 1954	66
1955	66 and 2 months
1956	66 and 4 months
1957	66 and 6 months
1958	66 and 8 months
1959	66 and 10 months
1960 and later	Age 67

received if you had waited until age 65. For those who will retire later, and for whom the "normal" retirement age to collect full Social Security benefits will be higher, the reduction will be greater if you begin taking your benefits at 62.

It's generally accepted that most people who have stopped working will be better off if they begin collecting Social Security as early as possible. If you wait until age 65 to begin collecting, it will take nearly 12 years—until you are 77—before you've received as much in benefits as you would have received if you had started early. That's just to receive the same amount of cash, without considering any cost-of-living adjustments to the benefit or the time value of the money. The bottom line is, if you don't live to 77, you will collect more by starting early. If you live longer, you will collect more by waiting until normal retirement age.

There's one major problem with the suggestion that you begin collecting as early as possible. If you begin receiving Social Security benefits before your normal retirement age and you continue to work, you may have your benefits reduced or eliminated. In 2000, retirees between age 62 and 65 will lose $1 in benefits for every $2 earned above $10,080.

If you are receiving Social Security benefits and have reached your normal retirement age, however, you can earn as much as you want from work without any reduction in your benefit. Effective 2000, the earnings limit for Social Security was eliminated for those who have reached their normal retirement age.

Remember, the trade-off in all of these decisions is that the longer you wait, the less time you have to collect.

HOW MUCH WILL YOUR SOCIAL SECURITY BENEFIT BE?

Your Social Security benefit depends on your earnings history. To be eligible to receive any Social Security benefit on your own earnings record, you must have paid into the system for 40 quarters—which takes about 10 years to accumulate.

To figure your exact benefit, the Social Security Administration computes your average earnings for 35 years, adjusted for inflation. To qualify for the maximum benefit, you need to have earned the maximum salary taxable for 35 years. For 2000, Social Security taxes are withheld on the first $76,200.

Below are listed the average 2000 benefits for selected categories of Social Security beneficiaries.

Beneficiary	Average Benefit
All retired workers	$ 804
Aged couple	$1,348
Widow(er) and 2 children	$1,611
Aged widow(er) alone	$ 775
All disabled workers	$ 754
Worker who has maximum taxable earnings and retires at 65	$1,433

Remember, you must *request* your Social Security benefits; they do not begin automatically. Three months before you plan to begin taking benefits, you need to call the Social Security Administration or visit a Social Security office and complete the necessary paperwork. There are over 1,000 Social Security offices across the country. Find them at the Social Security Web site: www.ssa.gov.

HOW DO YOU KNOW HOW MUCH SOCIAL SECURITY YOU'RE ENTITLED TO AS OF TODAY?

Each year beginning in 2000 around your birthday month, you will automatically receive your personal Social Security Statement from the Social Security Administration (SSA). This used to be called a Personal Earnings and Benefit Estimate Statement, or PEBES. It's a good idea to review your statement carefully. It will show your earnings history, so you can verify the accuracy of the information. If you don't receive your annual statement, you can call 1-800-772-1213 to request a Form SSA-7004. Simply follow the voice prompts to key in the necessary information using a touch-tone phone. Within four weeks you will receive a simple form to fill out and return to Social Security. You can also visit www.ssa.gov to obtain your statement.

In addition to your earnings history, your statement will show a history of your contributions to Social Security, what your estimated retirement benefit will be, what benefit you would be entitled to if you became disabled today, and what benefit your spouse and/or child(ren) would be entitled to you if you were to die today. You may want to log on to www.ssa.gov, where you will find a wealth of information—probably much more than you need—on Social Security. In addition, the site offers two calculators—a quick version and a detailed version—that will help you estimate your Social Security benefit. The request form is shown in Figure 8.4.

Delayed Retirement Credit

For each year you delay receiving Social Security past your normal retirement age, your Social Security benefit is increased by a fixed percentage. For example, for people turning 65 in 2000 or 2001, the increase is 6% for each full year they delay receiving their benefit past age 65. (This increase is in addition to adding another year of earnings, which may knock out a lower year in a person's 35-year wage history and also increase the benefit.) The Delayed Retirement Credit hits a peak of 8% for those reaching the normal retirement age in 2008 and thereafter.

FIGURE 8.4   REQUEST FOR SOCIAL SECURITY EARNINGS AND BENEFIT ESTIMATE.

Request for Earnings and Benefit Estimate Statement

☐ Please check this box if you want to get your statement in Spanish instead of English.

Please print or type your answers. When you have completed the form, fold it and mail it to us.

1. Name shown on your Social Security card:

_____
First Name _____ Middle Initial
_____
Last Name Only

2. Your Social Security number as shown on your card:
☐☐☐ - ☐☐ - ☐☐☐☐

3. Your date of birth
☐☐ ☐☐ ☐☐
Month Day Year

4. Other Social Security numbers you have used:
☐☐☐ - ☐☐ - ☐☐☐☐
☐☐☐ - ☐☐ - ☐☐☐☐

5. Your sex: ☐ Male   ☐ Female

6. Other names you have used (including a maiden name):
_____

For items 7 and 9 show only earnings covered by Social Security. Do NOT include wages from State, local or Federal Government employment that are NOT covered for Social Security or that are covered ONLY by Medicare.

7. Show your actual earnings (wages and/or net self-employment income) for last year and your estimated earnings for this year.

A. Last year's actual earnings: *(Dollars Only)*
$ ☐☐☐ , ☐☐☐ . ☐☐

B. This year's estimated earnings: *(Dollars Only)*
$ ☐☐☐ , ☐☐☐ . ☐☐

8. Show the age at which you plan to stop working.
☐☐ *(Show only one age)*

9. Below, show the average yearly amount (not your total future lifetime earnings) that you think you will earn between now and when you plan to stop working. Include cost-of-living, performance or scheduled pay increases or bonuses.

If you expect to earn significantly more or less in the future due to promotions, job changes, part-time work, or an absence from the work force, enter the amount that most closely reflects your future average yearly earnings.

If you don't expect any significant changes, show the same amount you are earning now (the amount in 7B).

Future average yearly earnings: *(Dollars Only)*
$ ☐☐☐ , ☐☐☐ . ☐☐

10. Address where you want us to send the statement.

_____
Name

_____
Street Address (Include Apt. No., P.O. Box, or Rural Route)

_____
City   State   Zip Code

Notice:
I am asking for information about my own Social Security record or the record of a person I am authorized to represent. I understand that when requesting information on a deceased person, I must include proof of death and relationship or appointment. I further understand that if I deliberately request information under false pretenses, I may be guilty of a Federal crime and could be fined and/or imprisoned. I authorize you to use a contractor to send the statement of earnings and benefit estimate to the person named in item 10.

▲

Please sign your name (Do Not Print)

_____
Date   (Area Code) Daytime Telephone No.

TRAPS, OBSTACLES, TOOLS, AND HELPERS

Try to avoid the following traps and obstacles, and use the following tools and helpers.

- Assuming that current Social Security benefit rules will not change before or during your retirement
- Not communicating your opinion about Social Security's future to your congressional representatives
- Delaying Social Security benefits past age 62 if you stop working by then
- Starting to collect Social Security benefits and then working and exceeding the annual earnings limitation
- Believing that Social Security benefits are always tax-free
- Relying on the government to automatically notify you when to apply for benefits

- Complex Social Security rules
- Federal and state taxation of benefits
- Earnings limitation on working after you begin receiving Social Security benefits before reaching your normal retirement age

- Personal Social Security Statements
- Social Security Administration toll-free number (1-800-772-1213) and over 1,000 local offices
- Social Security on-line retirement planner that lets you compute estimates of your future Social Security retirement benefits
- Social Security Web site: www.ssa.gov

- Current automatic annual cost-of-living adjustments (COLAs) that protect Social Security benefits against inflation (the COLA for 2000 was 2.4%.)
- Nonretirement benefits, including survivor, children, disability, and death benefits provided without proof of insurability

ACTION ITEMS

Item	Priority*	Completed
1. Select an estimated Social Security retirement benefit for your most reasonable retirement planning scenario, and calculate your funding gap. (Recalculate using 75% of this benefit, then 50% of this benefit. If you want to determine the worst-case scenario, calculate using no Social Security benefit.)		
2. Examine your Personal Social Security Statement that you receive each year to make sure your earnings history has been entered accurately. Errors will have an effect on your benefit estimate. If you don't receive your annual statement, call the Social Security Administration or visit the SSA Web site at www.ssa.gov.		
3. Apply for your benefits three months before you want them.		
4. Calculate any short-term reduction in Social Security benefits from work you will do after beginning to receive benefits but before you reach your normal retirement age.		
5. If you are a long way from retirement, begin a serious retirement savings program to mitigate against potential benefit reductions in Social Security.		

*A, B, C, or N/A, with A being the highest priority.

INSURANCE ISSUES

Among the most crucial issues to consider when you retire are your insurance needs. Many people depend on employer-provided insurance policies to cover their health, their life, and any potential disability. Upon retirement, for most people, "you're on your own."

Addressing insurance needs carefully will help you retire with a minimum of anxiety about the future; on the other hand, ignoring or underestimating these issues may cause you substantial worries—and perhaps big trouble—in your later years.

You must look at potential insurance needs in four areas:

1. Health insurance, either a full insurance policy or a supplement to Medicare if you have reached age 65
2. Life insurance
3. Long-term care insurance
4. Liability and property insurance

HEALTH INSURANCE AND "MEDIGAP" POLICIES

Believing that Medicare provides comprehensive health insurance, including prescription drugs, dental care, eyeglasses, and custodial care.

"What do I need health insurance for? I have Medicare."

Too many Americans fall for this retirement health care insurance myth. Although Medicare will address many of your health insurance concerns after you turn 65, the truth is that Medicare coverage is limited. It leaves you exposed in several ways, including deductibles and copayments. And not all doctors accept Medicare as payment in full.

Medicare has two parts: Part A pays for hospital services and Part B for doctors' services. Medicare Part A can help pay for inpatient hospital care, inpatient care in a skilled nursing facility, home health care, and hospice care. Part A is financed during your working years through the FICA tax, with 1.45% of your compensation withheld and designated for this insurance (2.9% for the self-employed).

If you plan to retire at age 65, you simply contact the Social Security Administration about three months prior to your 65th birthday. The Social Security Administration will enroll you in Medicare. If you're already receiving Social Security benefits when you turn 65, you'll be contacted by the SSA and automatically enrolled in Medicare Part A on your 65th birthday. There is no premium or fee for Part A.

Coverage under Medicare is described in terms of a "benefit period." A benefit period begins on the first day you receive service as an inpatient in a hospital and ends after you've been out of the hospital or skilled nursing facility for 60 days in a row, or remain in a skilled nursing facility but do not receive skilled care there for 60 days in a row.

Medicare doesn't pay for custodial care—that is, care that could be given by someone who isn't medically skilled, such as help with dressing, walking, or eating. However, if you're confined to your home and meet certain other conditions, Medicare Part A can pay the full approved cost of home health care visits from a Medicare-participating home health agency. No prior hospital stay is required, and there's no limit on the number of covered visits. Note, however, that coverage is for part-time or intermittent care only. Moreover, there's no coverage for services primarily to assist in daily living, as noted above.

Figure 9.1 shows services covered under Medicare Part A during any benefit period. As you can see, an illness or accident that requires a lengthy hospital stay or a number of benefit periods in one calendar year can be costly in terms of deductibles and copayments.

Medicare Part B helps pay for doctors' services and many other medical services and supplies that aren't covered by Medicare Part A. Where you receive these services—hospital, clinic, or home—is irrelevant.

FIGURE 9.1 MEDICARE PART A: HOSPITAL INSURANCE—COVERED SERVICES PER BENEFIT PERIOD.[a]

SERVICES	BENEFIT	MEDICARE PAYS[b]	YOU PAY[b]
HOSPITALIZATION Semiprivate room and board, general nursing, and miscellaneous hospital services and supplies.	First 60 days	All but $776	$776
	61st to 90th day	All but $194 a day	$194 a day
	91st to 150th day[c]	All but $388 a day	$388 a day
	Beyond 150 days	Nothing	All costs
POSTHOSPITAL SKILLED NURSING FACILITY CARE You must have been in a hospital for at least 3 days, enter a Medicare-approved facility generally within 30 days after hospital discharge, and meet other program requirements.[d]	First 20 days	100% of approved amount	Nothing
	Additional 80 days	All but $97 a day	Up to $97 a day
	Beyond 100 days	Nothing	All costs
HOME HEALTH CARE Medically necessary skilled care, home health aide services, medical supplies, etc.	Part-time or inter-mittent nursing care and other services for as long as you meet criteria for benefits.	100% of approved amount; 80% of approved amount for durable medical equipment.	Nothing for services; 20% of approved amount for durable medical equipment.
HOSPICE CARE Full scope of pain relief and support services available to the terminally ill.	As long as doctor certifies need.	All but limited costs for outpatient drugs and inpatient respite care.	Limited cost sharing for outpatient drugs and inpatient respite care.
BLOOD	Blood	All but first 3 pints per calendar year.	For first 3 pints.[e]

[a]Benefit period begins on the first day you receive service as an inpatient in a hospital and ends after you have been out of the hospital or skilled nursing facility for 60 days in a row or remain in a skilled nursing facility but do not receive skilled care there for 60 days in a row.
[b]These figures are for 2000 and are subject to change each year.
[c]60 reserve days may be used only once.
[d]Neither Medicare nor Medigap insurance will pay for most nursing home care.
[e]To the extent that the blood deductible is met under one part of Medicare during the calendar year, it does not have to be met under the other part. Numbers are for 2000.

■ 127

Part B is optional and is offered when you become entitled to Part A. You're enrolled in Part B automatically when you become entitled to Part A. If you do not want Part B, you must elect not to take it. There is a monthly premium—$45.50 in 2000—and you will be billed unless you decline coverage.

There's a $100 annual deductible before Medicare Part B begins paying for covered services. The $100 deductible must represent services or supplies covered by Medicare. It must also be based on the Medicare-approved amounts, not necessarily the actual charges billed by the physician or medical supplier. The approved amount for physicians' services is determined by the Health Care Financing Agency and set forth in a national fee schedule. Medicare pays 80% of the approved amount.

In addition to Medicare coinsurance, you pay for charges that exceed the amount approved by Medicare unless the doctor or supplier agrees to accept Medicare's approved amount as full payment. (In some states, doctors who accept Medicare are required to accept it as full payment.) Some healthcare providers do not accept Medicare patients.

Figure 9.2 shows the payments for services under Part B and your responsibility for deductibles and copayments. Note that the Medicare-approved rate for many doctors' services is below what many doctors charge for their services. Unless the doctor explicitly says he or she will accept Medicare as full payment, you must pay the difference between the fee and the Medicare-approved rate.

Although Medicare pays for many of your healthcare needs after you turn 65, there are limitations and exposures. For example, Medicare does not cover:

- Care in a skilled-nursing facility beyond 100 days per benefit period
- Custodial care—probably the type of care most commonly required by those in a nursing home
- Out-of-pocket prescription drugs
- Medical tests for (and cost of) eyeglasses or hearing aids
- Care received outside the United States

The way to cover these limitations and exposures is through the purchase of so-called Medigap insurance, sold by private insurance companies, designed to fill the gaps between Medicare benefits and the coverage you desire.

Horror stories about not being able to find appropriate Medigap insurance are no longer the norm. Federal law requires that insurers offer no more than 10 standard Medigap policies. Each policy must provide at least a "core"

FIGURE 9.2 MEDICARE PART B: MEDICAL INSURANCE—COVERED SERVICES PER CALENDAR YEAR.

SERVICES	BENEFIT	MEDICARE PAYS	YOU PAY
MEDICAL EXPENSE Physicians' services, inpatient and outpatient medical and surgical services and supplies, physical and speech therapy, diagnostic tests, durable medical equipment, etc.	Medicare pays for medical services in or out of the hospital.	80% of approved amount (after $100 deductible); 50% of approved charges for most outpatient mental health services.	$100 deductible,[a] plus 20% of approved amount and charges above approved amount.[b] 50% of approved charges for mental health services.
CLINICAL LABORATORY SERVICES	Blood tests, biopsies, urinalysis, etc.	Generally, 100% of approved amount.	Nothing for services.
HOME HEALTH CARE Medically necessary skilled care, home health aide services, medical supplies, etc.	Part-time or intermittent nursing care and other services for as long as you meet criteria for benefits.	100% of approved amount; 80% of approved amount for durable medical equipment.	Nothing for services; 20% of approved amount for durable medical equipment.
OUTPATIENT HOSPITAL TREATMENT Reasonable and necessary services for the diagnosis or treatment of an illness or injury.	Unlimited if medically necessary.	80% of approved amount (after $100 deductible).	Subject to deductible plus 20% of billed amount.
BLOOD	Blood	80% of approved amount (after $100 deductible and starting with fourth pint).	First 3 pints plus 20% of approved amount for additional pints (after $100 deductible).[c]

[a]Once you have had $100 of expense for covered services, the Part B deductible does not apply to other covered services you receive for the rest of the year.
[b]The amount by which a physician's charge can exceed the Medicare-approved amount is limited by law.
[c]To the extent that the blood deductible is met under one part of Medicare during the calendar year, it does not have to be met under the other part.

of basic benefits. A plan with only the "core" benefits is designated Plan A. The succession of standard plans—designated B through J—adds more benefits to the core. Insurers that sell Medigap policies in any state must make at least Plan A available within the state. Beyond that, they can offer whatever plans they want.

Figure 9.3 shows the various benefits offered under the 10 standard Medigap plans. The plans are defined in detail in Appendix III.

FIGURE 9.3 TEN STANDARD MEDICARE SUPPLEMENT PLANS.

CORE BENEFITS	PLAN A	PLAN B	PLAN C	PLAN D	PLAN E	PLAN F	PLAN G	PLAN H	PLAN I	PLAN J
Part A hospital (days 61–90)	X	X	X	X	X	X	X	X	X	X
Lifetime reserve days (91–150)	X	X	X	X	X	X	X	X	X	X
365 Life hospital days, 100%	X	X	X	X	X	X	X	X	X	X
Parts A and B blood	X	X	X	X	X	X	X	X	X	X
Part B coinsurance, 20%	X	X	X	X	X	X	X	X	X	X
ADDITIONAL BENEFITS	**A**	**B**	**C**	**D**	**E**	**F**	**G**	**H**	**I**	**J**
Skilled nursing facility coinsurance (days 21–100)			X	X	X	X	X	X	X	X
Part A deductible		X	X	X	X	X	X	X	X	X
Part B deductible			X			X				X
Part B excess charges						100%	80%		100%	100%
Foreign travel emergency			X	X	X	X	X	X	X	X
At-home recovery				X			X		X	X
Prescription drugs								1	1	2
Preventive medical care					X					X

Core benefits pay the patient's share of Medicare's approved amount for physician services (generally 20%) after $100 annual deductible, the patient's cost of a long hospital stay ($194 a day for days 61–90, $388 a day for days 91–150, approved costs not paid by Medicare after day 150 to a total of 365 days lifetime), and charges for the first 3 pints of blood not covered by Medicare.

Two prescription drug benefits are offered:

1. A "basic" benefit with $250 annual deductible, 50% coinsurance, and a $1,250 maximum annual benefit (plans H and I above)
2. An "extended" benefit (plan J above) containing a $250 annual deductible, 50% coinsurance, and a $3,000 maximum annual benefit

Each of the 10 plans has a letter designation ranging from A through J. Insurance companies are not permitted to change these designations or to substitute other names or titles. They may, however, add names or titles to these letter designations. While companies are not required to offer all the plans, they all must make plan A available if they sell any of the other nine in a state. Numbers are for 2000.

SELECTING AN APPROPRIATE PLAN

Standardized Medigap policies make comparison shopping easy.

Shopping for a Medigap policy is easier now than ever before. You should select your plan according to three criteria:

1. The plan itself (meaning the set of features and benefits that is right for you)
2. Service
3. Price

Although these three criteria are obviously interrelated, we'll look at each of them separately.

The Plan. You should study each benefit, then select a policy that includes the benefits you consider worthwhile and excludes the ones you don't need or want. On the one hand, you could just select the basic plan (Plan A) and self-insure for the additional benefits offered in plans B through J. This kind of "stop-loss" approach probably isn't advisable, however. Here are some general guidelines that may be more helpful. Benefits that insurance professionals generally recommend include:

• The skilled nursing home copayment ($97 in 2000)
• Part A hospital deductible ($776 in 2000 for the 60 days in the hospital)
• Foreign travel emergency benefits

Benefits that are generally considered less worthwhile include:

• The Part B deductible of $100 (which is likely to cost as much as the benefit is worth)
• Preventive care
• At-home recovery benefits

Coverage for Part B excess doctor expenses may also be less worthwhile. First, this coverage comes into play only if the physician doesn't accept Medicare's payment as full payment. Second, the law restricts the amount that physicians can charge over the Medicare-approved payment.

You should also consider the prescription drug benefits in the context of their pricing and their value to you. If you're healthy today, a long time may pass before you reap any benefit from the prescription drug benefit. Given the 50% basic prescription drug benefit, you would not reach the maximum benefit until you spent $2,750 per year on medications ($250 deductible plus your copayment of 50% of the next $2,500 worth of prescription drugs). The extended benefit is maximized at an expenditure of $6,250 per year.

Service. Although you might expect price to be the next most important criterion, you're probably better off long term by identifying an insurer that has distinguished itself for policyholder service. Here are some relevant questions to ask:

- How does the insurer manage claims?
- How does the insurer coordinate Medicare claims with its Medigap policy?
- Is coordination done electronically, or are forms necessary?
- Is there a toll-free telephone number for customer service?

Price. Once you've identified the Medigap plan (or plans) that interest you, and once you've identified one or more companies worthy of your business, you should compare prices. As always, the price differential between two providers is probably something you can attribute to some value added from the higher-priced provider.

Not purchasing Medigap insurance because you assume that your former employer's health insurance will continue to cover you can be one of your biggest mistakes in retirement. In 1994, only one-third of retirees and their dependents were covered by a former employer's group health plan. The number of new retirees covered by such plans continues to fall.

If your employer does extend coverage to retirees, that insurance will be your primary coverage and Medicare will be your secondary coverage. But even in this instance, you may still have some gaps in coverage.

Extending Benefits Under COBRA

The Consolidated Omnibus Budget Reconciliation Act of 1985 (COBRA) mandated that companies with 20 or more employees allow former employees and/or dependents to continue buying the company's group health policy following one of four qualifying events: an employee's death, retirement, entitlement to Medicare, or termination for reasons other than gross misconduct.

Underestimating the cost of COBRA coverage after you leave your employer.

If you retire from a company prior to age 65, the company is required to allow you to continue your group health coverage for 18 months at no more than 102% of the premium the company would pay. While this may be a significant savings over the cost of private insurance, it still can be quite costly. When you become eligible for Medicare, the company's obligation to you in this regard ends, but not to your spouse. Under the provisions of COBRA, the company is obligated to continue your spouse's coverage for a total of up to 36 months if he or she is not yet eligible for Medicare.

If your eligibility or your spouse's eligibility to purchase your employer-sponsored insurance ends before you or your spouse turn 65, you may be able to convert the employer's group policy into an individual policy with no proof of insurability and no waiver of coverage for preexisting conditions. Typically, you must convert to an individual policy within 30 days of the date your group coverage ends.

POSTRETIREMENT LIFE INSURANCE MAY NOT BE A WASTE OF MONEY

- Aggressive insurance agents who use misleading sales practices
- Artificial rules of thumb (like five times your pay) to determine how much life insurance you need

For years, cash-value life insurance has received a bad rap. It has been seen as a bad investment and, for those in retirement, a waste of money. The cry of "buy term and invest the rest" has been heard across the land.

In truth, while cash-value life insurance is not the best investment tool, it has other important uses, both before your retirement and as a retirement and estate-planning tool.

The most fundamental need for life insurance may be to provide adequate income for your surviving spouse. Consider what the surviving spouse's cash flow and capital would look like if you or your spouse were to die tomorrow. Would your spouse have enough money to live comfortably? Would you be able to live in comfort financially if your spouse were to die instead?

Existing cash-value policies may be valuable tax-deferred assets from which you can withdraw funds for income or medical care. Dividends from a policy that no longer requires cash premiums can be used to pay health insurance premiums after retirement. An existing policy may also be "annuitized" by exchanging it for an annuity to create another steady income stream. We'll discuss "buying out" a policy to cover expenses related to a terminal illness in more detail in Chapter 12.

This situation will be especially true if your retirement income will be comprised substantially of a pension and Social Security. Upon your death, the pension benefit payable to your spouse is likely to decrease by as much as 50%, and the Social Security benefit paid to your surviving spouse will also decrease. If your spouse still has a long life expectancy at the time of your death, this loss of income could cause serious problems.

It's important to do this analysis for a few different time periods—today, three years down the road, at the time when any employer-paid life insurance terminates for either of you, and at the end of the projected life expectancy of the older partner.

The Consumer Federation of America (CFA) can help compare the benefits of buying cash-value policies or lower-premium term insurance. The CFA can be reached at (202) 387-0087.

If you find you need postretirement life insurance, you have three options:

1. Convert group term coverage to an individual permanent policy.
2. Maintain or enhance existing cash-value insurance.
3. Acquire new coverage.

Most insurance professionals counsel against converting group term policies to individual policies if you are healthy enough to look elsewhere.

You can't convert at nonsmoker or preferred rates. If you are healthy at retirement, it's better to look to the open market for a new policy.

You may have one or more cash-value policies, such as an individual whole life, universal life, or variable life, or a group universal life policy. Where your cash flow, insurability, and policy terms permit, you may want to increase your premiums, or use the policy's dividends to purchase more insurance. There are several benefits associated with putting more money into the policy:

- The death benefit may grow.
- If your health has deteriorated, using dividends to purchase more insurance may be the only way to buy more insurance economically.
- The cash value will continue to grow tax-deferred.
- The increased cash value will increase the amount against which you can borrow or take partial surrenders for additional cash flow.

Pension Maximization

You can also use cash-value life insurance to maximize your pension. Here's how. Suppose your company's pension has a survivor annuity that allows your spouse to continue receiving benefits after you die (at a reduced rate). If you choose this option, you will receive a lower monthly pension benefit while you are alive than if you choose to base your benefit only on your life expectancy.

The concept of pension maximization involves your planning to take a higher pension benefit (with either a corresponding lower survivor benefit or no survivor benefit) and assuring the desired survivor benefit with life insurance.

Pension maximization is typically not advisable if you wait until retirement to purchase insurance. Often the premium will be too expensive for the amount of insurance your spouse will need to provide the targeted income, which could be provided by purchasing an annuity for his or her lifetime with the insurance proceeds, for example. However, pension maximization can be a viable strategy if the insurance is fully paid by retirement or any remaining premiums are quite manageable because the policy was taken out years before.

The risks of pension maximization are borne by the spouse. He or she takes the risk that there will be enough insurance proceeds to provide the necessary survivor income; that the insurer will remain solvent; that the insured spouse will pay the premiums; and so forth.

Also, pension maximization is a tricky technique, and calls for some calculations. You should consult a financial planner or insurance specialist to help you through the options. Also, if you and your spouse divorce, there will be some unique issues to address. Pension maximization works out best if your spouse is in poor health and likely to die before you do. You can take the higher benefit and carry the life insurance only as necessary.

Term Insurance

If additional life insurance is needed to create supplemental income for your spouse after your death but not for any cash needs during your lifetime, you should consider purchasing term insurance.Term insurance provides a death benefit of a stated amount for a stated duration or term. At the end of the term, the coverage expires. There is no cash value or savings element associated with a term policy. There are two basic types of individual term insurance policies on the market today: annual renewable term and level premium term. With annual renewable term (ART), you pay the premium every year and the policy remains in force. The benefit stays level, but the premium increases every year. Level premium term offers premiums that remain level and guaranteed for a period of 5, 10, 15, or 20 years. At the end of the guarantee period, you must "reenter" or medically requalify for another period of equal duration at excellent guaranteed rates.

Many term policies allow you to convert from term to cash-value insurance without evidence of insurability. The chief advantage here is that a temporary policy becomes permanent, an option particularly useful to policyholders whose health may have deteriorated at some point while holding term insurance. A prospective purchaser should always determine for how long the conversion feature is valid. This can be a trap for the unwary, particularly the younger insured who may ordinarily decide to convert at an age that is well beyond the policy year mandated by the contract.

Group term insurance is pure yearly renewable term insurance offered to employees on a group basis. While there is generally no individual underwriting, the participant must be a full-time employee. Coverage usually is available in a fixed amount for all employees or in a certain amount by position or in multiples of compensation. Group term coverage may extend beyond retirement, though at reduced amounts. An employee who leaves the employer may convert the group term coverage to individual coverage without evidence of insurability under certain conditions. The conversion must be made within 31 days after terminating employment.

Using Life Insurance in Estate Planning

Life insurance is increasingly being used as an estate planning tool, especially for those with estates worth more than $1 million. We'll discuss this in greater detail in Chapter 10, where we talk about linking your retirement planning more closely with your estate planning.

LONG-TERM CARE INSURANCE

Underinsuring against truly catastrophic risks, especially disability, major health, long-term care, and personal liability.

Perhaps no other insurance option causes as much anguish or confusion as long-term care (LTC) insurance. Long-term care is the kind of help you need if you're unable to care for yourself because of a prolonged illness or disability. Long-term care encompasses services ranging from care in a nursing facility to assistance in daily activities at home.

Statistics show that there is a relatively high probability that you'll spend some time in a nursing home if you are 65 or older. Yet Medicare and Medigap insurance are unlikely to cover the expenses associated with LTC.

Many insurance specialists believe that if your net worth is less than about $200,000, the cost of LTC is prohibitive, and that if your net worth is more than about $1.5 million, you might as well self-insure. It's the people with modest to good-size net worth—the vast majority of Americans today—who need to decide if they want to carry the risk of LTC expenses themselves or share that risk with others by purchasing insurance.

It wasn't too long ago that LTC policies were prohibitively expensive and did not offer very good coverage. But the insurance industry is continually working to create more affordable and better policies. Standardization of LTC policies does not yet exist, as it does with Medigap policies. So if you decide to explore the LTC market, you need to be very thorough and probably should seek some professional assistance from a financial planner or an insurance broker who can deal with any number of companies.

If you decide to pursue the LTC insurance option, begin by looking at policies that offer the most expansive (*not expensive*) coverage. You should

State Medicaid programs that partner with private LTC insurance providers to offer coverage to middle-income residents.

look at policies that cover all levels of care: skilled, intermediate, custodial, and home care. The better policies today offer such expansive coverage.

In addressing this issue, consider the following questions:

- Should you purchase an LTC policy?
- If so, how should you evaluate alternative LTC policies?

We'll divide our discussion into four sections:

1. What do we mean by LTC?
2. Deciding whether you need LTC.
3. Group LTC policies.
4. Should you purchase an LTC policy?

What Do We Mean by Long-Term Care?

LTC is assistance needed to help you care for yourself when you cannot because of a prolonged illness or disability. LTC encompasses services ranging from a skilled nursing facility to assistance in daily activities at home. While typically associated with skilled nursing care provided in a nursing home, LTC more properly includes services at several levels of care, including the following:

- *Skilled nursing care:* Acute nursing and rehabilitative care given by a registered nurse or therapist, usually daily (around the clock) and supervised by a physician.
- *Intermediate nursing care:* Occasional nursing and rehabilitative care under supervision of skilled medical personnel. This level of care differs from skilled care in that it is not on a 24-hour basis.
- *Custodial care:* Assistance in performing activities of daily living. This level of care is often given by nonmedical personnel, whether in nursing homes, adult day-care centers, or your home.
- *Home care:* This can include part-time skilled care, therapy, homemakers' assistance, home health aides' care, and other forms of assistance in your own home. Many people feel it is important to have home care coverage.

Deciding Whether You Need LTC

Although the general need for LTC is statistically significant, your own individual need is more difficult to assess. Bear in mind that LTC may be necessary for a variety of reasons that range from arthritis to Alzheimer's to accidents. Whether you or your spouse will need LTC depends on your current state of health, your family health history, and a variety of other factors, many of them unpredictable. These are issues you should discuss with your physician as well as with your insurance agent.

From a cost standpoint, the situation is somewhat more predictable. The cost of a nursing home stay varies by geographical location but ranges from about $30,000 to as much as $70,000 a year.

Group LTC Policies

Some employers are now offering group LTC policies. These policies are typically employee-paid and offer coverage, limits, and exclusions that are similar to those for individual policies. Premiums can be highly competitive; you may be able to cover not only yourself but also your spouse (and often your parents and in-laws as well) under the policy. Your coverage is also portable—you can keep the coverage even if you leave your employer.

Should You Purchase an LTC Policy?

If you feel that your circumstances might warrant purchase of an LTC policy, you should consider the following factors.

Affordability. Premiums for someone in his or her early to mid-60s are likely to range from $2,000 to $4,000 annually, depending on the insured's exact age, benefit amounts, benefit period, elimination period, and so forth. You should ask your insurance agent to show you the relative costs of various policies.

Attitude toward receiving public assistance. What are your sentiments on this subject? If you end up needing LTC but lack the funds to pay private care givers, are you comfortable with the notion of receiving care through Medicaid?

Family history. If your parents required LTC during their lifetimes, you're statistically more likely to need LTC, thus making the case for LTC insurance more compelling.

Availability, reliability, and desirability of care by family members. Do you have relatives who can provide adequate LTC in your home? Do you want to be cared for by (and be dependent on) a family member? Some people may find this an acceptable option; others may find it unappealing. Even if you're comfortable with the possibility, are your relatives sufficiently skilled, patient, and generous to provide you with the required level of care?

Attitude toward leaving an estate for your heirs. An LTC policy can be a "stop-loss" mechanism that could preserve at least some portion of your estate for your heirs. Given the costs associated with LTC, insurance coverage could limit the drain on your assets if you require LTC.

Flexibility in later years. You may have a notion of moving to a congregate care facility in a few years. The facility may or may not provide LTC as a part of its program. For this reason, you may want your own policy to cover you in the interim.

Broader (and better) choices for care. You may find that because of your net worth, income level, and LTC policy, you'll have greater choice of LTC facilities than some people with comparable or more limited assets who have no LTC insurance.

It's difficult to determine a precise combination of benefit amounts, elimination period, inflation riders, and so forth. One way to deal with this decision is to determine how much of the LTC risk you can reasonably retain and then transfer the balance of the risk to the insurer.

For example, you might decide to retain the risks of a brief period of care but insure for some portion of the risk of extended care. Thus a longer elimination period and a benefit amount that's a reasonable percentage of today's daily costs would be appropriate. A benefit period of at least three years would also serve you well, for it will give your assets time to compound and allow you and your family time to plan for possible asset transfers. Remember that LTC policies typically require that you pay the premium for the rest of your life. In many policies, you forfeit all benefits if you stop paying premiums; in others you may accrue a reduced benefit if you pay the premium for a specified term.

A WORD ABOUT LIABILITY AND PROPERTY INSURANCE

At the retirement stage in life many people have "burned the mortgage" or will soon do so. But it's still important to retain adequate insurance coverage, both on damage caused to your home and other property, and against the possibility of a claim against you for personal liability.

Make sure to check your liability limits. And if you do not have an excess liability or umbrella policy, talk to your insurance agent and/or advisor.

TRAPS, OBSTACLES, TOOLS, AND HELPERS

Try to avoid the following traps and obstacles, and use the following tools and helpers.

- Overinsuring against risks you can afford to retain
- Underinsuring against truly catastrophic risks, especially disability, major health, LTC, and personal liability
- Having duplicate coverage for risks, especially health insurance where both spouses work
- Assuming that current Medicare benefit rules will not change before or during your retirement
- Not communicating your opinion about Medicare's future to your congressional representative
- Believing that Medicare provides comprehensive health insurance, including prescription drugs, dental care, eyeglasses, and custodial care
- Underestimating the cost of COBRA coverage after you leave your employer
- Using life insurance to maximize your pension without analyzing the trade-offs

- Aggressive insurance agents who use misleading sales practices
- Rules of thumb (like five times your pay) to determine how much life insurance you need
- Complex insurance policy provisions
- High front-end expenses, sales commissions, and surrender charges on annuities, especially variable annuities
- Healthcare providers who do not accept Medicare
- New federal rules severely restricting "Medicaid trusts"
- Credit life, flight, hospital indemnity, and dread disease insurance

- Financial planning software that helps determine objectively how much life, disability, and other forms of insurance you need
- Insurance needs worksheets
- Insurance counseling services provided by state departments of insurance or area agencies on aging
- Consumer Federation of America (CFA)

- Flexible spending accounts
- Standardized Medigap policies to help with comparison shopping
- Federal prohibition against insurance companies requiring medical evidence of insurability during the first six months after you sign up for Medicare Part B
- Employer-provided group insurance plans
- Employer-provided disability benefits in defined-benefit retirement plans
- State Medicaid programs that partner with private LTC insurance providers to offer coverage to middle-income residents
- Tax deductibility of LTC insurance premiums
- Insurance company discounts to policyholders based on age or years of experience

ACTION ITEMS

Item	Priority*	Completed
1. Identify and analyze all of your financial risks, including job termination, death, health, disability, casualty/theft and personal liability. For each risk, determine whether you can avoid it, reduce it, accept it, or insure against it. For each risk you want to shift through insurance and examine your current coverage to determine if it is too little, too much, or has gaps. Consult an agent to review this.		
2. Ask your employer if your health insurance coverage continues in retirement. (In particular, make sure you understand how the company's retiree health insurance coordinates with Medicare benefits after you reach age 65. Does your employer provide you with the same level of overall coverage as active employees after "carving out" what Medicare pays? Does your employer apply its active employee coverage rules to whatever amount Medicare does not cover? Does your employer recognize Medicare health maintenance organizations (HMOs)? Does your		

ACTION ITEMS (continued)

Item	Priority*	Completed
employer just set aside an amount of money or credits to be used to purchase retiree health insurance each year?) Remember that your employer's plans and policies can change.		
3. If you are leaving your job prior to Medicare eligibility, find out from the company benefits office the cost of group health coverage under COBRA. (Also ask if you can convert your group policy to an individual policy without proof of insurability and without waivers of preexisting condition coverage after the COBRA coverage ends.)		
4. Ask your employer if your life insurance coverage continues, and, if so, for how long and at what death benefit level. (Consider replacing the coverage, especially if it does not continue, either by purchasing new insurance at a reasonable rate—if you are insurable—or by converting the group plan to an individual policy.)		
5. Consult with an independent financial advisor to determine whether pension maximization makes sense for you and your dependents. (Pay particular attention to the expenses involved in the life insurance policy that will provide substitute benefits to the survivor; the tax consequences for you and your survivor; and the impact of preexisting health conditions on the cost of insurance. Get an after-tax, present-value analysis showing the impact of pension maximization on your net income while alive and the survivor's net income after your death.)		
6. Ask your employer to describe what disability benefits, if any, are provided in your defined-benefit retirement plan. (If there are benefits, find out what the definition of disability is under the plan, how the benefit is calculated, and whether the benefit is payable immediately upon disability without any reduction for age.)		
7. Make sure all your healthcare providers accept Medicare. (Ask your doctor if he or she is a "par-		

ACTION ITEMS (continued)

Item	Priority*	Completed
ticipating physician," who agrees to charge you no more than Medicare's approved charge for all services. This is sometimes referred to as "accepting Medicare assignment.")		
8. Discuss the pros and cons of LTC insurance with family members, healthcare providers, and financial advisors.		
9. Check liability limits and coverage on your homeowner's or renter's insurance and your automobile insurance. Decide whether to purchase an excess-liability or umbrella policy to protect assets against lawsuits.		
10. If you decide to purchase an annuity, before doing so make sure the insurance company describes clearly and in writing: the interest rate or other factors used to calculate monthly payments, the provisions affecting your ability to cash in the policy, and all administrative charges and expenses.		
11. Document the value of all insured property with receipts, canceled checks, photographs, and videotapes to expedite insurance claims. (Keep all documentation in a safe, fire-proof location.)		

*A, B, C, or N/A, with A being the highest priority.

10

PERSONAL AND TRANSITIONAL ISSUES

When someone asks, "What do you do?", he or she usually means, "What do you do for a living?" or "What is your job, your occupation?"

We often think of our work as defining who we are.

You are an engineer. Someone else is a mechanic, a salesperson, a teacher, or a lawyer. Retirement can be traumatic if you define yourself entirely by your job. It's like giving up your identity. Since many of life's friendships are made at work, retiring not only means having to earn in a different way, it means having to define yourself and many of your relationships in a different way and create new relationships.

To say "I'm retired" is for many people equivalent to saying "I don't do anything anymore, and I'm not sure who or what I am."

Obviously, there are people who approach retirement with a great deal of excitement. It is something they have anticipated for a long time and are eager to experience. It means freedom to explore and create new tomorrows.

Others approach retirement with fear and anxiety. They are entering the unknown, and they do so with a sense of reluctance.

When you retire from work, you do not retire from life, and life is dynamic. It is always changing. Because many of us are retiring earlier and can expect to live longer, we can expect to spend 20, 30, or more years in retirement. So, retiring is the start of a series of new life changes. One way to think about your first years of retirement is that you are going through the first stage of "reinventing" yourself—the first of many stages you'll go through during your retirement.

Putting off planning for the transition to retirement until "after" something else happens: you get a bonus . . . you reach 50 . . . the kids get out of school . . . you pay off debt . . .

Take a look at Figures 10.1 and 10.2. Do these simple exercises on a scratch pad. They might help you to think about the positives of retiring.

For many people, a "phased approach" to retirement might make sense. In order to stay healthy—mentally, emotionally, and physically—it's important to have something to get up and out of bed for in the morning; something that is social, exciting, and meaningful. That's why so many professionals end up as consultants when they retire. And why retired executive programs, in which executives offer advice at low or no charge to small and medium-size businesses, are so popular. And why community colleges and large universities have so many older adjunct faculty members. And why

---

FIGURE 10.1   BELIEFS ABOUT GETTING OLDER.

A. "For me, getting older means . . . "
   1. _____
   2. _____
   3. _____

B. Close your eyes and imagine yourself at various ages. What do you see?
   At age 70, I am:_____
   At age 80, I am:_____
   At age 90, I am:_____

C. Name a person 65 or older whom you admire or have admired.

   _____

   What is so special about that person? _____

   _____

   How can that person be a role model for you? _____

   _____

FIGURE 10.2   ENDINGS AND BEGINNINGS.

Endings:

What will be missing in your life when you retire? Examples: paycheck, alarm clock, 90-minute commute, laptop computer.

What will be missing?	Will you be sorry it is gone?	
	Yes	No
1. _____	____	____
2. _____	____	____
3. _____	____	____
4. _____	____	____
5. _____	____	____
6. _____	____	____
7. _____	____	____

Beginnings:

What will you miss from your work environment?	What can you replace it with?
Examples: Managing projects	Volunteering in activities that need management skills
1. _____	_____
2. _____	_____
3. _____	_____
4. _____	_____
5. _____	_____
6. _____	_____
7. _____	_____

More if necessary . . .

large home-improvement stores are filled with retired plumbers, electricians, and carpenters in second careers as salespeople.

In today's tight labor market, employers are increasing the flexibility of work schedules to help retain employees longer—making part-time employment, sabbaticals, and other programs available not just to workers with young families but to older workers as well. All this means that you might not even have to change employers to phase into retirement. Or you may find a new employer in your line of work who offers a flexible work schedule.

Working by choice is far more satisfying than working out of necessity. Even if you think today that you will always want to work because you love the way you earn your living, it is a good idea to put yourself in a position to make that choice in the future.

CREATE A PLAN OF BALANCED LIVING

One of the best ways to make the retirement transition easier is to begin preparing for it well in advance and make it a gradual change rather than an abrupt one. The key may lie in what we call "balanced living."

It's a matter of learning to enjoy today and at the same time live with the confidence that you are doing what is necessary to have the freedom to choose tomorrow. If you are overly concerned about tomorrow and are obsessed with denying yourself today, the chances are you will be unable to enjoy tomorrow when it comes.

More than just financial preparation is required for a comfortable and fulfilling retirement. There are a host of mental, emotional, and social adjustments associated with a major change like retiring.

For some, retiring means quitting work altogether. For others, it simply means slowing down. You may work for a cause and not be paid at all, or you may work harder and earn more than ever but work at something you have always wanted to do because now you have the freedom to do so. You may take a risk on your own business, or you may work part time in a low-paying position at something you have always done for free in your spare time.

One retiree described the absolute joy he experienced when, after choosing to work part time during retirement at a job where he had a tyrant for a boss, he walked in one day and said, "I quit!"

He had never had the freedom to do that during his preretirement working life when he needed a steady paycheck to meet expenses and save for retirement. Because he liked the work, he found another job doing the same thing, with a boss he liked, and is now happy as a part-time retiree.

Use Figure 10.3 to help you think through the kind of work opportunities you might want to explore in retirement.

CHECK OUT OPPORTUNITIES BEFORE YOU LEAP

Suppose you visualize a very different lifestyle in retirement. Perhaps you see yourself living in a different city or state, or even a different country. You may have been there and loved it, so you've created a mental picture of yourself there.

FIGURE 10.3 ACTION PLANNING STEPS FOR WORKING IN RETIREMENT.

1. Type of paid work (part time, full time, own business, consulting or freelancing on project basis)

   _____

   _____

2. Where?   _____

3. When?   _____

4. Why?   _____

5. What do you need to do now to prepare for your future paid work activity? _____

   _____

   _____

6. With whom do you need to discuss this? _____

   _____

7. What special training do you need? _____

   _____

   _____

8. What are your immediate next steps? _____

   _____

Selling your family home too quickly after retirement before settling your lifestyle plans.

Rather than just picking up and moving, you should probably make an extended visit, say one to three months. This gives you a chance to find out if life there really is terrific, or if you've been caught up by the grass-is-always-greener syndrome. If your job allows, don't wait until you retire to do so—lump all your vacation time together into a "minisabbatical" a couple of years before retirement.

Make sure when you're there that you talk to people who have lived there all their lives as well as people who moved there later in life. Don't just ask about what they like to do—find out if what *you* like to do is available! The golf may be great but if you have to get on a plane to visit an art museum or to eat good ethnic food, it may not be the place for you. What if it's a place that family and friends just will not be able to get to easily or frequently? The more you can touch, taste, and experience what you've pictured as your own private paradise, the more likely you will make a smooth transition from the working years to the retirement years.

Figure 10.4 should help you think through the issues involved in making a relocation decision. You might want to do this exercise for two or three different locations.

The same is as true for activities and business opportunities as it is for location. For instance, you may not have to retire in order to go back to school. Elderhostel (www.elderhostel.org or 877-426-8056), an international educational and travel organization, sponsors hundreds of one- to two-week educational retreats each year. You can join the program at age 55.

FIGURE 10.4 CHOOSING WHERE YOU WILL LIVE.

A. Name your location choice: _____

B. Name your choice of housing style in that location (single-family home, condominium, rental apartment, houseboat, etc.).

_____

C. Will this location and housing style support your physical and mental health (climate, low crime rate, clean environment, etc.)?

_____

D. Can you find work near your housing choice? _____

_____

E. Can you enjoy your kind of leisure near your housing choice?

_____

F. Can you have the relationships you want and need near your housing choice? _____

G. If you are in a close relationship, does the other person support your choice and is he or she willing to live with you there?

_____

H. What will be the quality of the community support systems at your retirement housing location?

Worship? _____

Healthcare? _____

Emergency? _____

Library? _____

Culture and Art? _____

Senior Center? _____

Shopping? _____

Transportation? _____

Communications and technology? _____

Spending two or three weeks a year in intensive study of subjects you choose may leave you refreshed and excited enough to work longer and be more productive. Or take one evening course each semester.

You can start the business you've always dreamed of before you retire. If you like it, and if it is successful, you might retire early. If it turns out that being your own boss isn't all that it's cracked up to be, drop it. You've learned something.

Take a course in grandparenting. Become a small animal rehabilitator. Take up cross-country skiing. Whatever your dream may be, try it out first.

There are two more exercises you can do to help you think through your options. They're similar to Figure 10.3, the action planning steps for work. These action planning steps for volunteer work and leisure are shown in Figures 10.5 and 10.6.

Couples need to do retirement planning together. If your company has mandatory retirement at age 60 and your spouse or life partner wants to keep working for five years after that to maximize retirement benefits, you may have conflicting expectations. If your life partner dreams of starting a small business and you want to move to a warmer climate in order to play tennis every day, you may be headed for a problem. If you want to simplify life and pare down in retirement but your spouse or life partner feels differently, you will have to negotiate a lifestyle you both can live with.

FIGURE 10.5   ACTION PLANNING STEPS FOR VOLUNTEER WORK.

1. What skills, experiences, or special interests do you have?

   _____

2. Would you work better as part of a group or on your own?

   _____

3. Would you rather work with children or with adults?

   _____

4. What do you need to do now to prepare for your volunteer work activities?

   _____

5. With whom do you need to discuss this?

   _____

6. What special training will you need?

   _____

7. What are your immediate next steps?

   _____

Figure 10.6   Action planning steps for leisure.

1. Type of leisure? _____

2. Where? _____

3. When? _____

4. With whom? _____

5. Why? _____

6. What do you need to do now to prepare for your leisure activity?

   _____

7. With whom do you need to discuss this?

   _____

8. What special training do you need?

   _____

9. What are your immediate next steps?

   _____

EXAMPLE

■ Emmie and George were married almost 45 years before they both stopped working for pay. George had always promised he'd sell his toy soldier collection to supplement their retirement income. But when the time came to actually sell, he found parting with his miniature armies more difficult than he thought it would be—both practically and emotionally—until Emmie and George discovered on-line auctions. Now they sell the figures to collectors around the world—people interested in giving the collection a new life—and receive top dollar for them. ■

CLARIFYING YOUR VALUES

One place to start planning for retirement is to understand the values in your life. Figure 10.7 is an exercise that many people have found revealing not only to help them think through, for themselves and others with whom they share their lives, the "softer" issues of retirement but also to lay the foundation for the financial decisions that are discussed throughout this book.

While circumstances may force a change of plans, or you may just change your mind, you and the significant person who shares your life need to openly discuss some potentially tough issues:

1. *How will I spend my time in retirement?* Whether you plan to spend your retirement alone, with someone, or with a group of people, it may be important to create a daily schedule in retirement to replace

FIGURE 10.7 CLARIFYING YOUR VALUES.

This is a sample of 15 key values people typically want to experience for themselves.

Assume you have to give up 10 of these values. Which would they be? Mark them with an X in the left colum.

Now rank the five remaining values from highest (1) to lowest (5), placing the numbers in the left column.

_____ Achievement — To accomplish something important in life, be involved in significant activities, succeed at what I am doing

_____ Aesthetics — To be able to appreciate and enjoy beauty for beauty's sake, be artistically creative

_____ Authority/power — To be a key decision maker directing priorities, the activities of other people, and/or allocation and use of general resources

_____ Adventure — To experience variety and excitement and be able to respond to challenging opportunities

_____ Autonomy — To be independent, have freedom, be able to live where I want to live and do what I want to do

_____ Health — To be physically, mentally, and emotionally well, feel energetic, and maintain a sense of well-being

_____ Integrity — To be honest and straightforward, just and fair

_____ Intimacy/friendship/ love — To have close personal relationships, experience affection, share life with family and friends

_____ Pleasure — To experience enjoyment and personal satisfaction from the activities in which I participate

_____ Recognition — To be seen as successful, receiving acknowledgment for achievements

_____ Security — To feel stable and comfortable with few changes or anxieties in my life

_____ Service — To contribute to the quality of life for other people and be involved in improving society or the world

_____ Spiritual Growth — To have communication or harmony with the infinite source of life

_____ Wealth — To acquire an abundance of money and/or material possessions, be financially independent

_____ Wisdom — To have insight, be able to pursue new knowledge, have clear judgment, and be able to use common sense in life situations

Source: Adapted from Ken Rouse, *Putting Money in Its Place* (Dubuque, IA: Kendall Hunt, 1993).

the one left behind at work. Some people find it difficult to deal with unstructured time after many years in a work routine.

It's exciting in the abstract to think about all the extra time you will have after retirement. Create a plan to make that time as worthwhile as possible. Think through how you will "invest" that time in activities that involve other people or in ways that nurture you. Allocate time to play as well as time to work at something that keeps you productive— whether you earn money from it or not. And don't be stingy on down-time, time to rest and recharge so that your activities don't become too much like "work." Remember, in order to remain energetic, you need to take care of yourself.

E X A M P L E

■ At 62, Phil is behind his grandchildren in his Web skills. But to keep in touch with them, he bought a Web TV and exchanges e-mails and pictures with them regularly. And when he and the kids are to-gether, they visit Web sites. One of their favorite sites is Moneyo-polis (www.moneyopolis.org), where they can play a game that solves real-life financial problems using math skills. ■

2. *Where will I (we) live?* There are a host of issues that go into answering this question. You may want to live near children or siblings, not always easy in these days of far-flung families. You may need to live near aging and frail parents, an increasing possibility for today's "sandwich gener-ation" of younger retirees.

How important to you is the area of the country in which you live? Do you love the four seasons, or would you rather have more uniform— probably warmer—conditions? Do you like mountains, desert, ocean, the tropics? Do you like city life or the country? Lots of noise and action or peace and quiet? Will you spend all or part of your retirement in another country?

Do you want to own or rent? Do you want to live in a single-family home, semidetached, or high-rise? Do you want to live in a planned community, a community specifically for retired people? Increasingly, the first move you make in retirement is not the last move of your life. Aside from those who stay healthy well into later life, the increasing number of life-care, assisted-living, and other living arrangements makes it likely that retirees who make a living transition early in their retirement will move one more time.

Does the community welcome retired people? Will you be able to take advantage of special senior programs at cultural institutions, enter-tainment and retail establishments, or restaurants? Are there activities readily available for you to enjoy?

Moving to a low-income-tax state without considering property taxes, sales taxes, fees, and other costs that have an effect on your budget.

When making any relocation, don't forget to take into consideration the total tax burden of the state to which you wish to move. Figure 10.8 is a map of the United States showing no/low-income-tax states (less than 4%) and those with moderate to high state income taxes. But state income taxes aren't the only taxes that go into the total tax burden; consider also sales taxes, personal property taxes, and state inheritance taxes.

Especially for single or widowed retirees, the question of shared-living arrangements comes up. Are you willing to share your living space, and if so, with whom—a sibling, a child, a friend, a renter who pays rent in the form of labor by shoveling your driveway, cutting your lawn, or doing other chores you no longer can or want to do?

SPEND YOUR LAST DOLLAR ON YOUR LAST DAY

One stand-up comic says he wants to live long enough to become a burden to his kids. In reality, that's probably not a very exciting thought for either him or his children.

Perhaps perfect retirement planning is to time both life and financial resources to run out simultaneously so you can spend your last dollar on your last day, doing something you had always wanted to do but just hadn't got around to.

Given that no one knows when his or her last day will be, and that having money in old age is better than not having money, most of us will leave something to heirs.

LINK RETIREMENT PLANNING WITH ESTATE PLANNING

As you make the transition into retirement, it's important that you link your retirement planning more tightly with your estate planning. Figure 10.9 is an action planning list for your estate.

Failing to review life insurance and retirement funds to make sure the appropriate beneficiary is named.

FIGURE 10.8 PERSONAL INCOME TAX RATES ACROSS THE COUNTRY.

U.S. TAX RATES

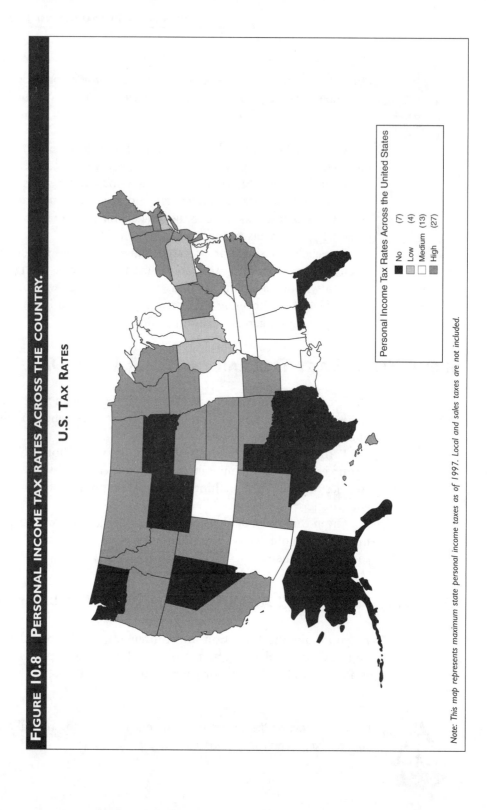

Personal Income Tax Rates Across the United States

■ No	(7)
▨ Low	(4)
□ Medium	(13)
▦ High	(27)

Note: This map represents maximum state personal income taxes as of 1997. Local and sales taxes are not included.

FIGURE 10.9   ACTION STEPS FOR PLANNING YOUR ESTATE.

Ask yourself the following questions, then consider your tax and legal plan. After completing these action-planning steps, you'll be ready to see a lawyer and begin drawing up a complete estate plan.

1. Do you have a will?   Yes _____   No_____
   If no, why not? _____

2. If you do have a will, when did you last review it? _____

3. Has your situation (family, business, investments) changed significantly since the last time you reviewed your will? If it has, what changes do you need to make in your will?
   _____
   _____
   _____

4. Do you understand how to integrate these changes with overall planning? What are some good reasons for setting up a trust?
   _____
   _____
   _____

5. Do you know how you want your assets distributed when you die? Describe the distribution.
   _____
   _____
   _____

6. Have you considered any special needs that your survivors might have? What might those be?
   _____
   _____

7. Is your life insurance adequate? How could it be better?
   _____
   _____

8. Have you integrated life insurance with your overall financial plan? How do you feel about it?
   _____
   _____

9. Do you have a durable power of attorney? Should you?
   _____

10. Do your parents have durable powers of attorney? Should they?
    _____

11. Do you have a living will? Should you?
    _____

12. Do you have a medical power of attorney (sometimes called an advanced medical directive or health care proxy)? Should you?
    _____

13. If you were to die, who should take care of your minor children? What if that person died?
    _____
    _____

14. Name the person who should administer your last affairs, file final tax returns, and follow your last instructions (executor).
    _____
    _____

This is not only the time to check the adequacy of your life insurance but also to make sure you have designated the appropriate beneficiary. You also need to make sure your retirement plan assets have properly designated beneficiaries—your tax-deferred retirement savings accounts, pensions that are calculated on a two-life basis, individual and group life insurance policies, annuities, IRAs, and stocks or stock options.

If you or you and your spouse have assets that will put your estate above the threshold at which federal estate taxes are due ($675,000 per person in 2000 and increasing thereafter), you may want to create a trust for those assets. Trusts are complex, and you should generally seek professional assistance in creating one.

You should also determine if you have or wish to have a living will, a durable power of attorney, and a durable medical power of attorney (which might be known in your state as a healthcare proxy or an advanced medical directive), so that someone can make not only financial but medical decisions on your behalf should you become incapacitated.

Remember, if you relocate to another state, all of these documents—will, living will, power of attorney, and medical power of attorney—need to be reviewed to make sure they comply with state laws, and redone or amended if they do not.

You should have all of your vital records organized. One of the biggest mistakes made by retirees is putting off the necessary discussion about death. As you age, the likelihood grows that either you or your life partner will be left alone at some point.

While the death of a spouse or life partner can never be "planned for," understanding the financial and lifestyle consequences—that there will be enough on which to live—can make the emotional distress somewhat more bearable. It's important to talk to your spouse or life partner and other loved ones—children, nieces and nephews, even older grandchildren—about what will happen when you die.

If you have been the major organizer of the family's financial affairs, you may want to write a letter to your spouse or life partner detailing where the various records are, whom to call upon your death, whom to ask for assistance in filing the necessary requests for death benefits, and so on. Figure 10.10 is a template of just such a vital records organizer.

FIGURE 10.10 VITAL RECORDS ORGANIZER.

These pages should be completed as soon as possible. Update annually. Distribute copies to your attorney and to a close relative or friend.

Name

Current Address

Date moved to this address   Date of residence in this state

Additional residence address

Dates living at this address

Date of Birth   Place of Birth   Organ donor?

Religious   Name/Phone of   Social Security
Affiliation   Clergyman   Number

Military Veteran? ☐ Yes ☐ No   If yes, Service dates from: to:

Currently Married? ☐ Yes ☐ No   If yes, date of marriage

Name and address of spouse

Previously married? ☐ Yes ☐ No   Date of Divorce or Death of Previous Spouse

Name and address of former spouse

Place of divorce   Who brought the action?

Was divorce contested?   Location of divorce papers

Prenuptial agreement ☐ Yes ☐ No   Location of agreement

Children	Name	Birth Date	Address	Phone

Parents	Name	Birth Date	Address	Phone

Immediate relatives that are incompetent and in your care

Name   Location of vital papers

Address   Location of Power of Attorney

FIGURE 10.10   VITAL RECORDS ORGANIZER. *(continued)*

Others	Name	Address	Phone
Accountant			
Attorney			
Doctor			
Employer			
Insurance Agent(s)			
Stockbroker			

Individuals to be notified in the event of my death:

☐ Spouse   ☐ Others _____

☐ Children   _____

☐ Parents   _____

☐ Attorney   _____

☐ Employer   _____

My Will

Original   Location_____ Date Signed_____

Copy   Location_____ Executor_____

Trusts

Yours   Location_____

Others   Location_____

Bank Accounts—Name and address of bank	Type of Account	Account Number

Safe Deposit Box—Name and address of bank	Box Number	Location of Key

FIGURE 10.10   VITAL RECORDS ORGANIZER. (continued)

Location of securities, stocks, and bonds

Credit Cards—Company	Account Number	Location of Card

Debts Owed—To Whom	Location of Records	Amount	Dates to be Paid

Other Property— Location	Value	Original Price	Mortgage	Type of Ownership	Location of Deed

Insurance— Carrier	Agent	Policy Number	Location of Policy	Principal Amount	Beneficiary
Life (yours)					
Life (another)					
Auto					

Figure 10.10 Vital Records Organizer. *(continued)*

Insurance—Carrier	Agent	Policy Number	Location of Policy	Principal Amount	Beneficiary
Home					
Health					

Benefits/Compensation Provided upon Death by Employer

How Benefits are payable

Company contact person   Phone

Company Stock Programs   Amount   Location of Papers

Location of Other Records

Birth Certificate

Marriage Certificate

Military Discharge

Citizenship Papers

Tax Returns

Where copies can be found

Gift Taxes

Income—State

Income—Federal

Organizations to Which You Belong

Name   Address

Your Affiliation   Benefits

Name   Address

Your Affiliation   Benefits

Name   Address

Your Affiliation   Benefits

Name   Address

Your Affiliation   Benefits

FIGURE 10.10   VITAL RECORDS ORGANIZER. *(continued)*

Notes

_____

_____

_____

_____

_____

_____

_____

_____

_____

_____

_____

_____

_____

_____

_____

_____

_____

_____

Believing your estate is not large enough to warrant an estate plan.

Don't underestimate the size of your estate. Remember, your estate includes all of your assets, including your share of ownership in your home, your car or cars, life insurance policies, tax-deferred retirement savings, and so on.

Although parts of your estate, such as life insurance death benefits and tax-deferred retirement savings, will pass to your beneficiaries outside of probate, and in many states the first spouse to die does not even need to have his or her will probated, if everything is left to a spouse, all items are normally included in the estate for estate tax computation purposes.

**E
X
A
M
P
L
E**

■ Glenn and Nancy have a home they bought 30 years ago for $60,000 and about $40,000 in personal savings. They have not thought much about their "estate." However, when they made a list of their assets on paper, they were surprised to discover that at current market values, their assets far exceeded the $675,000 threshold in the year 2000, and so they would need to create an estate plan to avoid unnecessary estate taxes. Here's a list of their current assets:

Home value today	$ 250,000
Personal savings	40,000
Pension plan benefits	225,000
401(k), Keogh, and IRA	350,000
Life insurance death benefit	260,000
Total Estate Value	$ 1,125,000

By incorporating special provisions in their wills that would create "marital" and "nonmarital" or "credit shelter" trusts upon their death, Glenn and Nancy were able to eliminate the potential estate tax while providing lifetime benefits to each spouse's survivor. Without an estate plan, the federal estate taxes would have been as much as $200,000 to $250,000. ■

Remember, if you don't plan for the disposition of your own estate, someone else will do it for you, usually a court-appointed administrator. It's impossible after death to communicate your wishes, so it is important to get your wishes in writing today.

TRAPS

Another potential trap is not clearly spelling out your wishes regarding the use of life support or other extraordinary means of keeping you alive should you become incapacitated as well as your desires to provide your organs as a donor. Most states now recognize a "living will" in which you state your wishes in the event of terminal illness. If you do not want to be kept alive by extraordinary means, you can also let that be known. You can also create a "health care power of attorney," under which you allow others to make such medical decisions for you. Such explicit direction can make your final days more comfortable and more tolerable for your loved ones. For more information, contact the Choice in Dying organization (212-336-5540 or 800-989-9455).

Using Life Insurance to Pay Estate Taxes

Couples who are fortunate enough to grow old together and who have amassed relatively sizable estates are increasingly turning to so-called survivorship or "second-to-die" life insurance policies as a way to cover the costs of both federal and state death taxes.

There is no federal estate tax due on estates that are left to a surviving spouse—either outright or in a qualifying trust. But when the second spouse dies, the taxes can be quite large. The second spouse can pass up to $675,000 of assets in 2000 without federal estate taxes (providing he or she has not used up all or a portion of this exclusion by making large gifts during his or her lifetime). After that, the federal tax begins at 37% and progresses up to 55%. This limit will increase each year until it reaches $1,000,000.

The second-to-die life insurance is often purchased with a face amount equal to the value of the total estate. It doubles the value of the estate, but provides enough cash at the death of the surviving spouse so that estate taxes can be paid, allowing the estate's other assets to be passed to heirs intact. This is especially important in estates that include nonliquid assets such as real estate, artwork and collectibles, or even family businesses. With some creative estate planning, it is possible to set up the life insurance in a trust arrangement, which reduces the overall estate tax. You should consult a professional for assistance in this regard.

TRAPS, OBSTACLES, TOOLS, AND HELPERS

You should try to avoid the following traps and obstacles, and use the following tools and helpers.

- Equating retirement with withdrawal from an active, productive life
- Not considering the needs and interests of family members and others who may be affected by your retirement, and not communicating with them as part of your planning
- Relocating in retirement without carefully considering all of the financial and social consequences
- Believing your estate is not large enough to warrant an estate plan
- Not spelling out your wishes regarding organ donations, life support, or other medical affairs in legally valid ways

- Self-imposed age stereotypes that limit personal potential
- Avoiding discussions about incapacity and death
- Complex federal and state estate and inheritance tax laws and rules

- Belief system worksheet
- Employer-sponsored retirement planning outplacement, and career transition services
- Location choice worksheet
- Vital records organizer
- Time in retirement to "reinvent" yourself

- Phasing into retirement
- Thinking of retirement as having stages
- Consulting and second-career opportunities
- "Balanced-living" perspective
- Elderhostel and similar adult education programs
- Senior citizen centers sponsored by local communities and government agencies
- Sense of humor

ACTION ITEMS

Item	Priority*	Completed
1. Complete the exercises provided in this chapter. Start early by doing them now. Make a lifestyle plan. You and your spouse or life partner need to establish how you will spend your resources, both time and money.		
2. Make a list of your assets and consult a professional to determine the most appropriate estate plan.		
3. Plan to take some time now to "rehearse" retirement. Make sure you like to do the things you dream will make your retirement years fulfilling: volunteering, learning new skills, going back to school, traveling, or sports.		

ACTION ITEMS *(continued)*		
Item	**Priority***	**Completed**
4. Make an extended visit of at least one month to a place you are considering as a relocation destination. (Go "off season" for at least part of the time. Get the local newspaper while you are there, and then subscribe to the paper for three months when you return home. Talk with people who have lived there all of their lives as well as newcomers. Attend local events. See if your family and friends will visit you there.)		
5. Put together a personal physical and mental health promotion plan, including exercise, diet, and stress reduction. Consult your physician on these.		
6. Clearly spell out your wishes regarding choice-of-death options, including use of life-saving, artificial life support, and feeding. If you relocate to another state, have all of these documents, including wills, trusts, powers of attorney, living wills, and health-care proxies, reviewed by a licensed attorney to make sure they conform to the laws of the new state.		
7. Review all of your beneficiary designations to make sure they are up to date and consistent with your overall estate planning goals. This is one area that people overlook most. Ask your lawyer to review them as well. This is key.		
8. Organize your vital papers. (Make sure that whoever needs to know—your spouse or life partner, other family members, executor, other financial professionals—has a letter of instruction as to where all of these documents are. Documents include: investment records; credit cards; insurance policies; bank accounts; marriage certificate; military discharge papers; mortgage documents; insurance policies; wills and trusts; pension documents; other legal documents; burial arrangements; and names, addresses, and phone numbers of financial advisors.)		
9. Take advantage of retirement planning programs offered through your or your spouse's or life partner's employer. These programs often address a		

ACTION ITEMS *(continued)*		
Item	**Priority***	**Completed**

broad range of transition issues, both financial and nonfinancial.
10. Remember the following eight things as you make your transition into retirement.[†]
   a. Exercise regularly.
   b. Eat well.
   c. Get enough rest and sleep.
   d. Keep a sense of humor.
   e. Set goals and be creative.
   f. Be self-sufficient.
   g. Help others.
   h. Maintain your energy.		

[†]Adapted from Dr. Walter M. Bortz II, *We Live Too Short and Die Too Long* (New York: Bantam, 1992).		

*A, B, C, or N/A, with A being the highest priority.

11

SPENDING IN RETIREMENT

Here you are. You've finally left the last job in your career. You've "retired"!

How much money do you need, and how will you spend it? In Chapter 3, we touched on what we call "the myth of replacement ratio." Remember, the replacement ratio is the rule of thumb that says you will need 60 to 80% of your preretirement after-tax income—in current dollars—in order to maintain the lifestyle to which you have grown accustomed.

Why do we consider the concept of replacement ratio a myth? There are two main reasons. First, everyone has a different lifestyle, and therefore everyone needs a different amount of money to maintain that lifestyle. Second, and equally important, we believe that financial needs in retirement have a natural ebb and flow, that they change over time based on changing needs.

EVERY LIFESTYLE IS DIFFERENT

Every lifestyle is different because every household is different. In each household live people with different likes and dislikes, different needs and different aspirations.

For instance, of the authors of this book, some live in the New York metropolitan area, others in greater Chicago, and Phoenix. Our housing costs are very different. Our commuting costs are different. We each pay different levels of state and local taxes.

We range in age from our 30s to our 60s. Some have grown children, others school-age children, and still others no children. Some are married, some are not. Some have spouses who work outside the home, some don't.

Our personal tastes are also different, as are our abilities outside of our jobs and how we like to spend our time away from work. One of us drives a 13-year-old car, another a car that is 19 years old. Another leases a new car every three years. One of us is handy and built his own addition on his house. Another has a very artistic child, and most of the artwork in his home is the product of that child's efforts—he has no home decorating costs. Another is an artist herself—with award-winning exhibits. One likes to travel overseas for every vacation; another likes to take the week close to home and play golf with his wife and friends.

Let's further assume that, since we are involved in financial planning, none of us lives beyond his or her means. We have each created a lifestyle in which we do as much of what we like to do as is possible within the income available.

When we retire, each of us will need a different percentage of current income to maintain that lifestyle. And each one of us will have a different level of expenses we no longer have to worry about.

Some Expenses Disappear

Let's look closely at the current expenses that might end when you retire.

Some taxes vanish. You will still pay income taxes on your investment income, assuming the present tax system remains. But when you stop working, you will stop paying the 7.65% withholding tax for Social Security and Medicare on earnings (15.3% if self-employed).

Some aspects of savings will be eliminated as well. You will no longer be sheltering a portion of your pay in your 401(k), 403(b), or 457 account. Because you should shelter the maximum allowed (e.g., $10,500 in 2000 in 401(k) plans) as soon in your working life as possible and certainly in the last 10 to 15 years before retirement, your final preretirement lifestyle will account for that. In addition, if you've been saving through an IRA or making payments into a universal life insurance policy with an annuity tied to it, these payments can now stop and you can flip these investments to become income producers.

Additional costs that are eliminated for most of us when we retire are commuting costs, uniform or dry-cleaning costs and some clothing costs, and incidental work costs such as parking at the office, lunches, snacks, contributions to buy gifts and cards for coworkers, and so on. And, in some cases, you can choose to live in a less costly region of the country, since you are no longer "tied" down to your home because of your job.

In short, the lifestyle you have created before retirement—partially driven by the costs associated with your work, your saving habits, and the costs of living in your region—determine what you will need in postretirement income to maintain a comparable standard of living.

RETIREMENT HAS THREE SPENDING PHASES

The second reason why replacement ratio is a myth is that your expenses in retirement do not increase in a linear fashion, consistent with inflation.

Simply determining what you will need in your first year of retirement, then factoring in inflation.

You may accuse us of falling into this trap earlier in this book. It's appropriate, when you are younger and trying to figure out how much you need to accumulate for the retirement you want, to have some gauge, some easy way to estimate. For that, we use the inflation-adjusted first-year need.

But as you get closer to retirement, and especially as you actually enter that phase of life, it's important to get more precise about what your spending needs will be.

If you look at the spending patterns of this generation of retirees, you will notice something quite different from what you might assume. By this generation of retirees we mean people between 60 and 90 in 2000, people who have retired since about 1970. The bulk of this generation of retirees is the first to retire with a truly comfortable standard of living, for a number of reasons.

- They earned all of their income in a period when Social Security was in place and have the highest possible benefit given their working income.
- They are the last generation to enjoy widespread benefits from defined-benefit pensions, which some companies have modified and a smaller number of companies have started since the late 1980s. Many have also enjoyed company-provided retiree health insurance.
- To one extent or another, depending on their age and working income, they were able to take advantage of IRAs, 401(k)s, 403(b)s, 457s, SEPs, and Keoghs.
- Those who owned homes saw the largest increase in real estate values ever in the years between 1970 and 1990.
- Finally, they are the first generation to obtain the benefits of huge advances in medical science and the personal health and wellness boom that has raised life expectancies.

This generation of retirees is living far longer than any previous generation. And their spending habits in retirement are showing a pattern that should hold up for those of us who will retire in the next 25 years.

What we are seeing is that there are really three distinct periods of retirement, with three different spending patterns, as shown in Figure 11.1.

Thinking of your inflation rate as the Consumer Price Index (CPI).

In truth, you need to analyze your spending to determine the rate of inflation in your own "market basket of goods."

As a simple example, the cost of energy measured by the CPI does not accurately reflect the costs of home heating oil for those who use it, the majority of whom live in the Northeast. Because of changes in refining patterns and "just-in-time" stocking by oil companies, home heating oil costs were as much as 30% higher in some local markets in December 1996 than they were in December 1995, despite the similarity of the early winter weather. And cutbacks in OPEC oil production during the winter of 1999–2000 sent home heating costs through the ceiling.

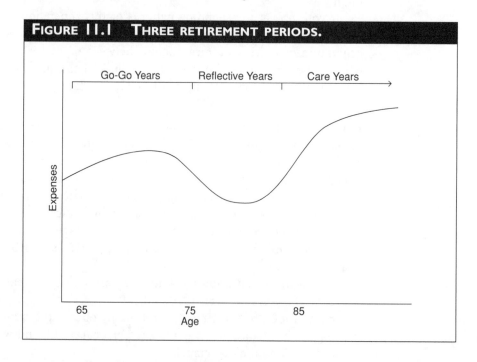

FIGURE 11.1   THREE RETIREMENT PERIODS.

Another example that many elderly people cite is the cost of prescription medication. While the costs of many drugs people use decline over time, new drugs that sometimes do a better job are always coming on the market. If doctors prescribe new, expensive brand-name drugs to replace drugs currently being used, costs soar for the individual patient. Keep in mind that Medicare does not currently cover prescription drug costs, although proposals are being considered to expand Medicare coverage to do so.

Here's a third example: Auto insurance is a cost that fluctuates greatly from state to state. Even though policy costs may not be regulated, other regulations might increase costs, such as new laws in some states that require insured owners to carry increased limits of liability for damage caused by uninsured or underinsured motorists.

The Go-Go Years

The first period, which lasts anywhere from a year or two to as many as 10 years from the beginning of retirement, we call the *go-go years*. This is when retirees—at least those who feel they can afford it—throw caution to the wind and spend. They let loose and fulfill all the pent-up demand that was built up during their years of saving for retirement.

They go on trips, sometimes to far-off places, sometimes to see the kids if they live in other cities, sometimes to Elderhostel programs or other educational adventures. They go on safaris and archeological digs. They buy an RV and spend two years driving across the country. They go on month-long golf vacations to play the old course at St. Andrews, Scotland. They travel back to the countries from which they or their predecessors emigrated.

During these years many retirees actually need more after-tax income than in their last year of work. This is especially true for retirees who are still carrying a mortgage on their home, a number that is growing all the time as people have had to refinance in their 40s or even 50s, in order to pay college tuition for their children.

The Reflective Years

The second period, which lasts from whenever the go-go years end until a retiree is 80 to 85, are the *reflective years*. People are slowing down. However, we hope they're not financially tapped out.

This is the time when people often consolidate their lifestyle. They may sell their home and downsize into an apartment or condominium. They may relocate to a place they discovered on their travels or somewhere near friends or family, often in a warmer climate and/or a low-tax state.

This is the time when people take advantage of what's around them, such as taking courses at local colleges or universities. Many of these schools offer discounts to older students and allow seniors to audit courses for little or no fee. Some take part in the growing number of cooperative education programs for retirees, where retirees themselves plan and teach the courses.

This is when people look to volunteer work to fill some of their time, becoming more active in their church or synagogue; becoming aides and assistants and surrogate grandparents in schools; and increasingly assisting their older and often more frail fellow retirees.

During this period, which for some can be as long as 20 years, people usually need *less income in real terms than in their final years of retirement*.

The Care Years

Finally, retirees enter the true twilight years. For most Americans who live to retire, this will occur after age 75; for an ever-increasing number, it occurs after age 85.

It is the time of life when, almost invariably, we will need some kind of assistance in our daily living. And that assistance, in whatever form it takes—nursing home, assisted-living apartment, life-care apartment, or even with family—is expensive.

For those who can afford up-market life-care facilities, as well as for those who are forced by increasing frailty into nursing home care, the care years mean expenses that *exceed those of the last year of work*.

PLAN FOR THE NEXT TWO PHASES OF YOUR RETIREMENT

Remember what we said earlier: You will spend everything you make, or you will entrust others to spend it for you.

If you spend early, you lose flexibility in planning at each later stage in your life. If you are forever frugal, chances are you will finally get to enjoy the fruits of your labor by spending your money on what's important to you.

Do aggressive planning for your next (nearest) phase of retirement, moderate planning for the phase you will enter after that, and modest planning for the phase that is three steps away.

While most 55-year-olds will not do serious planning for the care years, it is important for them to begin looking at how much money they will have at retirement and make a reasonable plan for the go-go years that leaves enough to live on and remain active during the reflective years.

Similarly, at 70 you need to ask yourself seriously whether there is enough to continue spending the way you are—assuming you're a real go-goer—for much longer and still have enough at the end of the road for the custodial care you may very well need.

As one friend who took a job at 60 after being self-employed as a consultant for six years said, "I was planning on retiring at 60, phasing out the consulting work. But I realized that if I work two more years for this company at my salary, with the benefits, and add to my retirement savings, I can live a lot more worry-free to 85. I can make it now. I can't go back and make it at 80."

PAYING IN TIME RATHER THAN MONEY

When you retire, you also have the opportunity to reduce your living costs by returning to some of the chores and services you used to pay someone else to do for you. There is no reason for a 70-year-old to shovel the driveway after a blizzard, but if you have a small, level lot with some shade you might want to go back to cutting your own grass. An hour or two a week behind a lawnmower, divided over two evenings, can provide you with as much exercise as two comparable sessions on a treadmill.

Similarly, you can take over the housecleaning chores that during your working life cost hundreds of dollars each year. You can also wash the car, paint the bedrooms that have been empty since the kids left, and generally make the house look nicer than it's been in years, either in preparation for sale or just to make it better for you.

In addition, having more time allows you to be a better shopper for the goods and services you need. Instead of zipping through the grocery store once a week as before, you can take the time to comparison shop, maybe even using two stores for the best buys—assuming you can save more than the cost of gas from one store to the next.

Without each of you having to be someplace different every day, you can also think about going from two cars to one. The savings in insurance, gas, and maintenance can easily be from $1,000 to $2,000.

DON'T BE TOO PROUD: TAKE ADVANTAGE OF YOUR AGE

American businesses know that the "gray market" is large, powerful, generally healthy, and often financially well off. And they all want your business!

Airlines, car rental agencies, trains, hotels, restaurants, and others all compete aggressively for your dollars by offering discounts. Often these discounts can be used against any price. For instance, having the ability to fly on midweek days and stay over Saturday nights can substantially lower air fare, and the senior discount would apply to this low fare. Senior discounts—many of which define seniors very generously, at over 50 or over 55—range from 5% to as much as 25%.

Some discounts apply on particular days or at particular off-peak hours. Recreation at town, city, or regional facilities is often free or greatly reduced for local seniors.

Your free time to shop for the best senior discounts can lower your costs—especially on discretionary entertainment—dramatically.

ANOTHER MYTH: ONE CAN LIVE FOR HALF THE PRICE OF TWO

Unfortunately for those of us who will be widowed at some point in our retirement, one person cannot live less expensively than two—at least not on a per-person basis. While total costs may decrease, the per-person costs typically increase, quite substantially.

You pay the same rent, or mortgage and property tax, whether one person is living in the home or two. A car costs the same to own and operate whether one person uses it or two. Costs may increase for family visits.

Of course, there are opportunities to reduce living costs after the death of a life partner. Make sure to change all insurance you cover to coverage for one person and to change the beneficiary on all of your life insurance and retirement funds. There can be a significant savings in Medigap plans and in auto insurance. And reduce from "couple" to "single" any membership in organizations such as health clubs, community centers, and so on.

HOW STATES TAX RETIREMENT INCOME

States take one of four approaches when it comes to taxing retirement income.

Approach 1. Some states have no income tax at all. Retirement income, whether received as a monthly check or a lump sum, will not be subject to income taxes in states that take this approach.

States with no income tax are: Alaska, Florida, Nevada, South Dakota, Texas, Washington, and Wyoming.

Approach 2. Some states have some form of income tax, but they do not treat retirement income as taxable. It is important, however, to check the state's definition of tax-free retirement income. Some states define it broadly as any income received from any type of retirement plan, such as a company plan, government plan, or IRA. Other states even define it as any income received from any source provided an individual is over a certain age.

Other states limit tax-free treatment to retirement income received from a qualified plan or government plan, and only if received as a monthly payment or annuity. Other states exclude from ordinary income subject to taxation part or all of a lump sum on which favorable federal tax treatment (10-year averaging, pre-1974 capital gain) is used.

States that take this approach are: Alabama, Hawaii, Illinois, Mississippi, New Hampshire, Pennsylvania, and Tennessee.

Approach 3. Some states tax retirement income but give a partial tax break if you are over a certain age. Eligibility ages range from 55 to 65.

For example, New York exempts from taxation up to $20,000 of annual pension and annuity income per individual over age 59½.

Make sure you check the eligibility age for such partial tax breaks, and once again check the definition of eligible retirement income.

Other states that take this approach are: Arkansas, Colorado, Delaware, Indiana, Louisiana, Maryland, Michigan, Montana, New Jersey, North Carolina, Oregon, South Carolina, Utah, Virginia, and West Virginia.

Approach 4. The final way states have of taxing retirement income is to give no special treatment at all to any type of retirement income. Retirement income of any kind is simply added to your other taxable income and taxed at the state's ordinary income tax rate.

Examples of states that take this approach are: Arizona, California, Connecticut, District of Columbia, Georgia, Idaho, Indiana, Iowa, Kansas, Kentucky, Maine, Massachusetts, Minnesota, Missouri, Nebraska, New Mexico, North Dakota, Oklahoma, Rhode Island, Vermont, and Wisconsin.

State tax laws and regulations often change. The best way to find out exactly how a particular state taxes various forms of retirement income is to obtain information, including a copy of a resident income tax return, with instructions, from the state's department or division of revenue. If the information from the state is unclear, you should consult an income-tax professional who practices in that state.

HOW STATES TAX SOCIAL SECURITY

Not all states follow the same rules as the Internal Revenue Service (IRS) when it comes to taxing Social Security benefits. Many states exempt Social Security from state taxation, even if it is subject to federal taxation. Other states subject different amounts of Social Security benefits to taxation and use different thresholds from the federal income tax triggers for single taxpayers, married couples filing jointly, and married individuals filing separately.

In Which State Do You Pay Taxes on Your Retirement Income?

The basic rule is that the state of your residence, or domicile, at the time you are receiving retirement income will subject that income to its tax system. When determining whether they can claim you as a resident, states look at evidence such as:

- How much time did you physically spend in the state during the tax year?
- Do you own residential property in the state?
- Are you registered to vote in the state?
- Is your driver's license from the state?
- Do you have automobiles registered in the state?
- What is your address on your federal income tax return?

Depending on these facts and circumstances, it is possible that two states can claim you as a resident and subject all of your retirement income to their tax systems. In that case, you may be able to obtain some tax credits from one state to offset part of the tax you paid to another state on the same retirement income.

Prior to 1996, some states subjected nonresidents to taxation on the amounts of retirement income that were earned while employed in those states. Some states with such "source taxes" were aggressively pursuing nonresidents and subjecting them to retroactive tax bills and penalties. A federal law now generally prevents states from taxing the retirement income of nonresidents.

Other State Taxes

In addition to examining a state's income tax rules, you should obtain information on the many other ways that states raise revenue from individuals. These various forms of state taxation include sales taxes, use taxes, personal service taxes, estate and inheritance taxes, and user fees.

CLOSING THE INCOME GAP

Let's face it. As much as we plan, some of us are not going to be able to generate enough income during retirement to cover our expenses. What are the options for closing the income gap?

1. *Consider postretirement employment.* You are still allowed to earn some income after beginning to collect Social Security benefits.

As we discussed in Chapter 9, if you are between ages 62 and 64 and collecting Social Security, you may earn $10,080 in 2000 before beginning to lose benefits. After that, you will lose $1 in benefits for every $2 earned. The Social Security earnings limit has been repealed for those who reach their normal retirement age. Once you reach your normal retirement age, you can have unlimited earned income without losing benefits.

2. *Consider tapping your home for income.* If you own your home, you can do this in two ways. The first is to sell your home. You can rent and use the entire proceeds to generate income. Or you can purchase a less expensive home, and use the difference between the purchase price of your new home and the sale price of your old home to generate income.

HELPERS

There is an exclusion from capital gains tax of $250,000 ($500,000 for joint filers) of gain for anyone selling his or her primary residence. The residence had to be owned and used as a primary residence for at least two years out of the five years prior to sale.

There is another option if you do not want to sell your home: a *reverse mortgage.* With a reverse mortgage, a bank essentially buys your home from you a little bit at a time by lending you money each month, using the equity in your home as collateral. When you sell your home, or when you die and your estate sells your home, the bank receives back the amount it has lent and interest that has accumulated on the loan.

3. *Turn your life insurance into cash.* You can, of course, cash in life insurance policies that have a cash value, such as whole life, universal life, and variable life policies. You can use this cash to cover living expenses, or buy an annuity with the cash, which will pay you a monthly income over your lifetime.

Many variable and universal policies can "flip" from life insurance policies to annuities. You can also borrow the cash value tax-free. Be sure to consult an insurance or financial planning professional before you cash in a policy or borrow against it.

For those who have been diagnosed with a terminal illness, or some chronic illnesses, many insurance companies are willing to give you an "accelerated death benefit," which in essence pays you a portion of the death benefit to which the policy's beneficiary would otherwise be entitled.

Another way to access life insurance funds is through a *viatical settlement*. In a viatical settlement, a qualified purchaser buys another individual's life insurance policy, at a discount from the death benefit. The purchaser then becomes the policy's beneficiary and receives the death benefit when the seller dies. The seller has use of a portion of the policy's death benefit during his or her lifetime.

Viatical settlements first became popular as a way for those afflicted with AIDS to pay for hospice or other custodial care in the last stages of their illness. The practice is growing to include other terminally ill life insurance owners, and is a way for elderly terminally ill people to pay for their care without their spouses having to drain all of their assets in order for the ill person to become eligible for Medicaid benefits.

Some life insurance carriers are buying back policies from chronically ill people as well, and viatical brokers are beginning to make a market in policies of chronically ill people. The discount from the face value is usually deeper for the chronically ill, given their longer expected life than those who are terminally ill.

Traps, Obstacles, Tools, and Helpers

Try to avoid the following traps and obstacles, and take advantage of the following tools and helpers.

- Determining what you will need in your first year of retirement and simply making a linear projection of expenses, factoring in inflation
- Assuming that the Consumer Price Index (CPI) accurately reflects the real impact of inflation on your retirement spending
- Believing that one person can live for half the price of two
- Spending more in early retirement years in response to higher rates of return on retirement investments
- Assuming that your retirement will be similar to that of previous generations

- Complacency
- Habits and routines
- Age denial
- Misinformation

- Financial planning software that helps you manage spending and project future expenses on a year-by-year basis
- Financial planning software with lease versus buy comparison modules
- Spending plan worksheets
- Employer-sponsored retiree clubs or associations
- Reverse mortgages, particularly those provided through the Federal Housing Administration of the U.S. Department of Housing and Urban Development (HUD)
- Viatical settlements and accelerated payments of life insurance death benefits
- Local skills—bartering and exchange programs

- Breaking retirement down into phases (go-go years, reflective years, and care years), with different anticipated spending needs in each phase
- Product and service discounts based on age
- Comparison shopping
- The money value of time
- Postretirement employment skills and opportunities
- Home-sale capital gain exclusion
- New favorable tax treatment of certain advance death benefits

ACTION ITEMS

Item	Priority*	Completed
1. Do aggressive planning for the first phase of retirement, being as specific as possible about spending categories. Do moderate planning for the next phase and modest planning for the third phase, with less-precision in each of these longer-term plans. As each phase gets closer, become more precise in planning.		

ACTION ITEMS *(continued)*		
Item	**Priority***	**Completed**
2. Create a retirement spending plan. Look at how you spend your money prior to and during retirement. For each category of expenses, estimate what is likely to happen at different points during retirement. Which categories will increase in cost? Which will decrease? Which will be eliminated? For those that you expect to increase, explore different ways to slow down the rate of increase.		
3. Calculate your own personal retirement inflation rate. Project the impact of inflation on each of your retirement spending categories by using inflation rates that are specific to each category and to your geographical area in retirement.		
4. Identify ways that you can continue to contribute to and build your nest egg during your early retirement years, without jeopardizing your lifestyle.		
5. Calculate a "cost of my time in retirement" index. This is done by dividing your net retirement income by hours awake. After you establish what an hour of your awake time is worth, divide this hourly rate into the price of any product or service before you buy it to determine whether it is worth buying. You can also use this index to determine whether you should "do it yourself" instead of paying someone else to do it for you.		
6. Examine different ways to turn passive assets, such as your home and life insurance policies, into active cash income. Explore each in consultation with a financial advisor who can help you objectively weigh tradeoffs.		
7. Conduct a "vendor relationship analysis" for each service provider you use to determine if you are getting the best value from each. Use this process regularly to assess, manage, and if necessary change these service relationships.		

*A, B, C, or N/A, with A being the highest priority.

12

INVESTING IN RETIREMENT

T here are three big traps you need to avoid when investing during your retirement.

Thinking that your time horizon for investments is the day you retire.

Too many people fall into this trap. An old investment myth states that you should steadily adjust your portfolio as you approach retirement, reducing your equity investments and increasing your fixed-income investments, until you are completely out of equities at the start of retirement and totally into income-producing bonds and CDs.

Nothing could be further from the truth. Your time horizon is not the start of retirement. Rather, your time horizon is the rest of your life. And since today's retiree has a life expectancy of another 18 years at age 65, your portfolio in retirement should be almost as focused on long-term growth as was the portfolio you built in expectation of retirement.

If you've been comfortable up to now with the market risk that exists in a portfolio with a significant portion invested in stocks, you should probably be carrying about 50% of your portfolio in equities on the day you retire. Over the next 10 years or so you should consider reducing that to about 25%. Your time horizon for investing really shouldn't be short-term until you are at least 80.

Believing that bonds and CDs are always better for producing income than equities.

This is really the flip side of the first trap. However, some mutual funds in the equity-income category pay regular dividends that rival some bonds, while the growth potential of the stocks in the fund adds another dimension to the investment. Also, many blue-chip and utility stocks pay dividends comparable to those offered by three- to five-year Treasury bonds, and again offer the potential for growth.

Remember, the interest rate offered on a longer-term bond or CD reflects the expected rate of inflation; but inflation fluctuates, and if it goes up, your interest or dividend may fall below the inflation rate. Inflation of just 4% cuts purchasing power by 50% over 18 years.

Thinking that principal is sacred; you should never touch your principal.

While it is true that most people should not touch their principal before age 75, the idea of never touching the principal leads many people to lock their entire portfolio into fixed-income investments, determine what those investments will return, and vow to "live on the income." Again, unless you're very wealthy and your fixed-income investments generate sufficient cash flows in your early retirement years, inflation will erode your purchasing power and you will have to either reduce your living standards or dip into your principal at inopportune times, possibly selling bonds for less than face value.

The better strategy is to plan how much you spend and create a portfolio that balances growth through equity investing and income through fixed-income investing, understanding that in years when the stock market performance is subpar, you will have to sell more equities to cover your expenses than in years when market performance is strong. However, keeping in mind that you are investing for the long haul, with a 15- to 20-year time horizon, or longer, you'll recall that over that time horizon, stocks historically have far outperformed fixed-income investments.

For more advanced planning, determine in rank order which equity investments you will shed each year, selling more growth-oriented stocks and retaining more dividend-producing stocks as you get older to increase your predictable cash flow while reducing your portfolio risk.

Many people fear their assets will not last during their lifetimes. Figure 12.1 presents a chart that illustrates the impact of time, amount of annual withdrawals, and investment return on how long your investment assets will last during your lifetime.

FIGURE 12.1 WILL YOU OUTLIVE YOUR ASSETS?

The row at the top lists annual rates of return from 1 to 12%. The column on the left lists withdrawal rates, from a high of 12% of principal a year at the top to 1% of principal at the bottom. Suppose you have accumulated $500,000 of assets and estimate your retirement expenses at $40,000. Divide $40,000 by $500,000 to get a withdrawal rate of 8%. If you read across that row, you will see that if you withdraw 8% annually, your $500,000 in assets will last 16 years if your rate of return is 7%. If you withdraw only 6%, or $30,000, your assets will last more than 25 years—obviously a strategy that may leave an estate to your heirs. The stars in the table represent a 50+-year time horizon.

Withdrawal	Rate of Return (%)											
	1	2	3	4	5	6	7	8	9	10	11	12
12	7	8	8	8	8	9	9	10	10	11	12	13
11	8	8	9	9	9	10	10	11	12	13	14	15
10	9	9	10	10	10	11	12	13	14	15	17	19
9	10	10	11	11	12	13	14	15	16	18	21	26
8	11	11	12	13	14	15	16	18	20	24	30	*
7	12	13	14	15	16	18	20	22	27	36	*	*
6	14	15	16	18	19	22	25	31	44	*	*	
5	17	18	20	22	24	29	36	*	*	*		
4	20	22	25	28	33	42	*	*	*			
3	25	28	33	39	*	*	*	*				
2	35	40	50	*	*	*	*					
1	*	*	*	*	*	*						

* = 50+ years.

Although Figure 12.1 adjusts for an annual inflation rate of 3%, *it makes no adjustment for taxes*. You must plan on paying taxes due on withdrawals from retirement accounts, interest and dividend income, and any earned income.

FOR THE EQUITY-AVERSE INVESTOR

Equity-averse investors—those who carried less than 60% of their retirement-accumulation portfolio in equities—will probably sleep better if they are essentially out of equities during their retirement.

You should consider using a technique called "laddering" your income-producing investments, essentially maintaining a rolling maturity date on your portfolio, so that every six months or so you have fixed-income investments maturing. This allows you to gain cash by closing out those investments at maturity rather than having to sell them into a fickle market. It also allows you to take advantage of changing interest rates, making investments in longer-term instruments when rates are higher and shorter-term investments when rates are lower.

Finally, it allows you to time investment maturities for when you will need them for major investments, such as a new car, a move, a special anniversary, or maybe a large gift to a grandchild for college, a wedding, or some other event.

U.S. SAVINGS BONDS

In the midst of an expanding array of investments available to you, "Series EE" and "Series I" U.S. savings bonds are two ways to save for goals.

Series EE Bonds

Series EE bonds are available in denominations of as little as $100. A Series EE bond is typically identified by its face value—the cash value it will reach in 17 years from its issue date—rather than its cost. Series EE bonds are sold at 50% of the face value of the bond. For example, a $100 Series EE bond is a bond with a $100 face value, but it costs you only $50. The maximum term for Series EE bonds is 30 years.

Series I Bonds

Series I bonds are issued in denominations of as little as $50. However, they are sold at face value, so a $50 Series I bond costs you $50. The earnings rate of Series I bonds is indexed for inflation—that is, it is calculated as a combination of a fixed rate of interest plus a semiannual inflation rate. The maximum term for Series I bonds is 30 years.

Tax Advantages

The interest you earn on Series EE and Series I savings bonds is exempt from state and local income taxes. Generally, unless you elect otherwise, you defer federal income tax on the interest until you cash in the bonds. This tax deferral means you can plan ahead for the best time to realize income for tax purposes.

Conservative Investments

Series EE and Series I savings bonds offer you a conservative investment opportunity and are fixed-income investments. More specifically, Series EE and Series I bonds are characterized by:

- *Liquidity.* Ideally, you will hold Series EE and Series I savings bonds for the long term. However, you can cash in a bond any time after you have owned it for six months. The interest earned on Series EE and Series I bonds is paid when the bonds are cashed. You will get back your principal plus interest due. If you cash in a bond before five years, a penalty equal to the last three months' interest will be subtracted from the cash value of the bond.
- *Stability.* Series EE and Series I savings bonds are backed by the U.S. Treasury. When you cash in your bonds, you will get back your principal and interest due. Also, your bonds can be replaced if lost, stolen, or destroyed. Unlike other government securities, only the registered owner, co-owner, or beneficiaries designated can cash in or redeem U.S. Savings Bonds.

While Series EE and Series I bonds pose no *market risk,* which involves the possibility of an investment's value going down, the Series EE bond may pose some *inflation risk.* This is the risk of not earning enough on your money to offset inflation over the long term. However, because savings bonds pose no market risk, you can use them to balance aggressive investments in your portfolio. Aggressive investments, such as stocks, are appropriate for long-term goals like retirement because they have the potential for a greater return over the long term. However, stocks also pose more market risk—risk that you can balance by investing some of your funds in savings bonds, which are fixed-income investments.

DOLLAR COST AVERAGING/MARKET TIMING

At some point, you may be faced with a situation of investing a large lump sum of money. You may feel unsure as to whether you should invest the lump sum all at once or whether you should invest it gradually over a period of time. This latter technique is referred to as *dollar cost averaging.*

Dollar cost averaging is an investing technique that typically results in a lower cost basis per share than the average price per share during the same period. Basically, for each time period (e.g., quarterly, monthly), the same dollar amount is invested in each of the funds or stocks selected. The purchase price of shares occurs at a different price each time because the market price of the security rises and falls to reflect fluctuation in prices of the underlying stock/bonds. When the market price is higher, you purchase fewer shares. When the market price is lower, you purchase more shares. Over time, this results in a lower average cost per share (see Figure 12.2).

At any given time, you might be tempted to wait to make changes to your investments based on your assessment of what the market is doing—going up or down. However, you should use caution when trying to time the market.

Market timing is generally a bad idea because investment studies show it is very hard to do accurately over a long term.

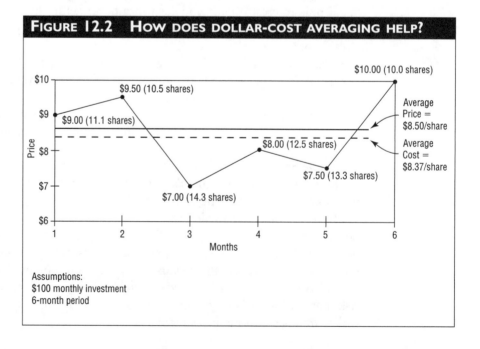

FIGURE 12.2 HOW DOES DOLLAR-COST AVERAGING HELP?

Assumptions:
$100 monthly investment
6-month period

ADVANTAGES OF MUTUAL FUNDS

One of the simplest methods of implementing your investment strategy is through the purchase of mutual funds. There are four key advantages to utilizing mutual funds in your overall investment portfolio:

1. *Diversification.* Because investors pool their money with other investors, mutual funds allow investors to take advantage of entire markets without having large sums of money. They are able to have a more diversified portfolio with a lower amount of risk.
2. *Professional management.* Individuals who manage mutual funds do this for a living. They watch the markets and study the companies on a daily basis. The typical investor does not have the time or the expertise to research and pick securities.
3. *Cost effective.* Even with investing in mutual funds, there is a cost. We review costs investing in mutual funds shortly; however, typically you will pay lower costs than if you had an individual money manager. Also, you are not paying transaction fees each time that a security is purchased within your portfolio. Instead, you are sharing the cost with the thousands of other investors in the fund.
4. *Flexibility.* Mutual funds are typically very liquid in the sense that you are able to purchase and sell funds easily. It is usually as easy as putting your order in. The transaction generally occurs on the same day. Therefore, funds provide a high amount of liquidity.

Funds are generally categorized by investment objective. The following is a list of some of the categories but by no means is it all inclusive.

- Aggressive growth
- Value
- Growth
- Growth and income
- Equity income
- Small company
- Global/world stock
- International stock
- Specialty
- Balanced/asset allocation
- Corporate bond
- Government bond
- International bond

- Municipal bond
- Index

With the thousands of mutual funds available, choosing which ones to buy can be confusing. Some of the key criteria you may use in evaluating mutual funds include the following:

- Ensure that fund objective meets the investment objective you are looking for. For example, if you are increasing your large-cap exposure, you should focus on reviewing only large-cap mutual funds.
- Review the three- and five-year performance periods, not just last year. A fund may have had a great performance over the last year but historically may not have performed very well.
- Check how long the fund manager has been with the fund. Is the current fund manager the one responsible for the historical performance of the fund? The fund may have performed very well over the last five years, but the current manager has only been around for one year. Therefore, the stellar performance is not due to the current manager but rather the prior manager.
- Be sure to compare performance to the appropriate index over the last one year, three years, and five years. For example, if you are reviewing a large-cap mutual fund, you should compare the performance to the S&P 500 index over the same time periods.
- Review the fees and expenses. Is it a load or no-load fund? If it is a load fund, ensure the performance overcomes the additional expenses.

The possible fees and expenses associated with mutual funds include the following:

- *Loads.* A fund may charge a front- or a back-end load. This translates into a sales charge at time of purchase or sale of the fund. It is typically a percentage of the value invested either at time of purchase or sale. If funds do charge a load, which is *not* always the case, they typically charge either a front end or a back end, but not both.
- *12b-1 fees.* Typically these cover the advertising and administrative fees of the fund.
- *Management fees.* These are the costs associated with paying the fund's money manager and the general costs of administering the fund. Typically, they range anywhere from 0.25 to 2% of the value of the fund each year.

Regardless of the fees, it is important to consider all fees before investing in a fund. Typically, you will find that the fees are summarized in one section of the prospectus.

SHOULD YOU CONSIDER TAX-FREE INVESTMENTS?

Tax-free investments are typically fixed-income investments where you make a loan to a state, city, or municipality for public works such as building roads, schools, bridges, and so on. These investments are usually called municipal bonds. The interest payments you receive are most often free of federal income tax. (They may or may not be subject to state income tax.) While it may sound great that the interest you earn on these investments is tax-free, that is not a reason by itself to invest in them. So, how do you determine if you should make tax-free investments?

Some key considerations in determining whether you should invest in tax-free investments include the following:

- Tax-free investments are not necessarily a "good" deal just because you don't pay tax on the earnings. Tax-free investments typically pay a lower interest rate than taxable investments since you don't pay tax on the earnings.
- Lower earnings from tax-free investments are typically calculated using the higher tax brackets that an individual faces.
- It is important to look at the quality of the underlying investment as well. Not all tax-free investments are high quality.
- *You should not invest tax-free in a tax-deferred account like an IRA* (because the income is still taxable when withdrawn).
- It is important to compare taxable and tax-exempt investments on a level playing field. To do so,
    Calculate equivalent yields for taxable and tax-exempt investments.
    Tax-exempt investments typically don't have comparable returns until you are in the higher tax brackets (31, 36, or 39.6%).
    Remember that you still have to look at the quality of the investment.

ACCUMULATE—EVEN AS YOU COLLECT

If you continue to work after you begin collecting Social Security benefits, it's important that you continue to make contributions to your tax-deferred retirement plans, such as IRAs, Keogh/SEPs, or 401(k)s, right up until age 70½, when you must begin taking withdrawals. You can continue to contribute to a Roth IRA even after age 70½. For those who continue to work past age 70½, you do not need to begin withdrawing from your employer-sponsored tax-deferred retirement plans, and you can keep accumulating. This rule does not apply if you are a 5% owner of the company that sponsors the plan; 5% owners must begin taking withdrawals by April 1 of the year after they turn 70½ even if they continue to work.

And you must begin taking withdrawals from IRAs (other than Roth IRAs) by April 1 of the year following the year in which you turn 70½, even if you continue to work.

THE WARY INVESTOR

Financial scammers have long targeted elderly people. Flim-flams come in all shapes and sizes. You need to be as wary in your investing as you are in purchasing any other products or services.

Learn to recognize a scam. Watch out for some of these tricks used by con artists to steal money, and don't fall into their traps.

Real Estate Frauds

These often start with "no-obligation" invitations to listen to a sales pitch. Sometimes a gift is included—dinner, a television set, even a trip. The presentation usually includes a slide show or video of beautiful tracts of land in the hills or nearby lakes. But often the land the salespeople are selling is desert, swamp, or steep mountains. Lots often go for as little as $2,000 an acre, but for unbuildable land.

Home Improvement Scams

Legitimate home improvement contractors don't sell their services door to door. If you need work done on your home, it's best to seek tradespeople through referral by neighbors or colleagues, then to get at least two—preferably more—quotes from these contractors before purchasing their services.

Con artists often undercut prices of legitimate contractors, but they usually demand that you sign a contract immediately and hand over a check as well.

Some home improvement scammers pose as building inspectors. Once inside your home, they find violations that must be corrected immediately—for a fee, of course. In reality, few if any municipalities send building inspectors door to door. Always ask for identification, write down the information of the identification, and tell the person to wait outside while you call your city or town's building department. Chances are when you go back to the door, the "inspector" will be gone.

Medical Quackery
Promises of cures for diseases and run-of-the-mill afflictions of old age are surefire ways for con artists to make money. Preying on the hopes and fears of people in pain and distress, they rake in literally billions of dollars a year in this country.

Medical swindlers quote "doctors" who often have no degrees, sell bogus products, and actually distract people from seeking the medical assistance they need. Be wary of direct-mail marketing, door-to-door pamphleteers, or invitations to health lectures by practitioners you can't readily check out.

Be careful as well of mail that assures you that you are a guaranteed winner or that offers a free vacation. Only trust your car to a dealer, a mechanic who comes to you by way of referral (and preferably who lives in the community), or one of the increasingly popular national repair chains.

Some con artists don't even try to sell you anything. The entire con consists of getting inside your home, where they can steal from you and often injure you. Ask for identification from anyone who comes to your door posing as an inspector or a factory representative, or someone who just wants to check something. Thieves also arrive posing as friends of one of your children or simply looking to get out of the rain or cold while waiting for a bus. Don't let them in.

Beyond the scams pulled by people you don't know, you still need to assess your broker just as you would assess someone who came to your door offering to clean your rugs or fix your roof.

Here are a few simple helpers.

Never have all your investments in a discretionary account.

People who invest your money for you, either money managers or brokers to whom you give discretion, do things their way and not yours. They are professionals, and they make their living taking risks.

In general, you should give discretion to money managers who charge as a fee a fixed percentage of the money they manage for you. They therefore have an incentive to make your investments grow in order to increase their fee. You should not give trading discretion to a broker who earns his or her living from commissions by buying and selling investments. This person's incentive is to trade, regardless of whether the trade improves your investment portfolio or detracts from it.

And, if you are going to allow someone to invest for you, never give that person *more money than you can afford to lose.*

Manage your team of professional advisors.

You are the proverbial 600-pound gorilla. Brokers, investment advisors, accountants, financial planners, and lawyers all work for *you* in making your retirement more enjoyable and profitable. Make sure they are working for you first and for themselves second. If they aren't listening, if they don't respond to questions, if they don't return phone calls, *get someone else.*

This is especially important for a person who has been widowed and is dealing with advisors who had dealt with his or her spouse. Just because the broker went to college with your husband doesn't mean he will manage the account, or make suggestions to you about the way you manage the account, in a way that is appropriate. Be wary of so-called fee-based advisors selling asset management services to widows and widowers under the guise of a survivor counseling program. A "fee-only" firm does not receive any commission. Ask for the firm's ADV form (required for a federally registered investment advisor). The ADV form will disclose how the organization truly makes money. You may do better by putting together your own team of advisors. An increasing number of women in law, accounting, and financial planning are making a practice specializing in working for women. But, of course, don't simply assume that a woman advisor will always have your interests in mind. Check credentials and references and monitor performance as you would for a man.

Read investment documents and contracts with professional advisors closely.

Before you sign, read. And, give yourself time to reread and ask questions. If you don't want to give discretion in investing to someone, make sure your brokerage contract does not have a discretion clause or that you cross it out. Make sure you understand the fee structures of your attorney, accountant, broker, and financial planner and that the fee structure is outlined explicitly in your contract with the advisor.

Read your monthly brokerage account statements before you put them in the drawer. It is not unheard of for unauthorized trades to be made on accounts where the broker does not have discretion. Keep a record of the trades you ask your broker to make, and check them against the statement. If you suspect your broker is trading without your consent, call the office where your broker works and ask to speak immediately with the compliance officer. The worst you'll have to do is apologize for misreading the statement or misunderstanding a transaction.

CHOOSING A FINANCIAL PLANNER

The financial planning field in the United States has been growing rapidly. However, because of the many types of planners, it's important that you understand the basics of financial planning.

There is no single definition of financial planning that is universally accepted. Various definitions of what constitutes a comprehensive financial plan include the following:

- The identification of specific goals and precise objectives, their ranking, and a time frame for their achievement
- The understanding and use of the time value of money
- The selection of critical assumptions to be used in long-range projections—for example, inflation, rate of return, marginal tax rate, and mortality
- The development of a statement of financial position, showing different categories of assets, liabilities, and net worth
- The development and analysis of a cash-flow statement, showing all sources and uses of funds
- The development and analysis of an income tax statement, showing all taxable income, adjustments, exemptions, deductions, marginal tax rate, and any special tax situations—for example, receipt of a lump-sum distribution from a qualified plan or alternative minimum tax for both federal and state tax liability calculation purposes
- The examination of financial risks—for example, death, disability, illness, property, personal liability, and business, if applicable—and the review of current levels of insurance and exposure
- The review of current investments and alternatives and the analysis of suitability for each identified objective, considering such factors as growth, income, liquidity, safety, and tax consequences
- The projection of funds needed and specific resources available in the future to meet each identified objective
- The identification of assets includable in an estate and the analysis of their control, disposition, and taxation
- The identification of issues and shortfalls in connection with each objective and the listing of recommendations for action to be taken

- The scheduling of actions to be taken to implement recommendations, including priorities, dates, and responsible parties

Some people claim that virtually any of these activities constitutes financial planning. Others contend that true financial planning must be comprehensive and therefore include all of these elements.

Training and Certification of Planners

Unlike other fields, such as law and medicine, financial planners do not have to receive specific training or meet licensing agreements. In 1979, an estimated 25,000 people said they were financial planners. Today, about 400,000 make the same claim. That is why it is important that you seek out a planner with whom you feel you will be comfortable. You should look for a planner who has completed specialized coursework. The following are designations used by planners who meet certain criteria:

- A *Certified Financial Planner* (CFP) is someone who has passed an exam given by the College for Financial Planning based in Denver, Colorado.
- A *Personal Financial Specialist* (PFS) is a designation given to Certified Public Accountants who have passed an exam and have several years of experience providing financial planning to clients.
- A *Chartered Financial Analyst* (CFA) is someone who has passed a test on finance and investments given by the Financial Analysts Federation.

To find a planner, you can ask friends or advisors, such as your attorney, for recommendations. If you feel more comfortable approaching someone on your own, you can contact the following organizations for referrals in your area:

American Institute of Certified Public Accountants
(888) 777-7077

The Financial Planning Association
(800) 282-7526

Society of Financial Service Professionals
(888) 243-2258

Whatever the source of referrals, it's important that you interview planners before choosing one. Be certain that you know whether the planner is part of a fee-only firm, a fee-based firm (which also gets commissions), or a pure commission-based firm. Among the questions you should ask are these:

- How long have you been in practice?
- What is your area of expertise?
- What are your credentials?
- What is your typical client profile? Can I speak to some clients whose background is similar to mine?
- May I have a sample of a financial plan you have written?
- May I have a copy of your ADV, Part II (this is a report the planner must file with the Securities and Exchange Commission)?
- How are you compensated?

There are three typical ways that financial planners charge for their services.

1. *Hourly rates.* The amount of time it takes a planner to work on a client's financial situation determines the cost of the service. Hourly fees generally range from $50 to $500. Solo practitioners tend to be at the lower end of the scale, with senior planners affiliated with large national firms at the higher end. Most practitioners who charge by the hour are fee-only practitioners, although some also earn a commission on the products they sell to their clients.

2. *Flat fees.* The common range for a comprehensive personalized financial plan is from $1,500 to $10,000. Within this category, some planners work on a fee-only basis; many practitioners at the low end of the scale also derive commissions from the products they sell to clients.

3. *Fixed percentage.* The amount of money on which a client seeks advice determines the cost under this method. Practitioners generally charge from 2 to 5% of the client's assets. Clients with smaller amounts of money will usually pay a higher percentage. Some of these advisors actually manage assets also.

You can check up on advisors through the following organizations:

CFP Board of Standards
Phone: (888) 237-6275
Web: www.cfp-board.org
What it does: Confirms if a planner is certified and can tell you if he or she has been disciplined.

National Association of Insurance Commissioners
Phone: (816) 842-3600
Web: www.naic.org
What it does: Gets the number for your state insurance commissioner to check licenses and rules violations.

National Association of Securities Dealers
Phone: (800) 289-9999
What it does: Gets the disciplinary history of a registered representative or broker dealer.

North American Securities Administration Associations
Phone: (202) 737-0900
What it does: Gets the number of your state securities commissioner, checks a planner's licenses, and asks about disciplinary actions.

Securities and Exchange Commission
Phone: (800) 732-0330
What it does: Checks whether the planner is a registered investment advisor and gets any other information available.

National Fraud Exchange Mortgage Asset Research Institute
Phone: (800) 822-0416
What it does: Provides a one-stop background check on stock brokers, financial planners and advisors, real estate agents, trust advisors, and mortgage officers. Cost: $39 for one name; $20 per person thereafter.

INVESTING IN HUMAN CAPITAL

One of the best investments anyone can make is in human capital, your own or someone else's. As we have repeatedly said, retirement planning isn't solely about money.

Think about the pleasure and fulfillment you can get by making an investment in your own physical or mental health, your education, or your spiritual growth. Classes, educational weeks at Elderhostel, religious retreats, Tai Chi in the park, or even sessions with a personal fitness trainer can add to your enjoyment of your retirement.

The way many retirees invest in the human capital of others is through gifts to grandchildren for education. Of course, since it's a gift you won't get a monetary return, but again you will get an emotional return on your investment. Those without children or grandchildren get this same kind of return by making donations to scholarships at colleges and universities.

On the other hand, getting a monetary return may not be as unrealistic as it seems. With low-interest loans and grants becoming more difficult for college students to obtain, the day may not be far off when private individuals will finance college for students they don't know, agreeing to take either fixed loan repayments or possibly even a variable rate of return based on the student's future earnings. Think of it—human venture capital!

DOING WELL WHILE DOING GOOD

Nonprofit institutions have already begun marketing investments to the increasingly affluent retired population through charitable annuities. They work like this:

You buy a charitable annuity through a museum, a university, or some other nonprofit organization. A portion of your investment is considered a donation for the purpose of current income taxes. The principal is invested and you receive monthly checks. At the time of your death, the principal goes to the institution that sold you the annuity. Your rate of return, as with any annuity, varies depending on your age when you purchased the annuity.

Most institutions sell these annuities in amounts as little as $5,000. The only real downside to these annuities is that the money is not available at your death to be passed to heirs. However, for people who were thinking about making charitable bequests in their estate plans, purchasing an annuity beforehand gets them the benefit of an income-tax deduction now, instead of a reduction of estate taxes later.

TRAPS, OBSTACLES, TOOLS, AND HELPERS

Try to avoid the following traps and obstacles, and take advantage of the tools and helpers.

- Thinking that your time horizon for retirement investment is the day you retire
- Believing that bonds and CDs are always better for protecting income than equities
- Panicking and selling stocks in response to market drops
- Focusing on yield instead of total return
- Being loyal to a bank, insurance company, or other financial institution that is not giving you the best deals on your money
- Investing in high-cost bond and money market funds with annual expenses that significantly reduce your rate of return
- Believing that you should never dip into your principal during retirement
- Having all of your retirement investments in a discretionary account
- Signing any contract without independent review and explanation

- Rules of thumb (like 100% minus your age) to determine how much of your retirement portfolio should be invested in stocks
- Fraudulent practices, scams, and telemarketers that target retirees, including real estate, home improvement, life and dread disease insurance, medical quackery, and phony charities
- Confidence games
- Confusing and deceptive promotional literature and documents
- Complex and inconsistent compensation arrangements used by financial advisors

- Financial planning software with investment planning modules
- Inflation-indexed U.S. bonds and other Treasury securities available for purchase directly from the Federal Reserve without a sales charge
- State and local consumer protection agencies, attorney general offices, and better business bureaus
- Law enforcement units that specialize in retiree victimization crimes
- Direct Stock Purchase Plan Clearinghouse (1-800-774-4117), which lists companies that sell their stock directly to the public without having to use a broker
- Financial planner certification confirmation from the CFP Board of Standards (1-888-237-6275)
- Registered Investment Advisor confirmation and information from the Securities and Exchange Commission (1-800-732-0330)

- Asset allocation
- Dividend reinvestment plans
- Laddering technique for fixed-income investing
- Automated phone systems to find out daily information about mutual fund investments
- Managing your own team of financial specialists, including accountants, brokers, insurance agents, attorneys, and financial planners

ACTION ITEMS

Item	Priority*	Completed
1. Monitor the growth of your retirement savings based on your most reasonable estimated annual rate of return. Make adjustments if your actual performance consistently lags behind your assumptions for a given time period.		
2. Rank your retirement investments according to their liquidity and tax consequences to determine in advance the order in which you will tap them to meet retirement spending needs.		
3. Establish your overall retirement asset allocation among cash, bonds, and stocks. Decide whether you want to further establish targets within stocks among large-company, small-company, international, and other equity subclasses.		
4. Decide how frequently you will rebalance your portfolio in retirement to maintain your desired asset allocation targets.		
5. Determine how much money you will need to have in highly liquid cash investments to meet spending needs and avoid having to sell equity investments in a bear market.		
6. Read carefully the prospectus for each fund in which you invest. Pay particular attention to annual expenses, commissions, up-front loads, back-end sales charges, 12b-1 marketing fees, and fund sales requirements, including signature guarantees. Shop around for similar funds to which you can switch that offer lower expenses, no sales commissions, and few restrictions.		
7. Put together your team of financial advisors. Make sure your spouse or life partner as well as other family members knows the role of each person on your team, his or her expertise, and the overall coordination role that you play. In forming your team, select advisors who develop a professional relationship with clients rather than those who develop primarily a commercial relationship.		

*A, B, C, or N/A, with A being the highest priority.

13

ALTERNATIVE RETIREMENT SCENARIOS AND POSTRETIREMENT OPPORTUNITIES

Time creates opportunities. In retirement, there should be more time to do what you choose to do. However, your days can quickly be filled with unimportant matters if you don't have a plan for what to do with your time.

Try this exercise: Write down on a piece of paper. "I have always wanted to . . ." Leave the paper for a few minutes, take a walk, pour a glass of juice or a cup of coffee, then sit down and make a list of the things you have always wanted to do.

Include in the list anything that comes to mind, even if it seems trivial. Don't limit yourself by categories, say "sports." Don't let cost influence your thinking.

If your list looks random—say, "go to a baseball fantasy camp, write a children's book, fish for marlin, act in community theater, open a craft store, finish a college degree," and so on—that's fine. You've decided on the size of the frame in which you can now paint your retirement masterpiece.

Now that you've created the frame, you have to split your task in two parts. One is to rank-order the list, from top to bottom. What would you do if you could only do one thing? And why? How about the top two, three, and so on? The second part of your task is to decide the retirement scenario into which you will put your activities.

By "retirement scenario" we mean whether you will completely retire from work and begin enjoying all the items on your list or whether you will go into semiretirement, working part time at your present position, or taking another part-time position; and moving through the items on your list more slowly. Will you use retirement as an opportunity to change your occupation, in which case you may have to delay taking part in the items on your list? Or you may want to use the items on your list as a guide for the kind of new career you will seek. Perhaps you want to develop a former hobby—or one on your list for which you've never had time—into a money-making business. Again, when choosing your ideal scenario, don't be guided by financial considerations; rather be guided by your desires.

LOOK INSIDE FOR ANSWERS

Most people don't get at the truth of what will work for them—in retirement as well as in other aspects of their lives—unless they look at it from the inside out. Ask yourself these questions about the items on your list as well as about your work: "How do I feel when I do this? Is it frustrating? Is it rewarding?"

Ask also: "What are the things I've done during my life that have given me the most pleasure?"

Sit back for a while and replay the course of your adult life. Don't look for the things you could have done better. Look at the good decisions you made, and how you made them. Chances are you are like most of us—some of our best decisions are made by saying, either clearly stated or just felt, "That works for me" or "That sounds like fun." How many of us have moved from one job to another because we said, "That looks like a real opportunity. Sure there's risk involved. But hey, no pain, no gain"?

Remember, now that you're in the retirement phase of your life, the pressure is off to earn a paycheck. If you try something and it doesn't work out, you're no longer boxed in by the need to save for retirement—and college for the kids, and a new home, and . . . You can pick up and go, and say, "It wasn't for me."

GET DOWN TO THE NITTY-GRITTY

Now that you have a rank-ordered list and a preferred scenario, it is time to get back to what's doable. At this point, you need to ask yourself a series of "business-decision" questions about the items of high priority.

1. *Do I need to get any special training, or accumulate any specialized knowledge to take part in this activity?*

If you've decided you want to restore old cars, for instance, you can pick up the required knowledge in a variety of ways. You could take a course at a local community technical college or high school adult program. Or you could take a job in an auto-parts store and pick the brains of your colleagues and your customers. Or you could serve as an apprentice yourself to a person who restores cars, either someone you know or someone you meet through one of the dozens of car clubs or car magazines.

If you want to take up a new sport—say golf or tennis—it may be just a matter of a few lessons and then swinging away.

If you want to turn a hobby into a business, it may be worthwhile to take a business course at a community college or attend one of the many seminars for small business owners offered by colleges, chambers of commerce, and other organizations.

2. *What are the financial considerations of the choices I have ranked highly?*

You need to be specific about your choice. "Travel" won't do. A two-week car trip across the desert Southwest of the United States costs a lot less than a two-week trip to Southeast Asia or an African safari.

If you want to take up golf, you need to create a budget. How much do the clubs cost? How many lessons do you want to take? How often do you want to play? Do you want to play at a local public course, or do you want to travel to nicer courses within, say, two hours of home? How about Pebble Beach, Pinehurst, the TPC Stadium course at La Quinta—even the Old Course at St. Andrew's?

If you want to start your own business or purchase a small business or a franchise, you need to do some very serious homework. If it sounds like a surefire way to make easy money, it probably isn't. Even if you've made big-dollar financial decisions in your working life, it's important to get some professional advice from an objective party—someone you hire to review the business opportunity for you.

3. *Does my chosen activity require partners or other participants, or is it something I can do alone?*

Unless you like hitting a tennis ball off a wall, a sport requires others to play with you. Can you find them? Do you know any players? Are they players of your skill level? Is there an organization near your home that can help match you with others of your skill level? Does your spouse or partner want to get involved?

If you want to turn your cabinetmaking hobby into a business, do you need to take on a partner to help with installations, or will you just hire day help for that? If you like the woodwork but don't like the business part, should you find a partner to handle the business end, selling, negotiating, and collecting and keeping the books straight?

On the other hand, if you want to try writing the great american novel, you don't need anybody else.

4. *Most important, how does this fit in with family and lifestyle? Do these aspirations mesh with those of the significant people in my life?*

If you decide that what you really want to do is travel the world and chase the perfect wave but your spouse wants to buy a bookstore in a college town in New Hampshire, your wonderful marriage may be headed for challenges. But then again, maybe you want to baby-sit for your grandchildren, take them to museums and the circus, and let your spouse work from dawn till dusk on heavy machinery building an extension to your home.

"DOING NOTHING" DOESN'T SUIT MOST PEOPLE

Increasingly, surveys show that nearly half of those looking at retirement 5 or 10 years in the future say they plan to work part time during retirement. Their reasons vary, from wanting to stay busy doing something they really enjoy to feeling the need to earn additional income for their retirement lifestyle.

We know of two men who have retired twice but still refuse to quit. One took early retirement in his mid-50s from a major daily newspaper, where he had spent more than 20 years as an editor. He then spent 10 years as a full-time journalism professor. After retiring from that job in his late 60s, he puttered around for a year, doing a couple of editing jobs and fixing up his house in the country. Then he went back on the adjunct faculty at still another university. "The pay is terrible," he said, "but I'd probably teach for free. I just need to get out of the house and do things."

This man has hobbies; he loves to cook gourmet meals—his children sent him to a one-week cooking school taught by a world-class chef for his 65th birthday—and he loves the theater. But being with people—and especially young people working at the craft of journalism—is what makes the days worth getting up for.

Another man retired in his 60s after a career in social work, settlement house work, and administration of Jewish community centers and synagogues. He and his wife were looking for a new apartment, and they discovered that a housing complex for elderly people was looking for a director. He took the job, which included an apartment, and had a second career that lasted into his 70s. When he retired again, he and his wife moved to yet another apartment in a big building with a large number of elderly tenants but also a number of graduate students from local universities. Before long, the man had taken it upon himself to become the volunteer social director for the elderly contingent—calling bingo games, running card nights and dances, and organizing bus trips to the local theater. He did this until shortly before he died, at age 93.

A FEW "SPECIAL SITUATIONS"

There are a few circumstances that will seriously limit your ability to determine what you do in retirement.

One is health problems you or your life partner have. A health problem may be expensive to treat, it may limit your mobility, or it may cause you to relocate even if that would not be your first choice. A number of people choose to make a postretirement relocation to the desert Southwest rather than the muggier Southeast because the dry heat is better for their health.

A second situation that is increasingly being encountered by retirees, especially younger retirees, is the need to care for an elderly parent. We are really living in the first era of two-retired-generation households. We've only begun to feel the implications of this, both as individuals and as a society. But in 15 years, this will be such a common occurrence, we won't even list it as a "special situation" in the edition of this book published in 2015.

Also, your retirement options may be limited by the need to care for a disabled spouse or a disabled child. If you find yourself in this situation, it's important that you still sit down and make your list of "things I would like to do."

As this becomes a more common situation, organizations are being founded to provide long-term caretakers with "respite" from their efforts.

You need to do things for yourself, whether that's occasional travel or an afternoon a week at the beauty parlor or volunteering for your favorite charity or the gym or reading to a class of kindergartners.

The third situation that needs special attention is divorce. Divorce occurs in the retirement years more often than most of us would like to acknowledge. It may involve a long marriage that isn't strong enough to face the challenges of retirement. Or it may involve a postretirement marriage that lasts only a short time.

In either case, divorce creates a unique set of issues—from financial to family—that must be addressed by both parties with care and with concern for each other and their individual futures. While divorce is never easy, it is a manageable experience when two people acknowledge their mutual responsibilities for making the transition as smooth as possible.

TRAPS, OBSTACLES, TOOLS, AND HELPERS

Try to avoid the following traps and obstacles, and take advantage of the tools and helpers.

- Failing to explore and use continuous self-improvement techniques
- Underestimating the role of work and job-related status in your life
- Attributing to aging what you really can control
- Not diversifying your retirement activities
- Not considering the needs of others in your retirement plans

- Limited personal vision
- Equating what you do with who you are
- Sedentary living
- Looking for the silver bullet for a successful retirement
- Special situations that may seriously limit your ability to determine what you will do in retirement, including health problems, elder care, and family breakup

- Self-assessment worksheets
- Personal development courses and training programs
- Retirement living publications
- Discussion groups
- State and local agencies on aging funded and coordinated by the Administration on Aging of the U.S. Department of Health and Human Services

- Looking to successful retirement role models
- Volunteering

ACTION ITEMS

Item	Priority*	Completed
1. Create a wish list of all the things you would like to do in retirement—no limits. Then rank-order them.		
2. Determine the limits on wish-list items imposed by time, training, and financial considerations.		
3. Conduct an inventory of your personal skills. Determine which are already marketable as a source of volunteer or paid work. Determine which need to be upgraded through training, and explore specific self-improvement programs in which to enroll.		
4. Identify several retirement success models and why you believe they are successful. Interview them to find out what they believe has most contributed to their successful retirement.		
5. Put the other people in your life into the picture to see how your relationships affect all of your retirement decisions.		

*A, B, C, or N/A, with A being the highest priority.

14

RETIREMENT ISSUES AFFECTING EXECUTIVES

Against the backdrop of the Age Discrimination in Employment Act (1967, as amended), which set the mandatory retirement age in the United States at 70 and made it unlawful for employers to terminate anyone over age 39 on account of age, "early retirement windows" and other incentives to leave at or before the normal retirement age have become commonplace. Since the mid-1980s, when American businesses began simultaneously experiencing megamergers and downsizing on what seemed to be a daily basis, the subject of retirement for many executives has understandably become a matter of intense personal interest.

Whether you've reached retirement by choice or were subject to a forced early retirement due to company downsizing or other circumstance, it is crucial that you are aware of issues concerning your company's benefits. For example:

- Did you know that you may have a very short time during which to exercise any outstanding stock options you hold?
- Did you know that the federal government requires that you begin taking retirement plan distributions at a certain age?
- Did you know that there is a "penalty tax" for taking too little at any one time?
- Did you know that, generally, you are able to save a smaller percentage of pay in qualified retirement plans than lower-paid employees?

While the distribution laws are complex, so too can be company-specific rules that govern participation in your company's plans. We will take a look at these issues, giving an overview of the kinds of company retirement savings plans in which you may be participating and how you can make the most prudent decisions.

Stock Options

Stock options are an incentive to stimulate the efforts of key employees and strengthen their desire to remain with the company. Upon retirement, such incentives are no longer relevant.

Consequently, many companies reduce the time period during which retired employees may exercise their options or terminate the right to exercise options altogether. It is terribly important, therefore, to make sure that you keep track of stock option exercise dates. Consider the published case of Richard Gillman [as detailed in *Gillman v. Bally Mfg. Co.* 670 A.2d19 (N.J.)].

Richard Gillman served for many years as one of Bally Manufacturing Company's top executives. Ballys manufactures slot machines. In 1991 Bally granted Mr. Gillman options to buy 1 million shares of stock in the company.

Under the option agreements, the option had a 10-year life, as long as Mr. Gillman remained with Bally. The option agreement further provided that if he retired, the options could only be exercised within one year after retirement.

On January 8, 1993, Mr. Gillman retired. One year and 16 days later, on January 24, 1994, he attempted to exercise his options, but Bally refused. Mr. Gillman's inaction cost him millions of dollars.

Moral: *Read your stock-option agreements closely and adhere to them!*

There are several variations of stock incentive programs, including Non-Qualified Stock Options (NQSOs), Stock Appreciation Rights (SARs), and Incentive Stock Options (ISOs). Read your plan description to find out about any special conditions on your stock options or SARs, and consult your lawyer or financial advisor if you have questions.

Qualified Company Retirement Plans

Critical to maximizing your benefits from a company plan is gaining a solid understanding of what benefits are provided by the plan as well as the payout options made available to employees.

Qualified retirement plans include defined-benefit plans (often called pension plans) and defined-contribution plans such as 401(k), 403(b), and profit-sharing plans. These plans are called "qualified" because they qualify for certain tax advantages by meeting requirements of the Internal Revenue Code.

There are generally two choices for receiving benefits from a qualified plan—an annuity (lifetime payment) or a lump-sum distribution. These methods are detailed in Chapter 7 but are worth reviewing here. There are pluses and minuses with each payout option.

Lifetime Payment

+ The employee (and spouse or other beneficiary) receives a fixed monthly amount no matter how long he or she lives.
+ The employee is relieved of the investment burden.
− Payments stop at death unless the pension has "term certain" payments that continue for a predetermined period of time.
− Inflation will erode purchasing power if the payments are not indexed or variable.
− Access to assets is limited to monthly payments.

Lump-Sum Distribution

+ Distributed assets can be invested in a portfolio that offers a hedge against inflation.
+ There is full emergency access to proceeds at any time.
+ You can roll over all or part of the distribution into an IRA to extend the tax-deferral.
− The employee and beneficiary could outlive the funds.
− A large fund may present a temptation to overspend or make it difficult to plan a comfortable budget.
− The employee has the responsibility for investing a large sum of money.

TAX CONSEQUENCES

Under the Employee Retirement and Income Security Act of 1974 (ERISA), amounts deferred from current taxation into a qualified retirement plan are not supposed to be used for expenditures before retirement or deferred beyond the employee's life and passed to his or her estate. The intent of the law is to encourage saving for retirement. Thus, there are restrictions on distributions before retirement and substantial penalties for not taking distributions during the retirement years.

Both lifetime payments and lump-sum distributions from qualified plans are generally taxable as ordinary income. Certain special rules may apply if you receive a lump-sum which includes employer stock or if you were born before 1936. See Appendix I for more details.

Early Distributions

Early distributions are distributions from individual retirement accounts (IRAs) or from an employer's qualified retirement plan that you take before reaching age 59½. There is a 10% "penalty tax" for an early distribution unless the distribution meets one of several exceptions, including the following:

- Annuity-like payments for the life of the participant or the joint lives of the participant and a beneficiary. This exception ceases to apply if distributions are changed to another form before the participant reaches age 59½ or within five years from the first payment date, whichever is later.
- Distributions attributable to a participant's death or disability.
- Distributions to a participant who terminated employment in or after the year in which he or she reached age 55. This applies only to company plans, not to your IRA.

E X A M P L E

■ Katie and Tyson both accepted early-retirement buyout offers from their company late in 1999. Their cash settlement was considered taxable income for 1999.

At age 57, Katie decided to retire and take $100,000 of her 401(k) account as a lump-sum distribution early in 2000, rolling the rest over into her IRA. The $100,000 was taxable income for 2000 but not subject to the 10% excise tax.

Tyson, at 51, decided to purchase his own business. He needed $150,000, so he took a $250,000 lump-sum distribution from his 401(k). He paid a $25,000 (10%) penalty tax in addition to the ordinary income tax on the $250,000, which left him with just enough to purchase the business. ■

- Distributions to a participant used to pay deductible medical expenses (medical expenses that exceed 7.5% of your adjusted gross income).
- Distributions paid to another person designated in a qualified domestic-relations order, that is, splitting your plan with your spouse should you divorce.
- IRA exceptions for higher education expenses, $10,000 of first-time home-buyer expenses, and health insurance premiums if you're unemployed.

Minimum Distributions

Minimum distributions from any tax-deferred retirement plan you partici-pate in—qualified plans, IRAs (other than Roth IRAs), or SEPs/Keoghs for self-employed—must begin by April 1 of the year following the calendar year in which you reach 70½. However, if you continue to work past this time, you may defer having to take withdrawals from employer-sponsored plans until April 1 of the year after you retire, unless you are a 5% owner of the company that sponsors the plan. As long as the IRA account owner is alive, lifetime distributions from Roth IRAs are never required.

However, it is not necessary that your entire account be distributed at this time. Annuity distributions based on your life expectancy, or on your life expectancy and that of your spouse or another designated beneficiary, satisfy the distribution requirement.

EXAMPLE

■ Martin turned age 70½ on August 1, 1999; his wife, Fern, had already died. He has named his synagogue as his beneficiary (since the synagogue has no "life expectancy," he will use only his life expectancy in determining the minimum required distribution). Martin's life expectancy under the single-life expectancy table is 16 years, and he elects not to recalculate his life expectancy.

The account balance in his IRA as of December 31, 1998, was $200,000. He divides $200,000 by his 16-year life expectancy. The resulting amount, $12,500, is his minimum required distribution for 1999, and must be made by April 3, 2000 (April 1 was a Saturday). His required minimum distribution for 2000 will be determined by dividing the balance in his account as of December 31, 1999, by 15, and must be distributed by December 31, 2000. ■

If you fail to take the minimum distribution, there is a "penalty tax" of 50% of the difference between the actual distribution you took and the minimum distribution you should have taken.

Excess Distributions and Excess Accumulations

The 15% "penalty tax" imposed on excess distributions from, and excess accumulations in, retirement plans was repealed retroactive to January 1, 1997. The repeal of this tax should not, however, encourage you to with-draw excessive amounts. Distributions still are subject to income tax and reduce your tax-deferred assets.

While Social Security is discussed at length in Chapter 8, it's relevant to repeat the discussion of Social Security benefits taxation. Most executives can expect to pay federal income taxes on 85% of their Social Security benefits.

It's also important to note that you can be penalized if you take Social Security benefits and continue to work. If you begin receiving Social Security benefits before your normal retirement age and you continue to work, you may have your benefits reduced or eliminated. In 2000, retirees who have not yet reached their Social Security "full retirement age" will lose $1 of benefits for every $2 earned above $10,080. Recipients who reach full retirement age in 2000 lose $1 of benefits for every $3 they earn above $17,000 but only before the month that full retirement age is reached.

If you are receiving Social Security benefits and have reached your normal retirement age, however, you can earn as much as you want from work without any reduction in your benefit. Effective in 2000, the earnings limit for Social Security has been eliminated for those who have reached their normal retirement age. Prior to 2000 you had to reach age 70 to collect Social Security benefits without a limit on earnings.

Traps, Obstacles, Tools, and Helpers

Try to avoid the following traps and obstacles, and take advantage of the following tools and helpers.

- Not keeping good records about executive benefit programs
- Letting taxes alone drive your basic financial decisions
- Ignoring the emotional effects of retirement in your planning

- Complex and changing federal and state tax laws aimed at curbing executive tax-favored retirement plans
- Mandatory withholding on distributions that are not directly transferred to an IRA
- Additional tax on early distributions
- Minimum required distributions
- Potential means-testing or increases in taxes of government programs, particularly Social Security and Medicare

- Employer-sponsored financial counseling and outplacement programs
- Financial planning software with sophisticated tax and investment modules
- Service Corps. of Retired Executives (SCORE), a program in the U.S. Department of Commerce's Small Business Administration

- IRA rollovers
- Pre-1974 capital gains treatment
- Treatment of net unrealized appreciation on employer securities
- Substantially equal periodic payments exception to additional tax on early distributions from qualified plans and IRAs
- Exceptions to additional tax on early withdrawals from IRAs
- Nonqualified retirement and deferred compensation plans
- Incentive stock option (ISO) and nonqualified stock option (NQSO) plans
- Stock appreciation rights (SARs)

ACTION ITEMS

Item	Priority*	Completed
1. Make an appointment with your employer's benefit office to discuss all components of your benefit program. Make sure that all decisions that you must make are identified in advance so you can examine trade-offs in an unhurried manner. Inquire about and take advantage of any executive counseling services your employer has arranged.		
2. Identify the specific aspects and perquisites (i.e., "perqs") of your position at work that you will miss in retirement. Don't overlook everyday routines that you take for granted. Discuss these with your spouse, life partner, or others who have an interest in your retirement as well as with other executives who have retired from similar positions. Determine which of these features of your current position you can find substitutes for in retirement and which will have to be modified or even sacrificed.		

*A, B, C, or N/A, with A being the highest priority.

15

RETIREMENT ISSUES AFFECTING THE SELF-EMPLOYED

The biggest issue facing you as a self-employed individual is that you must take more of the initiative to create retirement possibilities. No one is providing a retirement plan. Social Security is the only forced savings plan, and its benefits are limited, as we have discussed.

Many self-employed people have a tendency to put all of their money into growing the business. After all, that is what they have chosen to do. They believe in the business and its potential for growth. But precisely because many self-employed people are involved in high-risk ventures, they, more than others, need to balance their passionate pursuit of the business's growth with regular savings. You can't depend on the proceeds from selling your business to provide a comfortable retirement.

Not diversifying financial holdings by setting up a qualified retirement plan.

Too often, those who work for themselves, either as sole-practitioner professionals or as owners of small businesses that may or may not have other employees, feel that as long as their business appreciates in value, they have no need to save for retirement. They figure that it is a better investment to invest in growing the business than in stocks, bonds, mutual funds, or other investments.

This can be very dangerous. Compare this to individuals who put all of their 401(k) savings into the stock of their employer. Showing loyalty is admirable, but it is also important to diversify. The truth is that harsh economic realities exist, and sometimes the business you own, or work for, is the victim of those realities. You may be adversely affected by factors you can't control. Regardless of how astute you are in your business, it is wise to hedge. Setting up a qualified plan is an excellent way to do that.

There are a number of tax-deferred retirement savings opportunities available to the self-employed. You can use an *individual retirement account* (IRA); a *Keogh* plan, an individually designed *qualified* plan; a *simplified employee pension* (SEP); or a *Savings Incentive Match Plan for Employees* (SIMPLE), a retirement vehicle created by Congress in 1996. These types of plans, which all qualify for tax-deferred treatment under the Internal Revenue Code, are discussed in detail in Chapter 6.

Keoghs, Simplified Employee Pensions (SEPs), and the New SIMPLEs

For the self-employed, there are a number of options. Some of the most widely used are in the family of plans called Keoghs. There are defined-benefit Keoghs and different versions of defined-contribution Keoghs.

For those who do not want to go through the paperwork of setting up and administering an individual Keogh plan, such as the annual one-page tax report—Form 5500EZ (for plans in which there are over $100,000 in assets)—there are simplified employee pension (SEP) plans offered by brokerages, banks, and other financial institutions, which basically allow you to have your own plan under their umbrella qualification. Paperwork for these SEPs is usually only a one- or two-page form for starting such a plan.

SEPs were designed to give small businesses and sole proprietorships the ability to accumulate retirement funds for themselves and their employees without the complexity and expense of administering a large, individually qualified plan. Any company can use a SEP.

Your contributions to SEP plans are always fully deductible, regardless of whether you or your spouse participate in another plan, and regardless of your total household income. SEPs are a terrific way to shelter some income from a business you run on the side while also working full time.

Keoghs are for sole proprietorships or partnerships. There are two varieties.

A *profit-sharing* Keogh plan allows you to contribute an amount up to 15% of your net self-employment earnings, up to a maximum of $25,500 in 2000. You can contribute a different percentage each year.

Your allowable contribution may actually be less than 15% of your income because you may only contribute to the plan 15% of total net earnings (earnings after expenses), minus your 15% contribution. For instance, if your self-employment income is $40,000 after your business expenses, you can put into your profit-sharing Keogh 15% × ($40,000 − your contribution). That amount works out to $5,217, which is actually 13.034% of $40,000. The same limit applies to a SEP.

$$15\% \times (\$40,000 - \$5,217) = \$34,783 \times 15\% = \$5,217$$

A *money-purchase* Keogh plan allows you to contribute up to 25% of your net self-employment earnings, up to a limit of $30,000 a year. While you can put away more in the money-purchase plan, the drawback is that you must state the amount of your contribution when you establish the plan and make the same percentage contribution each year. You trade the ability to shelter more income from current taxes and create a larger tax-deferred retirement account for reduced flexibility.

Of course, you can have it both ways by having one of each plan. You can commit to a fixed 10% contribution to your money-purchase plan, then make flexible contributions of up to 15% into your profit-sharing plan, up to a maximum contribution of $30,000 in both plans combined.

One important thing to remember: If you have employees, generally you must make the same proportionate payment into your Keogh or SEP plan for each of them as you do for yourself, unless you create an integrated, age-weighted plan or comparability plan, which takes some time and paperwork—and probably some professional assistance.

Another important thing. You manage all of the assets in the plan, so you have fiduciary responsibility for the money you are putting in the plan for your employees. This means that if you don't handle this responsibility well, you could be sued by one of your employees.

The salary-reduction SEP, or *SAR-SEP*, acts like a mini-401(k) and is available only to companies with less than 25 employees. It allows your employees to put aside up to 25% of pay, to increase or decrease their contribution, and to start it or stop it at any time. You as the employer may choose to match any portion of the employee's contribution. With a SAR-SEP, each of your employees manages his or her own account, relieving you of the fiduciary responsibility.

The limiting factor for how much you contribute to the plan is not so much the legal limit of 15%. Rather, it is the fact that you cannot put into the plan more than 125% of the average contribution your employees make. So if your employees made average contributions of 8% of their pay, you could contribute only 10% of yours.

No new SAR-SEPs can be created as of January 1, 1997. But those created on or before December 31, 1996 can continue to be funded.

Employers with 100 or fewer workers who each earn at least $5,000 and who have no other retirement plan may establish a Savings Incentive Match Plan for Employees (SIMPLE). The SIMPLE, which is not subject to some of the complicated rules that apply to other types of employer-sponsored retirement plans, can be set up using an IRA for each employee or a 401(k) model. The maximum annual pretax contribution an employee may make under a SIMPLE is $6,000.

With certain exceptions, employees who make at least $5,000 must be eligible to participate. Generally, the plan requires the employer to make a dollar-for-dollar matching contribution for every employee who elects to participate in the plan, to a maximum of 3% of each employee's pay, or a flat 2% of pay contribution to every employee, regardless of whether the employee elects to participate.

All contributions under a SIMPLE IRA must be 100% vested. Employer contributions under a SIMPLE 401(k) can be subject to a vesting schedule. However, you as a business owner would be required to satisfy certain nondiscrimination tests with respect to contributions, should you set up a vesting schedule.

Generating Retirement Value from Selling Your Business

To realize some value from your business, you will need to think about just what it is about your business that is valuable and whether the value you derive from your business is transferable as economic value to someone who purchases your business.

There are generally three elements of value to a small business or professional practice:

1. Value of property, equipment, or inventory
2. Value of a book of business from loyal clients, which can be transferred to a new owner
3. Value of goodwill in the name or reputation of the business

Property, Equipment, and Inventory

If you own the property from which you run your business, selling the property as part of the business can create a lump sum of money that can be invested to produce income.

Or you might want to lease the property to the person who purchases the business. For instance, when John sold his business, a wholesale distributorship of roofing, siding, and other home improvement products, he kept the property in a suburban industrial park and continued to lease it to his former company. He had purchased the property in the 1950s for less than $100,000, and it was worth over $2 million when he sold his business.

Leasing the property produced steady income throughout his life. In addition, later in life he transferred ownership of the property to a trust, the income from which benefited his grandchildren. In this way, he did not have to pay the capital gain tax that would have been due on the sale of the property, and his heirs did not have to pay any estate tax on the money he received from the sale.

The major problem with holding the property is the possibility that your former business will move and that you will have to seek another tenant. For John, whose property was in a vibrant industrial park with an excellent location, this was not a problem.

Selling equipment is another matter. Many small-business sales include the purchase of all the business's equipment. But for those who liquidate the business and "cash out," selling equipment may not really be viable. This is especially true for professionals who maintain their own practice. For instance, unless a physician has kept up with the latest in office technology, his or her exam tables and instruments are of little use to anyone else. Computer equipment changes so rapidly, it will be hard to find a buyer for the four desktops being offered by an insurance agent who is closing her doors. The same would be true for an attorney.

One option is donating this kind of equipment to a charitable or nonprofit organization, as defined by section 501(c)(3) of the Internal Revenue Code, and claiming the replacement value or the remaining basis as a tax deduction, whichever is lower. This may be more financially worthwhile than selling the equipment at a deep discount on the open market.

For those whose business maintains inventory, the inventory is usually sold as part of the business sale at its book value.

The "Business Book"

In most states, professionals are technically not allowed to "sell their book" of business. Physicians, attorneys, accountants, and the like must notify all clients or patients that they are retiring. They can recommend the person who is purchasing their practice, but they must transfer records to any individual who wishes to take his or her business elsewhere.

Because of this, the value of the clients you assume will remain with the new provider when you sell the business will be subject to negotiation. It is also difficult to estimate how much service any one client or patient will use and whether high-use clients or low-use clients will remain.

For businesses that sell products rather than services, this may be a simpler calculation to make, based on a percentage of gross sales. For instance, Jack wants to sell his business, which markets promotional items such as pens, canvas bags, coffee mugs, and the like. The business grosses about $1.2 million a year, has been growing slowly in the past few years, and has a client list that turns over frequently and often purchases based on price. Jack and his buyer negotiate the sale price of the business taking all of these factors into consideration.

Goodwill

Black's Law Dictionary defines goodwill as:

> The advantage or benefit which is acquired by an establishment, beyond the mere value of the capital, stocks, funds, or property employed therein, in consequence of the general public patronage and encouragement which it receives from constant or habitual customers, on account of its local position, or common celebrity, or reputation for affluence or punctuality, or from other accidental circumstances or necessities, or even from ancient partialities or prejudices. (Story, Partnerships sec. 99; *Haverly v. Elliott*, 39 Neb. 201, 57 N.W. 1010.)

To put it simply, goodwill is an intangible quality. The value of a business's goodwill varies greatly depending on the type of business and the type of clientele it has.

For instance, a national medium-size accounting firm wishes to buy your firm, which is local, and has a clientele of mostly local and regional businesses and some municipalities. Your firm has been growing reasonably well in the last few years, and you are increasingly making the "short list" of finalists for municipal auditing jobs. Your growing reputation, especially in a particular area of practice, may increase the value of your firm's goodwill.

On the other hand, there is little if any goodwill value in a business like Jack's, described above. He is selling commodity items to a customer list generated mostly from catalog distribution, which often purchases on price considerations.

Ownership-Transition Planning Alternatives

Assuming that you are not simply going to liquidate your business when you retire, here are three alternative approaches to plan for its eventual sale:

1. Choose someone as a key person to take over and continue the business.
2. Write a buy-sell agreement for the sale of the business in advance of retirement.
3. Take your chances that there will be an opportunity to sell when you wish to retire.

You can also hire outside management to operate the business while ownership is passed to heirs or transferred to your loved ones as gifts during your lifetime. Outside management can also run a business that is transferred to a charitable remainder trust. The most notable example of this is the *St. Petersburgh Times* newspaper in Florida, which is owned by a charitable trust established by the paper's late owner, Nelson Poyntner. Some of the paper's operating profits fund the Poyntner Institute, which runs seminars and workshops for working journalists and also funds journalism scholarships.

The first two options give you the chance to "groom a successor," either someone from inside the company or someone from outside who joins the company prior to your leaving with the understanding that he or she will buy the business from you at a particular time or over a period of time.

Insisting that the business stay in the family even if that is the worst possible situation for all involved.

Thinking about who will take over a business is a very emotional part of retirement planning. Many small business owners consider keeping the business in the family if possible. But that doesn't work for all families. In fact, it probably doesn't work for most families.

Individuals have different interests. Many have no desire to run the family business, or to have any day-to-day involvement at all, but still believe they are entitled to a share in the business's financial future as a matter of "fairness." Others have a great desire to be involved in the business but don't really have the aptitude. Then again, a family business sometimes gets embroiled in nonbusiness family issues.

In Boston, one son of the founder of the famous Legal Sea Food restaurant group sued his brother and parents for allegedly forcing him out of the corporation. He says the issue had nothing to do with the business, or how he was running the part of the business for which he had responsibility. Rather, he said, his mother simply didn't like his choice of spouse.

Choosing a nonfamily member from inside the company creates more of an arm's-length transaction but can also cause emotional trauma to those family members who might have hoped to carry the family's business forward.

Hiring from the outside for the specific purpose of creating a buyer-seller relationship in the future also has its difficulties. The person may have all of the proper qualifications for being an owner—both experience and financing—but you may simply not create and/or maintain a good relationship with him or her during the time you are working together prior to the sale. Often such differences cause an "agreement in principle" to fall apart, when it needn't. But some people are able to keep a level bearing and negotiate their differences.

For instance, a former client of one of the authors owned a business started by his grandfather, which was passed down to his father and then to him. None of his children were interested in carrying the business to a fourth generation. The man went looking for someone to come into his business who would want to buy it a few years later when he retired.

The person who came to him brought more than just desire; he brought management experience and capital. Within a few years, the new partner became the company's driving force. Personality conflicts cropped up between the two. It got to the point where they were thinking of dissolving their relationship. The man who joined the business now had a serious investment at stake, an investment of time, effort, and capital. But the man whose business it was still had ownership.

The coauthor was brought in as an impartial third party and asked to arbitrate the dispute. He said to the two of them, "Imagine that you are in the other person's place. What would it take for you to go or stay?" The owner, who was retiring, made a list of what he would need to take with him if he were leaving. The man who was being asked to leave made a list of what would be important to him if he were to stay. By backing off the legal and tax issues and getting at the emotional issues that bind up a long-time owner and an entrepreneurial investor, they were able to sort out their differences and come to an agreement for the sale and retirement.

Letting go of a business you have built with your time and sweat—sometimes from a startup—may be as emotionally difficult as having a child leave home. For some people it is more difficult. But just as with a child, who must be allowed to leave, grow, and find his or her own way, a business must be allowed to change hands, change focus, change direction, and grow in the way a new owner would like it to.

Here are two key helpers for people looking to sell their business at retirement.

Find a team "quarterback."

From among your team of advisors—banker, attorney, accountant, insurance agent, broker, and benefits specialist—choose one to be your "trusted advisor"—your team leader or quarterback. That person should be your contact person with all the specialists, making sure everyone is heading in the same direction.

Decide on an exit strategy and stick to it.

You may want to, or be asked to, retain a financial interest in the business for a while. You may want to, or be asked to, remain on the board of directors for a period of time. You may want to, or be asked to, take a position as a paid consultant for a period of time—often this is a way to secure an income stream for yourself during the period when a noncompetition clause is included in your sale contract. Or you may want to just mark a date on the calendar and on that date hand over the keys and leave.

Whatever your decision, whatever your plan, whatever the agreement you work out with the person or people who buy your business, it is important to look forward from that point. As a self-employed person, you created something of value. It served you well. You can now let go and create new opportunities in retirement with the resources you have developed.

TRAPS, OBSTACLES, TOOLS, AND HELPERS

Try to avoid the following traps and obstacles, and take advantage of the tools and helpers.

- Viewing the business itself as your sole retirement vehicle and consequently not diversifying financial holdings by setting up a qualified retirement plan
- Insisting that your business stay in the family regardless of circumstances
- Ignoring the emotional aspects of business ownership and transition

- Family members' interests and desires

- Ownership transition planning worksheets
- Independent financial advisors who specialize in family business planning

- Keogh plans
- Simplified Employee Pensions (SEPs)
- Savings Incentive Match Plan for Employees (SIMPLEs)
- Clear exit strategies

ACTION ITEMS

Item	Priority*	Completed
1. Explore your alternatives for a qualified retirement plan and set one up that works best for you and your business. Consult with an independent financial advisor. Analyze each planning option both as a vehicle for your business and as a vehicle for your personal retirement. Weigh trade-offs.		

ACTION ITEMS *(continued)*		
Item	**Priority***	**Completed**
2. Determine the most appropriate way of getting value out of your business when you decide to retire. Conduct a thorough valuation of the business, including property, books of business, and goodwill. Assess its transferability through a sale as part of your retirement plan. Assess the trade-offs of different exit options.		
3. Set a firm date for transferring or selling your business.		
4. Create an exit strategy from the business and an entrance strategy into your retirement.		

*A, B, C, or N/A, with A being the highest priority.

16

RETIREMENT ISSUES AFFECTING WOMEN

Consider the following statistics about women and their retirement needs and resources:

- Women outlive men. A 65-year-old woman in 2000 has a life expectancy of another 21.33 years; a man's life expectancy at age 65 is another 16.73 years.
- Women who are currently retired or nearing retirement are less likely to have been eligible for defined-benefit pensions than are men in their age groups. Only 32% of women retired today receive pension benefits, as opposed to 55% of men. And if they receive defined-benefit pensions, those pensions are usually lower than men's.
- Married women who are currently retired or nearing retirement are less likely to have worked throughout their adult lives than are their husbands. They are more likely to have worked part time, or worked seasonally, or had gaps in their employment history to raise children and care for family members. This is also true for single, divorced, or widowed women with children.
- Women who are currently retired or nearing retirement are less likely to have earned as much as men in their age groups—in 1997 women earned about 74.4% as much as men.
- Women retiring today are less likely to have participated in a defined-contribution retirement plan if their employer offered one. This is especially true for single women, who must spend more of their pay to meet daily living needs and have less put into personal savings for retirement.

- Men remain more confident investors. So, if women did participate in defined-contribution plans, they are likely to have contributed less than male coworkers and to have invested their accounts more conservatively.

For these and other reasons, women are more likely to outlive their money than are men. They are more likely to live at least part of their retirement years in poverty than are men. And, even if they have adequate retirement resources, women are more likely than men to fear spending their retirement poor.

Because of this, it's important that women understand what they have and how to make it last.

A Few Positives

There is, however, a positive side of this equation. Of women working today, fully 48% are covered by either a defined-benefit or defined-contribution retirement plan, compared to 51% of men. Also, among married women, 73% have retirement benefits through either their own work or their husband's. The retirement benefit rate for married households is far higher than for individuals of either gender.

For the generations farthest from retirement, women are ahead of men in the uptake on retirement benefits. In fact, women under 35 are more likely to be covered under either a defined-benefit or a defined-contribution than are men under 35; 40% of women are covered versus 39% of men. In businesses with fewer than 25 workers, 20% of women working full time, full year are covered versus 17% of men.

And a survey conducted by the Oppenheimer Funds shows that the gap between men and women in investing is narrowing with 64% of women more interested in investing today than they were five years ago. Among women in their 20s and early 30s, half report that they were encouraged to learn about investing while they were growing up.

What Else Gets in the Way

In general, among today's generation of retirees, women are less likely to have managed the family's financial planning than men. Although women are more likely than men to manage financial matters at home—such as paying the bills—men have traditionally concerned themselves more than women with long-term planning and investing. This is less true of families that are looking toward retirement after 2010.

Those currently approaching retirement are sometimes called the "sandwich generation," with their own needs and desires sandwiched between those of their older and often frail parents and their children, many of whom are still struggling with financial and emotional independence into their 30s. For some, it's really a club sandwich, as they add concerns about how their grandchildren's day-care and college education will be paid for. When these extended families have needs, it's often hard to say no, even though the price is depleting earnings or savings and thus threatening retirement security.

Women are now asking more questions about receiving an inheritance themselves—but lack confidence, compared to men, in how to invest a lump sum of money. At the same time, more women are concerned with leaving behind resources for the next generations as well as for charities. But this desire is not often matched with a real understanding of how to build up those resources or what it means for their lifestyle and spending in retirement.

Regardless of a woman's generation or personal circumstances, women report that they do not take the time to take care of themselves—and often lack the motivation to tackle short- or long-term money issues. As one current retiree put it: "Paying bills is not exactly relaxing, and it's not what I look forward to doing at the end of the day."

YOU'RE RETIRING? HERE'S WHAT YOU CAN DO FOR ME

One problem most women who are recently retired don't report is having trouble filling their time. But they do report a disconnect between what they are doing and what they thought they'd be doing. Time fills, but not always with what women say they want to be doing. Time has a way of filling itself—and lots of other people have an idea of what you can do in retirement, mostly for them.

We've all heard the horror stories about one-income couples after the husband retires; of husbands following wives around the house all day with nothing to do; of others who have never answered their own phone and bark at their wives to stop the ringing next to their ear. To say the least, retirement for a man who has worked outside of the home and a woman who has not can create a host of issues revolving around space, privacy, and "turf."

Nonworking women whose husbands are nearing retirement should work hard at beginning a dialogue over all of the issues involved with retirement. Many men who plan the financial aspects of their retirement with great detail don't put any thought into the physical, mental, and emotional elements of retiring. This gives wives a chance to "drive the retirement agenda."

Not making a list of the top 10 things you'd like to accomplish in your current phase of retirement.

It isn't only the couples in the so-called traditional families entering retirement who face these issues of discovering and reordering priorities and expectations for themselves and others. Retirement—and planning for it—is a chance for women to assess and take control of their lives. For example:

- Where do you want to live? Will it be near your siblings, friends, or children? Or someplace with good transportation access to the people important to you? Or just anyplace warmer? Or familiar?
- Do you want to be involved more closely with other people's lives? Would you care for grandchildren or nieces and nephews while their parents work? Do you want to reconnect with friends? Find new ones through volunteering or new careers?
- What are the new skills you'd like to acquire? Or old ones you'd like to resurrect? And would you like to earn an income from them? Or use them to relax?

Not understanding your retirement benefits and choices.

For those women who are in "preretirement," it is important to become more attuned to financial planning. Assess yourself first. Regardless of how you've faced money in the past, retirement planning gives you a good excuse to raise the bar—regardless of where it is now—on taking care of your own financial planning.

E X A M P L E ■ Janet is approaching her 50th birthday this year. She has a postgraduate degree in science and a good job where she is recognized as a leader in her field. Janet has a comfortable but modest lifestyle—accumulating savings and not overspending—in part because she's too busy to spend, as she juggles work, family, and personal enrichment. But she's never paid attention to planning her finances. And given her education and success in her field, it's somewhat embarrassing to her that she really hasn't focused on the financial aspects of her life. So now she's really uncertain about where she stands financially for her retirement. ■

In two-earner families, each person should take responsibility for his or her own retirement planning and investing, knowing what benefits are available and how to get them.

In single-earner families, where the man is the earner, it is important for a woman to understand what options her husband has for collecting his retirement benefits and how each option will affect her. This is important because, if her husband's pension is covered under ERISA, she must give written consent for her husband to take his pension without a 50% or better joint-and-survivor clause, or if he wants to name a child or someone else as beneficiary.

It's important also because, should the couple divorce, pension and other retirement benefits should be considered when making a settlement.

For single wage earners who have dependent children, it is important for women to understand what, if any, benefits from their retirement plans are payable to their children. In most traditional defined-benefit pension plans, children, even if they are minors, would not receive any benefits if the parent died, either while still working or after retirement. On the other hand, assets in a savings plan, defined-contribution plan, or cash-balance plan are usually available to any beneficiary named by the employee, including children.

For single wage earners without children, there are similar issues about the value of retirement benefits when they die. Traditional defined-benefit pension plans stop paying benefits at the death of the wage earner. So, if there are people who depend on your pension plan payments for income, they will need to replace that income after you die. However, the remaining assets from savings plans, defined-contribution plans, or cash-balance plans can be passed on to beneficiaries.

THE BIG QUESTIONS: LUMP SUM OR ANNUITY? SURVIVOR OPTION OR LARGER BENEFIT?

The most important questions regarding how to receive one's retirement "pension," sometimes called a pension defined-benefit plan "distribution," are:

1. Should the retiree take the benefit as a lump-sum distribution (if available) or an annuity?
2. If the annuity option is chosen, should the annuity pay only during the retiree's lifetime, or should it pay the spouse for his or her lifetime as well?

Although a defined-benefit pension plan can include a lump-sum option, it must include an option that pays the retiree monthly pension benefits during his or her lifetime, followed by the payment of survivor benefits for the spouse's lifetime if he or she lives longer than the retiree. In these plans, *the spouse must agree in writing* to allow the participant to receive a lump-sum distribution or a monthly benefit only during his or her lifetime.

This is a very important decision. We discussed the lump-sum versus monthly benefit question in detail in Chapter 6, but it makes sense to review it here.

The advantage of receiving a lump sum is that you have the option to invest the money in a way that you want. You can directly roll the lump sum into an individual retirement account (IRA) without paying tax, and the money can accumulate tax-deferred until you need to take it out. If you have other savings, you may not need to draw on this IRA until the mandatory age of 70½. A lump sum works if you and your spouse feel comfortable managing your own finances—making your own investments and creating a realistic spending plan that allows you to maintain financial flexibility.

Taking a lump-sum distribution and not rolling it over into an IRA.

The U.S. Labor Department reports that women retiring are *more likely* to take a lump-sum distribution than are men, and that of those who take a lump-sum distribution, women are *less likely* to roll over the distribution into an IRA to preserve its tax-deferred status. This robs them of future savings.

The advantage of taking an annuity is that you have a guaranteed monthly income, which you know in advance. You know if it will increase each year—most pensions do not, but remain flat over time. You don't have to worry about investment risk with these retirement funds. In short, these funds last as long as you live.

However, because of your former employer's or your spouse's former employer's obligation to manage retirement funds conservatively, the monthly pension might not equal what you could earn on the investments if they were invested in a diversified portfolio. In addition, inflation tends to erode the value of pensions over time. And you don't have flexibility to take out larger distributions, as you do with your own IRA, for major expenses like a relocation or a gift to a child or grandchild.

If you and/or your spouse choose to receive a monthly benefit, the next question is whether to base the benefit amount on only the retiree's life expectancy or on that of the retiree and his or her spouse. You need to understand the calculation done by your or your spouse's company before retirement very closely. Companies do not use the same actuarial or life expectancy tables that annuity and life insurance companies use. Some subsidize the survivor option, reducing the benefit less than would be the case under normal actuarial assumptions.

Remember, if you and your spouse choose the survivor option, the monthly benefit paid during the retiree's lifetime will be less than if the single-life option were chosen, in order to account for the survivor pension benefits that will be paid to the retiree's surviving spouse.

The decision to take or decline the survivor option is based on six variables:

1. How much longer do you expect to live—in terms of actuarial life expectancy—than your spouse? Remember, though, that you are a "population of one." Life expectancy tables based on large numbers of people don't really apply. You need to consider what-if scenarios when making this determination.
2. What are the other resources available to survivors, including investment portfolio, life insurance, their own retirement benefits, and so on?
3. What is the history, if any, of increases to the surviving spouse's pension benefit?
4. Is the survivor option tied to other benefits, such as medical benefits?
5. Is your spouse, or other survivor in your joint-and-survivor annuity, in poor health and likely to die before you? If so, does your pension have a "pop-up" provision, which would allow a joint-survivor benefit to pop-up to a single-life annuity in the event the employee's spouse predeceases the employee?

E X A M P L E

■ Ken and Marilyn elect a 75% joint-and-survivor (J&S) pension. Ken's pension without any benefit to Marilyn after he dies—a straight-life benefit— would be $1,000 per month. Ken is told that if he wants, he could instead receive a 75% J&S pension of $800 a month with a pop-up provision.

If Ken chooses the straight-life benefit, Marilyn's benefit after his death would be nothing. If Marilyn dies before Ken, his benefit would remain $1,000 per month.

If Ken chooses the 75% J&S benefit, during his lifetime, Ken gets $800 a month. If Ken dies before Marilyn, her monthly benefit after his death would be $600 (75% of $800). Under the pop-up provision, if Marilyn dies before Ken, his benefit would pop back up to $1,000. ■

6. Will the rules of your pension plan allow you to choose the person who will be your survivor receiving benefits?

A person who maintains a large amount of life insurance may not need to provide his or her spouse with a survivor pension benefit. The death benefit from the insurance, put into an income-generating portfolio, may bring in as much or more than the survivor pension benefit. This technique, taking the single-life pension benefit and buying or maintaining life insurance to provide for the survivor, is called "pension maximization." It works only when the life insurance premiums cost less per year than the after-tax difference between what the retiree gets in monthly benefits based on his or her life expectancy and what he or she would have received had he or she chosen the survivor benefits.

"HIS AND HERS" RETIREMENT FUNDS

For working women who are married, it is important that you manage your own retirement fund. Even if you allow your husband to manage the other investment and financial planning for the household, you should use your retirement money—whether it is in a 401(k), 403(b), or 457 plan at work, or your own IRA, SEP, or Keogh if you are self-employed—as an investment learning experience.

Diversifying retirement funds as a household rather than as an individual.

TRAPS

It's important that each of you diversify within your own retirement account rather than diversifying as a "household—"I'll keep my retirement account in high-flying stocks, you keep yours in bond" is not the right strategy.

This becomes noticeably important in case of divorce. If you've agreed to hold the conservative part of the retirement portfolio, and you divorce, you've got a fund that's probably worth a lot less than your husband's.

Creating your own team.

HELPERS

You might want to find your own professional advisor to help you manage your money. Employees report that their primary source of investment information is family and friends. But free advice is not always the best advice. Creating your own relationships with your own group of professionals and advisors is important, both for now and for the future. There is a growing list of women in the financial planning field who specialize in working with women on retirement planning as well as on handling the financial transition necessary after the death of a spouse or partner.

It's a fact that more women will be widows than men will be widowers. And more women will enter retirement alone than men. Understanding how to invest your funds for both the present and the future, in addition to understanding what your resources are—whether yours alone or shared with someone else—is too important to put off.

You might also want to seek out network for moral support. Look for friends and family members with whom you can talk about planning for the future and who will encourage you in your planning effort.

TRAPS, OBSTACLES, TOOLS, AND HELPERS

Try to avoid the following traps and obstacles, and take advantage of the tools and helpers.

- Using unisex life expectancy tables for retirement planning
- Not knowing the details of your or your spouse's or partner's retirement benefits, your legal rights involving survivor protection and waiver requirements, and choices in payment options
- Believing that one person can live at half the cost of two
- At one extreme, not getting involved in any aspect of your family's financial management; at the other extreme, being responsible for every aspect
- Diversifying retirement investments as a household rather than as an individual
- Not having a personal credit card to demonstrate creditworthiness
- Automatically turning into a conservative investor in retirement

- Lack of defined benefit pension coverage
- Traditional views of money and reluctance to be involved with money management
- Not taking the time to articulate financial goals, develop strategies, and execute them
- Multiple generational responsibilities and pressures
- Tax rules that provide less favorable treatment for married people than for single people

- Employer-sponsored financial and retirement planning programs that include family members as participants
- Employer-sponsored investment education and investment advice tools
- Publications directed at women and finances
- Older Women's League (730 11th Street NW, Washington DC, telephone 202-783-6686) and similar advocacy groups
- Support network: financial professional

- Spousal rights to preretirement and postretirement survivorship protection under ERISA plans
- Pension pop-up provisions that reduce the cost of survivorship protection in the event the spouse predeceases the retiree
- IRA rollover rules for surviving spouse beneficiaries
- IRA rules on nonworking spousal contribution
- Qualified domestic relations orders (QDROs) to protect divorced spouses
- Estate tax disclaimer rules
- Moral support network: family and friends

ACTION ITEMS

Item	Priority*	Completed
1. Assess your own financial experience. Are you: married or in a relationship, worked a full career, but haven't handled the money? Are you married, single, or in a relationship and have your personal financial house in order? Are you single or in a relationship, with a long-term career, but casual about money? Are you a stay-at-home mom with or without financial experience? Decide what support you need to motivate yourself to improve your financial savvy.		
2. Know your and your spouse's or partner's benefits. (If you don't work, know what benefits you're entitled to from your spouse's or partner's plans as if they were your own. Obtain summary plan descriptions from your spouse's or partner's employee benefits office. Make sure you read all benefit communications mailed to your home, sent to the worksite, or available on the company's human resource Web site. Get a telephone number for the benefits office and call with any questions.		
3. Get information on the healthcare benefits that might be available to you through the same employer from which you might get pension benefits.		
4. Take advantage of retirement planning education workshops, Web sites, and counseling offered by employers. Most are available not only to employees of the company but to others with whom the employee shares a financial interest in retirement. These resources are particularly good at describing the decisions and choices to be made by both you and your spouse or partner prior to retirement.		
5. Review with your spouse or partner all of the primary, secondary, and contingency beneficiary designations currently in effect in all the company benefit plans, insurance policies, and bank or brokerage		

ACTION ITEMS (continued)		
Item	**Priority***	**Completed**
accounts, including IRAs, to determine if they are consistent with your overall estate planning.		
6. Make sure you and your spouse or partner check with all prior employers to see if either of you has any vested pension benefits due and survivor benefits available at the time of death. Find out the procedure to claim such benefits. Keep former employers up to date on your address.		
7. Create your own financial team or involve yourself in the financial team that your spouse or partner has put together. Make sure the team includes people with whom you feel comfortable working and turning to for guidance.		
8. Put all of your household financial and legal papers in order. Make sure both you and your spouse or partner—as well as another trusted family member or friend—know where they are located and whom to call in the event of death or incapacitation.		
9. Switch household financial responsibilities (such as balancing the checkbook, paying bills, monitoring investments) for at least one month, so that both you and your spouse or partner are familiar with and appreciate the tasks each of you perform regarding finances.		
10. Periodically obtain and review your personal credit record from one of the major credit bureaus.		
11. If you're married, before your husband's retirement: • Review your husband's life insurance to make sure you (or an appropriate trust) are the beneficiary. Especially in closely held businesses, some of this insurance may have designated a partner or the company as the beneficiary as part of a business agreement. • Make sure your husband checks with former employers to see if he has any pension benefits coming from them.		

ACTION ITEMS *(continued)*		
Item	**Priority***	**Completed**
• If you are not yet 65 and you and your husband were covered by company health insurance, make sure to remain on the company plan under the provisions of COBRA. Even if your husband is eligible for Medicare, the company must allow you to buy insurance through its group plan for up to 36 months or until you become eligible for Medicare.		
12. If you work, manage your own retirement fund. If you have not worked outside the home, manage your own IRA, if you have one. If you do not have an IRA, take some of the family savings and actively manage it. Find financial advisors if you feel you need assistance.		
13. Diversify within your own portfolio, not just as a household.		
14. Start now to think about and plan for some of the extra measures you can take to compensate for some of the disadvantages women traditionally have when planning for retirement. For example, women live longer than men, have to plan for more assets to cover a longer life, but can take better advantage of the time value of money through compounding. Or more women enter retirement alone but don't have to spend it that way if they think about sharing living arrangements with a sibling or friend.		

*A, B, C, or N/A, with A being the highest priority.

17

RETIREMENT ISSUES AFFECTING NONTRADITIONAL FAMILIES

By the time many of us start planning for retirement, we find ourselves in what have come to be called "nontraditional" lifestyles and relationships. Over the past decades, some traditional images have begun to change. Even in traditional marriages, there is more variety in the roles each partner assumes. As the following statistics indicate, demographics are changing.

- In 1998, 26% of households consisted of a person living alone.
- In 1998, 1 in 5 men in their late 20s and 1 in 10 men in their 30s lived with their parents.
- For women, the figures are 1 in 8 in their late 20s and 1 in 22 in their 30s.
- In 1994, unmarried adults represented 39% of all adults, up from 28% in 1970.
- Divorced people were among the fastest-growing segment of the unmarried population, growing from 4 million in 1970 to 17 million in 1994. In 1998, divorced people represented 9.8% of the population.
- In 1998, unmarried couples made up about 10% of all households. This includes young people planning to marry, same-sex couples committed to lifelong relationships, and older people living together to share expenses but with no intention of marrying.

So, if it's no longer just the "traditional" married couple retiring together, who are these "nontraditional families"? The word "nontraditional," when used for relationships, can mean different things to different people. Indeed, whatever personal circumstance you are in besides marriage could be defined as nontraditional. That includes people who are divorced or get divorced in retirement, who never married, same-gender couples, and remarried or nonmarried couples living together. Family units in retirement increasingly include children—younger or older—for whom there is financial responsibility, for example: grandchildren, children conceived or adopted later in life, children who are disabled, and stepchildren. And there are more adults in these extended families, for example: grandparents, parents, siblings, and friends who are considered part of the family.

Most of the principles for retirement planning contained throughout this book can be applied or adapted to everyone, regardless of their definition of family, but there are some special circumstances for people who do not fall into the "traditional" category. The purpose of this chapter is to address some of those issues for nontraditional families who confront issues when planning for retirement that are significantly different from traditional families.

KNOW YOUR BENEFITS

Whether a nonspouse partner can receive benefits on the basis of your earnings depends on a number of factors. Looking at the simplest way of determining this, retirement accounts where you actually *own* the account—your IRA, a Keogh, or SEP if you are self-employed, or your employer-provided defined-contribution plan—become a part of your estate at death and can be left to anyone you choose if you are not married. If you are married and want your Keogh or defined-contribution plan account (but not your IRA) to go to someone other than your spouse, your spouse must agree to it in writing when you designate the beneficiary.

Unmarried couples should remember to name each other as beneficiaries for their IRAs.

Typically, a surviving spouse has two options for the deceased's IRA or qualified plan balance. Either it can be cashed out, or it can be directly rolled over to the surviving spouse's own IRA. Surviving nonspouses cannot do a direct rollover to their own IRA.

Employers are increasingly expanding benefit program eligibility to include nontraditional families. Check with your employer for eligibility requirements and administrative procedures.

Nonmarried partners, whether opposite sex or same sex, need to look carefully at each partner's employer-paid benefits to see if you have the same benefits as married partners. An increasing number of companies are offering these benefits to nonmarried partners. Now nontraditional families are being included for healthcare, group long-term care, group long-term disability, life insurance, time off, employee assistance programs, and survivor benefits for pensions.

Even where companies provide benefits to nontraditional partners, the conditions of eligibility differ from company to company. Some companies require evidence of a familylike situation or household. Some may require a minimal length of time during which the partners have shared their residence. Others require evidence of a financial and emotional commitment to each other. Some allow benefits for partners who are of the same sex but not for those who are of the opposite sex.

Regardless of the company or insurance plan rules, the tax treatment for nontraditional partners is different from spouses and children. The value of the benefit for the nontraditional partner is considered income and therefore is included in the employee's earnings for tax purposes. (That issue is covered in more detail later in this chapter.)

Some employers have also started to recognize contingent beneficiaries and to allow employees to include others for whom they have financial responsibility in some benefit programs. Children for whom you have financial responsibility can usually be covered under employer plans, but there may be special administrative requirements—this is particularly true for children who are disabled and/or no longer minors.

Consider making your partner the beneficiary for your employer-sponsored group life insurance, savings plan, and retirement plans (if eligible).

In addition, some state laws regarding family leave include nontraditional family members in their definition of eligible leaves.

Figure 17.1 illustrates typical differences between how nontraditional partners are treated compared to spouses. Because each employer plan is different, and because rules and laws covering these circumstances are controlled by a variety of government entities—local, state, and federal—we recommend that you check you specific situation with your employer as well as with advocacy groups for the latest updates.

FIGURE 17.1 NONTRADITIONAL PARTNERS.

Type of Benefit Plan Option	Spouse Coverage	Nonspouse Relative Coverage	Nontraditional Partner Coverage
Social Security			
• Retirement Benefit	YES	NO	NO
• Survivor Benefit	YES	YES	NO
• Medicare	YES	NO	NO
Defined-Benefit Pension Plan			
• Preretirement Survivor Benefit	YES	NO	NO
• Postretirement Joint & Survivor Benefit	YES	YES *	YES*
• Postretirement Term Certain Benefit	YES	YES*	YES*
Defined-Contribution Plan (401(k), 403(b), 457)			
• In-Service Death Benefit	YES	YES*	YES*
• Postretirement Death Benefit	YES	YES*	YES*
Employee Stock Ownership Plan			
• In-Service Death Benefit	YES	YES*	YES*
• Postretirement Death Benefit	YES	YES*	YES*
Individual Retirement Account			
• Death Benefit	YES	YES	YES
• Rollover after Death	YES	NO	NO
Life Insurance Death Benefit			
• Employer-Paid Basic	YES	YES	YES
• Employee-Paid Supplement	YES	YES	YES
• Dependent Life	YES	Varies	NO
Other Insurance Programs			
• Disability	NO	NO	NO

FIGURE 17.1 NONTRADITIONAL PARTNERS. *(continued)*

• Accidental Death & Dismemberment	Varies	Varies	NO
• Dependent Accident	YES	Varies	NO
• Long-Term Care	YES	YES (typically only if employee is covered)	NO
Health Benefits			
• Employer-Sponsored Retiree Health	YES	Varies	Varies
• COBRA Coverage	YES	YES	NO
• Flexible Spending Accounts	YES	YES	NO**
Paid Time Off			
• Death payout of Accumulated Balance	Varies	Varies	Varies
Work & Family Programs			
• Child Care	YES	YES	NO
• Dependent Care Reimbursement	YES	YES	NO**
• Dependent/Elder Care Referrals	YES	YES	NO
• Employee Assistance	YES	YES	Varies
• Family Leave	YES	YES	NO***
Lifecycle Benefits			
• Preretirement Planning	YES	Varies	Varies
• Financial Counseling	YES	Varies	Varies
• Survivor Counseling	YES	Varies	Varies
• Legal Services	YES	Varies	Varies
• Education Assistance	Varies	Varies	Varies

*If there is a legal spouse, then that spouse may be required to consent to coverage of the nonspouse relative or nontraditional partner.
**Since the IRS does not recognize nontraditional partners, pretax contributions to flexible spending accounts under Section 125 of the Internal Revenue Code cannot be made on behalf of such partners.
***Some state laws provide that a family leave may include nontraditional family members in their definition of eligible leaves.

If your employer does not extend benefits to nontraditional partners or extended family, don't let that stop you from planning for and getting together adequate savings, retirement income, and insurance programs. Look for ideas in the chapters of this book on Social Security, insurance, and tax-deferred savings for retirement.

NO REMARRIAGE HERE—WE'RE RETIRED

Increasingly, divorced or widowed retirees are "living together" rather than remarrying. What's the rationale for this? If it's fear of losing Social Security or other benefits, make sure to separate the myths from the facts and let information—not suppositions—drive your decision.

Many people think Social Security, especially for widowed nonworkers who are collecting Social Security benefits based on their late spouse's earnings, will stop if they remarry. But this isn't so. The truth here is that widows or widowers can continue to collect survivor benefits (100% of the deceased spouse's benefits) after remarriage that are often greater than the 50% (new) spousal benefit.

If you remarry before you are eligible to collect survivor benefits (age 60), you may not collect them, but if your second spouse dies, you may collect survivor benefits based on whichever spouse's earnings were greater. The Social Security Administration will calculate which will work best for you and pay you accordingly.

If you and your late spouse had a joint-and-survivor pension, and you are receiving survivor benefits, those are also safe. The federal government does not allow a plan to cut off your benefits, regardless of whether you remarry or live with someone else.

For widows or widowers of government employees, the situation is a little more difficult. Federal and military pensions suspend survivor benefits if the survivor remarries before age 55. Some municipal pensions for police and firefighters, however, suspend survivor benefits if there is a remarriage at any time.

Social Security benefits do not pass to the surviving partner at the death of one partner in a nontraditional family.

Healthcare and Long-Term Care

Health benefits for people who will retire in the next 10 years or who are retired now are probably changing faster—and have the potential to change even more—than any other type of employer- or government-sponsored benefits. So what we say here can only be a guideline. You need to check the particulars with your employer, former employer, and advocacy groups. Companies are allowed to change the rules of their retiree medical plans at their discretion. And government-sponsored programs are subject to changes in public policy.

Many retiree healthcare packages cover surviving spouses until they remarry. When they remarry, the plan can terminate their benefits. This is important to plan for because individual retirees often have difficulty purchasing private insurance prior to Medicare eligibility. Also, companies are not obliged to allow you to continue purchasing health insurance under the COBRA law if you remarry before becoming eligible for Medicare.

Long-term care needs present special problems. The law states that both spouses' assets must be used for the benefit of an ill spouse before he or she becomes eligible for Medicaid, the federal/state program that pays medical costs for the poor, including nursing home costs for many people. By cohabiting, the healthy partner protects his or her assets from being decimated by nursing home costs. This aspect of the law also works to the advantage of same-sex couples; they are considered independent individuals for Medicaid purposes.

If marriage is important to you, you can get around this problem by writing a prenuptial agreement in which you and your new spouse agree to carry long-term care insurance at your individual expense.

ANOTHER BIG REASON: TAXES

Taxes are another good reason for retired folks not to remarry. There is the so-called marriage penalty every married couple faces—higher taxes for those married and filing jointly than for two people living together and filing singly. This issue has been taken up in Congress and may be alleviated for those in the lower income brackets.

Seniors face another burden when it comes to the taxable portion of their Social Security benefits. If two people live together, they can each have up to $25,000 in provisional income—adjusted gross income plus tax-exempt interest plus 50% of Social Security benefits—before any Social Security benefits are taxed. A married couple, on the other hand, can only have a combined income of $32,000 before a portion of their Social Security benefit is taxed.

Estate Planning

Some people avoid remarriage because they say it complicates estate planning. But this need not be the case. A well-constructed will or living trust can be drawn up to make sure your estate passes to children from a previous marriage and to other desired recipients rather than your new spouse's family.

A Tax Matter That Hits Unmarrieds Harder

As we said, companies are increasingly offering benefits to unmarried couples—either same sex or opposite sex—that are comparable to those offered to married couples. It's important to remember that health benefits offered under these arrangements *are taxable to the employee receiving them.*

This is an instance where it makes sense for each partner to accept his or her own employer-paid health benefits and not to seek benefits through one partner's employer as a couple. Of course, if only one partner works for a company that offers health benefits, and they are offered on this basis, it makes sense to accept them and pay the tax.

In addition, the Internal Revenue Service does not recognize nontraditional partners. So pretax contributions to flexible spending accounts under Section 125 of the IRS Code cannot be made on behalf of such partners. Only the employee making the contributions can use them.

Other tax code benefits that nontradtional partners cannot take advantage of include joint tax filing and deducting a partner as a dependent. And nontraditional households face additional record keeping—for example, keeping track of the proportion of joint expenses, such as mortgage interest, property taxes, and donations.

OTHER CONSIDERATIONS FOR UNMARRIED COUPLES

Day-to-Day Budgeting

Like married couples, many unmarried couples create joint checking and/or savings accounts for basic expenses like housing, food, and travel. It's also a good idea to retain separate accounts. Married or not, it can be helpful to retain at least some financial independence with separate, individual accounts.

Living-Together Contract

Today more married couples are writing prenuptial agreements, so consider a similar living-together contract. These contracts are not enforceable in all states, so you will need to check locally. But, even without legal clout, you can use the contract to spell out how expenses are shared, who owns what property, and how items will be divided if you break up.

Power of Attorney

Healthcare proxies and durable powers of attorney for each partner will allow decisions to be made, in the event of an illness or accident that incapacitates one partner, by the other partner. In some places, unmarried partners are considered "strangers," and the well partner may be restricted from visits to a hospital that allows only traditional family visits.

Wills

Each partner should have a will drawn up by an expert with experience in nontraditional families. With a solid will, the chances of having others contest the distribution of the estate decreases. Also, when one partner dies, the other retains the rights not just to assets but also to make decisions in the short term about those assets.

Estate Planning

Some people assume that having a will is estate planning. Though they are related, estate planning is more than drafting a will. Planning your estate as an unmarried couple is important because you two cannot pass assets to each other at death without tax liability. For unmarried couples there is no marital deduction, which means property cannot be passed along tax-free. You should seek expert advice, particularly for real property, so property ownership is set up during your lifetime in a way that it passes to the survivors you want without challenge.

TRAPS, OBSTACLES, TOOLS, AND HELPERS

Try to avoid the following traps and obstacles, and use the following tools and helpers.

- Assuming that your benefit plan automatically covers any individuals who are dependent on you, regardless of their legal status
- Not knowing the details of your or your spouse's or partner's retirement and other benefits, your legal rights involving survivor protection and waiver requirements, and choices in payment options
- Not understanding the impact of state laws on nontraditional family members
- Remarrying without considering the possible loss of Social Security, government retirement, and income-tax benefits

- Absence of formal legal protection for nonspouse or nontraditional family dependents
- Federal tax rules that limit the provision of tax-free benefits to dependents
- Medicaid rules that require spouses to spend down assets as a condition for long-term care coverage
- Less-favorable tax consequences associated with distributions from tax-favored retirement plans to nonspouse beneficiaries

- Employer and government benefit tables
- Employer-sponsored financial and retirement planning programs that include family members as participants
- Employer-sponsored investment education advice tools
- Employer-sponsored retention and diversity programs

- Some tax rules that benefit unmarried taxpayers
- State laws recognizing same-sex marriages
- Knowing about and getting assistance from special advocacy groups

ACTION ITEMS

Item	Priority*	Completed
1. Review every benefit plan that covers you as the employee or other nontraditional family members as employees to determine which plans, if any, provide coverage for domestic partners or other nontraditional family members.		
2. Obtain summary plan descriptions from your employee benefits office. Make sure you read all		

ACTION ITEMS (continued)		
Item	**Priority***	**Completed**
benefit communications mailed to your home, sent to the worksite, or available on the company's human resource Web site. Make sure you have a telephone number for your benefits office. Share it with your partner for emergencies.		
3. Get information on the healthcare benefits that might be available to you or your family.		
4. Take advantage of retirement planning education workshops, Web sites, and counseling offered by employers. Most are available not only to employees of the company, but also to others with whom the employee shares a financial interest in retirement. These resources are particularly good at describing the decisions and choices to be made by both you and your partner prior to retirement.		
5. Review with your partner all of the primary, secondary, and contingency beneficiary designations currently in effect in all your company benefit plans, insurance policies and bank or brokerage accounts including IRAs to determine if they are consistent with your overall estate planning.		
6. Create your own financial team or involve yourself in the financial team. Make sure the team includes people with whom you feel comfortable working, turning to for guidance, and who have significant experience with people in situations similar to yours.		
7. Put all of your household financial and legal papers in order. Make sure both you and your partner—as well as another trusted family member or friend—know where they are located and whom to call in the event of either death or incapacitation. Make sure you've discussed your wishes with your extended family so that there are no surprises—and to minimize the noise from those not included as they might think they should be in your plans and benefit from your estate.		

ACTION ITEMS (continued)		
Item	**Priority***	**Completed**
8. Start now to think about and plan for some of the extra measures you can take to compensate for some of the disadvantages of being a nontraditional family when planning for retirement. For example, consider a living trust to avoid probate for your estate. Or double your personal savings for retirement if your partner cannot get benefits from your pension. Maximize the savings you can put into employer-sponsored savings plans—where you can designate anyone as a beneficiary. Consider alternative pension plans, like cash balance plans, and alternative distribution options, like lump sums, so that the value of your retirement income can live beyond you and pass on to whomever you designate.		
9. Before marrying or entering a relationship with someone who has been previously married, conduct a review of the employment and tax benefits he or she enjoyed in the previous marriage to determine their impact on your overall financial situation. Pay particular attention to benefits such as survivor pensions, retiree health insurance, and tax breaks. Explore the role of properly drafted prenuptial agreements and consult with a domestic relations specialist in the state where you will reside in retirement.		
10. Upon entering a new marriage or when in a relationship of long-term commitment, review all of your estate plans and other documents as well as your partner's. Make sure that they are consistent with each of your goals and objectives as well as for other family members. Also, make sure they conform to the laws of the state in which you will reside.		

*A, B, C, or N/A, with A being the highest priority.

18

RETIREMENT AND TECHNOLOGY

Imagine this retirement scenario sometime in the not-so-distant future.

You begin your day in front of your widescreen multimedia, multisensory console, viewing an electronic personal broadcast network digest of current newspaper and magazine articles on a preselected list of topics that interest you. You save those that are most relevant to you. You also enter a newsgroup for an on-line discussion forum on a particular topic, and you post questions and opinions on the forum's bulletin board.

You check your portfolio of stocks and mutual funds in your IRA to see how they've started the trading day. An alarm puts you on notice that one stock has reached what you had set as its peak price, so you e-mail instructions to your broker to sell.

You then check your e-mail to find out what family members, friends, and others are up to. You remember that it's the birthday of one of your grandchildren, so you find a cartoon, scan it, take a digital image of yourself and superimpose your head on a cartoon character, then e-mail your personally designed birthday card.

You search for and choose a virtual reality site. Today you feel like starting the day with an ocean swim in Maui, followed by 18 holes of golf on one of Palm Springs' most challenging courses. You take a digital tour of resort hotels to plan for your real trip in a couple of months.

You place an electronic order for lunch from a local restaurant and pay for it from your on-line cash account, getting a digital discount because of your age. You could have used frequent-purchaser credits that you have accumulated during your Web travels.

To prepare a report for a college course you are taking, you resume your on-line travels and find an electronic encyclopedia. You sign up for an instructor-led video supplement to the course and schedule its showing for yourself on any day and time you'd like.

You notice that the pain you developed a few days ago seems to be getting worse, so you access an on-line medical service. You enter your symptoms, and in a few minutes you receive a diagnosis and prescription generated by an expert medical system.

You check your e-mail again for replies to your earlier bulletin board messages. Finally, you enter a live chat room to discuss retirement issues, personal interests, leisure pursuits, and other subjects. You and one of the participants begin a focused dialogue and decide to continue your conversation in a private room. You exchange e-mail addresses and personal profiles. You find out that this person is planning a trip to one of the resorts you toured earlier, so you agree to exchange digitized photos. You print the photo out on a laser printer. You set a follow-up time to connect with your videophone for a visual and audio interchange.

INTRODUCTION TO THE INTERNET

Nearly 63 million U.S. residents used on-line services in 1999. And 14% of Internet users are over age 50.

If you are not yet one of them, here's a brief introduction for the novice, known in cyberspeak as a "newbie."

The Internet is a global network of computers that you can easily access. It has been called everything from the information superhighway to a massive electronic mall. Its most usable feature is the World Wide Web. Worldwide, there are over 102 million people accessing the Internet.

The Web is made up of electronic "pages" of text or graphics. A Web site is a collection of pages. Many organizations, including major companies, government agencies, and service firms, have sites, which are often referred to as "home pages." Individuals can also create and maintain their own home pages.

Many Web pages also provide links to other Web pages that deal with related topics. A "hypertext link" is marked on a Web page with different-color text or a graphic symbol. Point and click the cursor on this colored text or symbol with your mouse, and you are hooked up to another Web site.

Each Web site has an address, called its uniform resource locator (URL). Addresses follow a common format. For example, Ernst & Young's Web address is http://www.ey.com. Com means that the site is commercial. College and other educational institutions sites use "edu" and government sites use "gov."

To connect to the Web, most people use a modem. New computers typically come with a preinstalled modem, which can also act as a fax machine. You can use your normal phone line for a modem. You will, of course, incur local phone charges. If you have call waiting, you can disable it so that your on-line use will not be disconnected by an incoming call. The higher the modem speed (measured in kilobits per second), the faster will be the searching and downloading of information. A minimum of 28.8 kilobits per second is recommended. Alternatives to modem access are cable, DSL, satellite, and wireless application protocols (WAP). Broadband lines will offer speeds thousands of times faster than normal telephone dial-up.

You also need a commercial program to get access to the Web. On-line services, like America Online, CompuServe, Prodigy, AT&T WorldNet, EarthLink, MindSpring, and Microsoft Network, all include Web connections, as do Web search engines, also called browsers, like Netscape's Navigator and Microsoft's Internet Explorer. There are also thousands of smaller local Internet service providers (ISPs). A typical fee is $20 per month for unlimited use. You select a password that enables you to get on-line.

You can also access directories and indexes that sort sites based on your choice of category. An example of a Web directory is Yahoo! (http://www.yahoo.com), which catalogs thousands of new sites a week and provides hundreds of thousands of entries for which you can search either by broad topic (like retirement) or keyword (like retiree organizations in Fort Myers, Florida). Other examples of Web directories and indexes are AltaVista (http://www.altavista.digital.com); Excite (http://www.excite.com); Lycos (http://www.lycos.com); Magellan (http://www.mckinley.com); and the University of Michigan's Internet Public Library (http://ipl.sils.umich.edu/ref/).

Another feature of the Web is e-mail, which lets you send and receive electronic messages to and from Web sites and other Web users.

SEARCHING FOR CONTENT

Searching for Internet information on a topic, often called surfing the Web, is still tedious and has been dubbed the "World Wide Wait." Most search tools require that you enter keywords and ask you what level of specificity you want and, sometimes, how long you are willing to wait for the search to be completed.

Search results often turn up many more "hits" than are relevant to your needs. You then have to click on each page to determine if it is on target. Many searches miss key articles on a given topic or important sites. Using words in your search like *and, or,* and *not* can help narrow the search and increase the accuracy of the results. Some search engines have advanced search features that increase the likelihood of relevant findings. Examples are: OOway (http://www.OOway.com); Fast Search (http://www.ussc.allthe web.com); and Google (http://www.google.com).

New and better search tools are being developed in response to user and media criticism. For example, Web scrapers and broadcast networks are enabling users to download information customized to their interests off-line onto their hard disks to save time and money.

Instead of the user trying to "pull" what he or she wants from sources of massive amounts of data, the newer devices "push" customized and updated information, based on a user-completed profile, directly to the user's personal computer. Examples of these newer tools are Freeloader (http://www.freeloader.com) and Pointcast (http://www.pointcast.com).

Although Web sites are continuously changing and their numbers are escalating, here's a collection of some of the best sites on retirement and related topics.

Retirement Planning

AARP Webplace (http://www.aarp.org): Information about the organization formerly known as the American Association of Retired Persons and re-sources of interest in all areas of retirement planning

ElderWeb (http://www.elderweb.com/index.html): Referral source for all aspects of aging

International Longevity Center (http://www.ilcusa.org): Research and policy on aging

Pension and Welfare Benefits Administration (http://www.dol.gov): A guide to the Department of Labor agency that oversees the Employee Retirement Income Security Act (ERISA) and private pension plans' compliance with legal requirements

Social Security Administration (http://www.ssa.gov): Includes an on-line Retirement Planner

WiseCity (http://www.wisecity.com): Lifestyle content for people over 50

General Personal Finance

Bank Rate Monitor (http://www.bankrate.com): Current data on credit cards, mortgages, home equity loans, and credit unions

Consumer Information Center (http://www.pueblo.gsa.gov): A service from the U.S. General Services Administration that provides free on-line consumer publications related to money, credit, and financial planning as well as hundreds of other topics

EDGAR (http://www.sec.gov/edgarhp.htm): Securities and Exchange Commission (SEC) filings by publicly traded companies

Ernst & Young (http://www.ey.com/pfc): Objective information on a broad range of personal finance topics, including comprehensive links to other sites on the Web

Taxes

Ernst & Young (http://www.ey.com/pfc)

Ernst & Young Tax & Financial Planning Corner (www.wiley.com/ey.html)

U.S. Internal Revenue Service (http://www.irs. gov)

Health

Merck Manual (http://www.merck.com/pubs/mmanual): A comprehensive, fully searchable medical manual

OnHealth (http://www.onhealth.com): A comprehensive listing of health topics

ThriveOnLine (http://www.thriveonline.com): Focuses on fitness, sexuality, nutrition, serenity, and weight

Wellness Web (http://www.wellweb.com): Reports on a broad range of health issues from the perspective of the patient and links to other Web health sites

WebMD (http://www.webmd.com): Breaking medical news for consumers and physicians

Lifelong Learning

Elderhostel (http://www.elderhostel.org): Not-for-profit organization with 25 years of experience providing high-quality, affordable, educational adventures for adults who are 55 and older

Housing

National Center for Home Equity Conversion (http://www.reverse.org): Consumer information on reverse mortgages from nonprofit national organization specializing in reverse mortgage education and analysis

Recreation and Travel

MapBlast! (http://www.proximus.com/myblast/index.mb): Displays street maps of any local address in the United States

Mr. Showbiz (http://www.mrshowbiz.com): Reviews movies, television programs, and music

Parknet (http://www.nps.gov): A complete guide to every national park in the United States, sponsored by the National Park Service

Third Age (http://www.thirdage.com): Comprehensive guide to all aspects of aging

WebTix Classified (http://www.tixs.com)): Ads from individual sellers and buyers of concert, theater, travel, sporting, and special event tickets

Social Services

New York City Department for the Aging (http://www.ci.nyc.ny.us/html/dfta/home.html): An example of electronic information and referrals to services provided by state and local agencies on aging. Every state and most major cities have agencies on aging that act as clearinghouses of public and private sources of services to individuals over a certain age

Technology

SeniorNet (http://www.seniornet.org): Nonprofit organization providing individuals 50 and older access to and education about computer technology and the Internet

Miscellaneous

Shareware (http://shareware.cnet.com): Catalogue of computer programs available for free or a nominal voluntary payment to the program's author

Speakers On-Line (http://speakers.com/database/speakersonline.asp). A collection of speakers' bureaus that can be searched by topic, location, and price

Switchboard (http://www.switchboard.com): Nationwide address and telephone listings to help you track down long-lost friends and locate businesses

Third Voice (http://www.thirdvoice.com): Lets Web users add sticky note–like comments to any site on the Web

TRAPS, OBSTACLES, TOOLS, AND HELPERS

Try to avoid the following traps and obstacles, and take advantage of the tools and helpers.

- Thinking of yourself as "too old" to learn computer technology

- Explosive growth and change in technology
- Inflexibility

- Internet sites geared toward retirement
- Employer-sponsored intranet sites, on company networks

- Growing interest among product and service providers in the booming retiree market
- Proliferation of "Introduction to Computer" classes at senior centers and through local councils on aging across the country

19

HEALTH COSTS AND CARE IN RETIREMENT

There's an old saying, "Without good health, what's wealth?" Lifelong planning for your physical health in retirement is as important as life-long planning for your financial health in retirement. Since we are not healthcare experts, in this chapter we are not giving you guidance on specific health issues, but we will show you how planning now for your physical health in retirement affects planning for you financial health in retirement and vice versa.

EXAMPLE

■ Al and his wife, Karen, knew years before their actual retirement that they wanted to relocate in retirement. With this goal in mind, they moved from Washington, DC, to New Mexico, and both planned to work there until retirement. But a few years short of their planned retirement date, Al was diagnosed with heart problems. He could no longer work and, instead of his regular pay, he had to live off long-term disability. Not only was their current income reduced, but the couple's planned retirement savings, pension, and retiree healthcare benefits would also be less than expected. Al's regret was that he had not paid attention to the telltale signs of his illness earlier—he was always too busy working and put off visits to his doctor for check ups. ■

LINK RETIREMENT PLANNING WITH HEALTHCARE PLANNING

For many people, learning to become a more informed consumer of healthcare is a new skill that needs to be acquired as they get older and plan for retirement. Many people are lucky enough to get through their working years without major healthcare problems, but as we get older and our bodies change, the chance of having more significant healthcare issues increases.

During preretirement years, most working people obtain healthcare coverage through their employers—who have done the work of selecting the insurance and managed care programs for their employees. Not only do employers screen the providers and choose the level of coverage, but they often pay for at least some of the cost of that coverage. While employees are responsible for deductibles, copayments, and some of the premiums, employers often pick up the majority of the premiums not only for their employees but also for their employees' families.

Failing to plan for your health in retirement—and not having adequate resources to pay for your healthcare after you stop working—puts your health in retirement at risk.

Often in retirement, the picture changes. Fewer employers continue to provide the same medical coverage for their retirees as they do for their active employees. In many cases, there are no routine medical benefits. Therefore, retirees must become more active consumers of medical care:

- Finding the right provider of coverage—either insurance or a managed care plan like a health maintenance organization (HMO)
- Understanding what is available from employer and government resources
- Deciding what level of coverage you and family members need
- Deciding whom you need to have coverage for: yourself, your spouse or partner, others who may remain dependent on you for healthcare costs during your retirement
- Paying for all or most of the coverage—particularly during early retirement before Medicare starts at age 65 under current law

Understand the balance between quality and costs for your healthcare. High costs are not necessarily an indication of good quality—and lower costs do not necessarily imply poor care.

Here are some steps you can use in considering your medical coverage in retirement:

- Decide what you need: Who, besides yourself, is dependent on you for their healthcare? What do you anticipate that their healthcare needs will be?
- Define the parameters of your top priorities for medical coverage: What benefits do you need? What level of quality is important? How much are you willing and able to pay?
- Determine the other key features of medical coverage that are important to you: How much paperwork do you want to deal with? How much choice of providers and facilities is important to you? How flexible do you want coverage to be, for example, allowing you to use alternative therapies? How convenient should it be in terms of location and how long you have to wait for appointments? Will you need care in more than one location? What information or resources do you want to be available to you? Do you want the providers to be proactive or reactive? How important is it to have an already existing medical condition (also called "preexisting condition') covered by the provider?
- Compare the answers to these questions to what is available to you from different insurers and managed care plans.
- Select your insurer or managed care plan.
- Reevaluate your decision annually.

Switching providers without checking to see if the new provider will cover a medical condition that you already have. Look to see what the "preexisting condition" clause is in any new insurance policy or managed care plan *before* you sign up. Do not switch plans until you are certain your current illness is covered by the new plan.

Also, in retirement the need for prescription drug, dental, vision, and hearing care changes—for most people it increases. Coverage for these services is limited under many employer-sponsored medical plans and government programs. So, be sure to take your needs in these areas into account as you do your retirement planning for healthcare. What will insurance pay for? What do you have to fund from other resources?

Chapter 9 contains information about the types of insurance programs available in retirement—both before and after Social Security and Medicare are available to you.

Two other insurance coverages are important to plan for while you are still actively employed because they will help protect the assets you might need later, in retirement, to pay for your healthcare expenses.

Most people make the mistake of thinking that long-term care coverage is only for the old. But it can be used just as effectively by people earlier in life—if they have the unfortunate need for assistance with daily living because of an accident or illness that strikes when younger. Without this coverage, savings that you earmarked for retirement might be needed to pay for care during your younger years.

Check with your employer while you are still working to see if you can purchase long-term care insurance on a group basis through payroll deductions. Purchased this way, the coverage often costs less and includes better benefits than those available as individual policies on the open market. As a parent, you might also be able to get coverage through your child's or in-law's employer plan.

Another important protection of your assets comes from long-term disability insurance, which is often provided by employers but may also be available through associations and in private policies. This insurance is designed to replace income that might stop if you are unable to work for extended periods of time—usually, longer than six months.

E
X
A
M
P
L
E

■ Most people are familiar with actor Christopher Reeve's horse riding accident, which left him paralyzed from the neck down. What they are less familiar with is that medical insurance does not cover the long-term rehabilitation and assistance with daily living that an injury like his requires. Nor does it replace income. ■

UNDERSTANDING WHO PAYS FOR WHAT

Most people do not understand the economics of the U.S. healthcare system—and for those who do, there is significant disagreement on what's right or wrong with the financing of the current healthcare system. But the one thing everyone seems to believe is that healthcare costs too much.

Not understanding the difference in the cost of medical coverage during "early" retirement versus "normal" retirement. During active working careers, we are collectively younger and healthier, so the cost of healthcare is less than when we are not working, older, and collectively in less good health. It is in these later years, once we are eligible for Medicare at age 65, that the government becomes the primary payer of our medical bills. Despite whatever out-of-pocket payments people on Medicare make for copayments, prescriptions, or Medicare Part B premiums, the government pays more of the overall cost of healthcare than retirees—collectively or individually.

But for people who are retired but not yet eligible for Medicare—the so-called early retirement years of 50 or 55 to 65—the situation is different. Many early retirees are caught by surprise with little or no medical coverage—or they have not planned for the expense of insurance or managed care plans. This is because in the early retirement years, the individual, not the former employer or the government, has the primary responsibility for the cost of healthcare coverage.

More and more people will be working at least part time in retirement. So check to see if your part-time employer offers medical coverage or other healthcare and work/family plans that you can use while you are working or after you "re-retire."

Be sure to understand your retirement medical coverage—both before and after age 65—*before* you process your retirement paperwork. You will find it harder and more expensive to get coverage on your own as you get older. You do not want to take the risk and enter retirement without healthcare coverage and "wait" for Medicare.

Some employers continue to make healthcare coverage available to early retirees by letting retirees stay in the active employees' healthcare plans. However, most early retirees will have to pay more for the coverage for themselves and their families than they did while they were active employees. Coverage under COBRA (see Chapter 9) is another alternative for early retirees, although it is available for only a limited period of time.

Proposals to expand Medicare coverage for pre-65 retirees have been introduced in Congress. Although none has gone far in the legislative process thus far, keep an eye on their progress, and make your voice heard with your congressional representative and senators.

New Type of Employer Retirement Medical Accounts for Retirees

Recently some employers are changing the form of financial support they provide to retirees for healthcare coverage from a "defined-benefit" approach— defining specific healthcare benefits in retirement—to a "defined-contribution" approach—instead, committing to a specific contribution toward future healthcare needs by setting aside a specific amount of money each year to fund for future expenses.

The money is put into a retirement medical account (which may be given different names by different employers) set up in each employee's name. It grows each year with interest credits and employer contributions, the latter of which continue as long as the employee remains active and the plan stays in effect.

This retirement medical account is different from a medical reimbursement account, also know as Flexible Spending Accounts (FSAs), which many employers make available to their active employees. FSAs allow employees to contribute a specific amount to the account each year from payroll deductions. The contributions can then be used to pay for otherwise nonreimbursed expenses during the same year. Employees save federal and, in most cases, state and local taxes on the money put into the FSA. If the money is not used during that year, under the use-it-or-lose-it federal rules governing these plans, it is forfeited to the employer. These FSAs are available only to active employees and, despite their rules, give most active employees with predictable medical expenses a chance to save on their taxes each year and pay for some medical expenses with pretax dollars.

Regardless of the type of funding your employer uses for retiree medical benefits, be sure you understand how your retirement medical benefits work, including administrative rules and requirements. For example, under some plans, you must collect your pension right away upon retiring to continue to get access to employer-sponsored retiree healthcare.

WHAT HEALTHCARE WILL COST IN THE FUTURE

There are many unknowns in planning for retirement—many things about which we have to make our best guess right now. One of the hardest to predict may be healthcare. We do not know now what our future health will be like or what our needs will be. We do not know now what advances will be made in medical science—what new procedures or drugs will change the medical choices open to us. And we do not know what any of this will cost.

But we do know that in recent history, the rate of medical inflation has been about twice that of other items, as measured by the Consumer Price Index. And we also know that as we get older, we will consume more healthcare than we did before we were retired. Both of these lead financial planners to recommend high estimates of healthcare expenses in retirement. That is, plan on costs being more!

Other factors that healthcare professionals say will impact our future healthcare costs are our environment and behaviors. In fact, they claim that the environment we live in or create for ourselves, along with our behavior—

Many healthcare professionals believe that one of the best predictors of your future healthcare needs may be as close as your own family. Genetic characteristics and family medical history are important to know about because they might help you know and control your health future. A Web site that can help you get information about and track your family's medical history is www.mayohealth.org/mayo/9612/htm/family.htm.

both of which are within our control—account for up to 70% of how long and how well we live.

Most healthcare professionals agree that, for the population as a whole, the high costs of healthcare are a result of the many people who did not take care of themselves early and then experience an expensive—and premature—medical decline.

Want to know what your "real age" is based on health factors that affect aging?

The professionals at Real Age have a quiz on almost 150 health factors that affect aging. Check your "real age" at their Web site: www.realage.com and get tips on nutrition, exercises, and healthful lifestyles.

PHASES OF HEALTHCARE NEEDS

Like other aspects of retirement, there is not a single phase for your health once you stop working but a *series* of phases. One example already discussed is that your share of healthcare costs in retirement will start at one level but change, probably increasing, as you move from your active retirement years to your later retirement years.

For many people who are still working, awareness of the physical health phases of retirement begins in their middle and later careers as they watch parents and other family members or friends grow older and have changing needs. Some surveys have shown that as many as half of workers say that they have rearranged their workday to care for an elderly family member.

Recognizing this, many employers have started to make eldercare resources available to their active employees, as part of their "work/life" programs. People planning for retirement can also use these resources to increase their own knowledge of eldercare issues and resources.

Employee Assistance Programs (EAPs) are provided by many employers. EAP services have been expanded in recent years to help people with eldercare issues. This includes help finding home care, assessing assisted care facilities, and understanding government programs. In some areas, eldercare managers are available to step in and coordinate services for the elderly or an at-need family member. Some employers are even evaluating the feasibility of on-site eldercare.

Planning for where you will live in retirement might also be an evolution. Most people want to remain active for as long as they can and plan to live in communities that support activities they enjoy. During the later years of retirement, activity might become more restricted, and, again, people seek communities supportive of their needs. In most parts of the country, adult communities (sometimes called "assisted living" or "continuing care" communities) for all levels of activity and needs are a rapidly growing part of the economy. If you are considering one of these communities, be sure to check on the level of healthcare support built into their services—from transportation to medical providers and assistance with daily activities to on-site care.

E X A M P L E

■ Aunt Phyllis was divorced at an early age and spent most of her life responsible for her own well-being. In her mid-50s, she moved into an apartment in her niece's home. At 65, over her family's protests, she left the apartment for a garden apartment complex sponsored by her church. Her reason: If she moved in there, she would be eligible for their assisted living residence, if she ever needed it, and not become a "burden" to her family. After many years as a community resident, she did spend her last two years in the assisted living facility. There she got the help she needed. She was proud of her independence and making her own decisions throughout her life. ■

Variations among retirement communities are multiplying in response to the demand for lifestyle choices. Two complexes in the same area that label themselves "continuing care communities" may offer very different services. Most communities charge a sizable entrance or application fee, plus monthly payments. Some will sell a unit to you; others will only rent. Fee arrangements, contract terms, and conditions vary considerably. These variations in services, costs, and payment plans can be quite confusing, especially if decisions must be made during a short period of time. The best time to explore your options is before you actually need them.

National organizations, such as the American Association of Homes and Services for the Aging (1-800-675-9253, www.aahsa.org), can provide you with information and materials to help you anticipate your needs and evaluate the range of retirement living options available.

During the last months of life, many people make the choice of using the services of a hospice to help manage living arrangements and medical needs. Hospices are designed to let people with terminal illnesses make their own choices in the last year or less of their life. They let people prepare for death with family and friends nearby in their own homes or a homelike setting. When considering your healthcare needs, if hospice care is consistent with your personal preferences, make sure that such services are covered by the healthcare coverage you choose.

POLITICS AND EMERGING HEALTHCARE COVERAGE

Clearly, the government—both federal and state, and in some areas, local—is actively involved in healthcare, particularly for retirees. This means that the discussions about your healthcare are not limited to what gets talked about in your home or in your physician's office. Some of that discussion goes on in a legislature somewhere.

More than a dozen states, including New York, Massachusetts, California, North Carolina, and Minnesota, offer resources to fill the prescription drug gap in Medicare. At least another dozen are considering legislation to do the same. Check locally and with advocacy groups like AARP for what you might be entitled to and what is on the agenda for your state legislature.

TAKE CARE OF YOURSELF

It is a little-known fact that most people remain active and healthy until the last year or so of their lives. But it takes planning—paying attention to yourself.

Throughout your working career, and in retirement, follow emerging healthcare issues, act in your own best interest, and become more self-reliant about your healthcare, taking advantage of new discoveries as well as time-tested approaches. Health information and research have always been relatively abundant in the United States, and now the Internet makes access to information possible for everyone, not just healthcare professionals (see Figure 19.1).

Routine physicals are sometimes not covered by medical insurance policies; they are routinely covered by managed care plans. In either case, do not skip them. In the long term, your medical expenses will be less if you practice preventive medicine.

Diagnostic testing for specific diseases is covered differently by each insurance plan and managed care plan. Know what the benefits and admin-

---

FIGURE 19.1 HEALTH-RELATED RESOURCES ON THE INTERNET.

In 2000, someone estimated that there were over 15,000 health-related resources on the Internet. Of course, not all are of equal value. Here are a few that experts recommend:

- www.healthfinder.gov
- www.familydoctor.org
- www.cdc.gov
- www.prevention.org
- www.merck.com/pubs/mmanual
- www.mayohealth.org

- www.fda.gov
- www.arthritis.org
- www.cancer.org
- www.americanheart.org
- www.aarp.org

---

istrative procedures are for your healthcare plan so that you can have tests when you need them—detecting early serious and expensive illnesses. And practice self-management by knowing what your personal schedule should be for testing.

E X A M P L E

■ Michael's busy legal practice kept him running—but that was not the only reason he did not take the time to get his routine physicals and tests. He simply did not like to go to the doctor. So, by the time his pain was so bad that he was forced to seek medical care, his prostate cancer was too far advanced to treat. ■

Other keys to good health management in retirement are eating well, maintaining a healthy weight, regular exercise, and not smoking—not just once you retire but throughout your life. If you take care of yourself, your healthcare needs—and expenses—in retirement could be less, not to mention your ability to maintain an active lifestyle longer.

Finally, healthcare professionals and people who study aging suggest that maintaining a positive image of the aging process is a key to long life. The latter part of your life is a great time to reinvent yourself. Planning what you will do and enjoying it is tied to good health—and good retirement planning.

HELPERS

Theoretically, at least, you should have the time to exercise in retirement. But many retirees seem more booked than they did when they were working. Establish your retirement exercise routine early. Use it as a way to spend time with friends—old or new—or as a way to get some time on your own.

Record your personal history—review your life and put it in down on paper or record it on tape. Include your goals for retirement.

TRAPS, OBSTACLES, TOOLS, AND HELPERS

Try to avoid the following traps and obstacles, and take advantage of the tools and helpers.

- Failing to pay attention to your health before retirement and thinking you can "catch up" with your health once you retire
- Not taking advantage of long-term care and long-term disability plans to protect assets that could be used for healthcare in retirement
- Believing that during your "early" retirement years the government or your former employer have primary responsibility for your healthcare coverage and expenses
- Thinking of your health in retirement as two phases—always healthy or always feeble

- Not being an informed consumer of healthcare
- Inadequate resources to pay for heathcare in retirement

- Employer-, government-, and association-sponsored medical plans for retirees
- Employer-sponsored resources, like medical accounts and savings plans to help fund healthcare costs in retirement
- Employing a "self-management" and "self-reliant" approach to your retirement healthcare needs
- Knowing your family's medical history, and recording your own for future generations

- State insurance departments and A.M. Best provide ratings for insurers
- Internet Web sites on health issues
- Retiree clubs run in conjunction with other retirees from your former employer or by advocacy groups like AARP
- Lifelong good health habits like nutrition and exercise

HELPERS

ACTION ITEMS

Item	Priority*	Completed
1. Become an active consumer of healthcare. Start now to learn what alternatives are open to you for healthcare coverage in retirement through your and your spouse's or partner's employer, an association you might belong to or could join, the government, and in your community.		
2. Learn now to ask questions about your health. Be your own advocate. New resources like the Internet make it easier than ever to find out about your health.		
3. Start to think about what healthcare needs you and your spouse or partner will have in retirement. Also think about whether there are other people— parents, disabled children or siblings, children who will still live at home—who will be dependent on you for the cost of their healthcare.		
4. Know how much healthcare will cost in retirement so that you can include the cost of your health in your financial projections for your retirement needs. At the same time, find out what resources you might be entitled to through your and your spouse's or partner's employer and the government so that you can take that into account in your planning as part of your retirement income.		
5. Record your own medical history and research your family's.		
6. Plan for what care you want to receive and where you want to receive it in retirement. Do not wait until you need it. For example, what will you do to		

ACTION ITEMS (continued)		
Item	**Priority***	**Completed**
get medical care if you plan to travel or spend long periods of time in a place other than your primary residence? What hospital would you like to be treated at in an emergency? 7. Confirm you desires in writing and discuss them with family members and your primary care physician. (See Chapter 17 regarding healthcare proxies.)		

*A, B, C, or N/A, with A being the highest priority.

Taxation of Qualified Retirement Plan Distributions

Ten-Year Averaging

If you take a lump-sum distribution from your qualified plan (and don't roll over any part of it), you may be eligible to elect to have it taxed using a special calculation called 10-year averaging. Averaging does not apply to IRA or 403(b) distributions. This method is only available if you were born before 1936.

Under this method, the taxable amount of the distribution is divided by 10. A tax is calculated on that amount, using the single taxpayer rate tables in effect in 1986. The tax is multiplied by 10, and you pay it in the year you take the distribution.

This method allows you to use the graduated tax rate tables a number of times, sometimes resulting in a lower tax than if you had paid ordinary tax on the distribution.

The tax law has special requirements for a distribution to be considered a lump-sum distribution.

1. It must be the entire balance of your account or benefit.
2. It must be paid:
   a. after you separate from service;
   b. after you turn 59½;

c. after you're disabled (only if you're self-employed); or
d. after your death.

You must have been participating in the plan for five years in order to be eligible for averaging (except for a distribution after death).

You can elect special averaging only once in your lifetime. If you receive more than one lump-sum distribution in a year, all of them must be taxed using special averaging; you can't use averaging for only one lump-sum distribution. Also, you can't use averaging if you rolled over any part of the distribution.

If you participated in the plan before 1974, and you were born before 1936, part of your distribution may be eligible for a special capital gains tax rate of 20%. Your plan administrator should be able to tell you what portion, if any, is eligible for this pre-1974 capital gains treatment.

LUMP-SUM DISTRIBUTION OF COMPANY STOCK

The law provides for special tax treatment if you receive employer-company stock as part of a lump-sum distribution from a qualified plan. These plans might include an Employee Stock Ownership Plan (ESOP), a stock bonus plan, or a 401(k) plan.

If you receive such a lump-sum distribution, you will not be taxed on the unrealized appreciation on the stock in the year of distribution unless you elect to be taxed. The unrealized appreciation is the difference between what the plan paid for the stock and the stock's value on the date of distribution.

For instance, let's say your plan distributes $250,000 worth of employee stock, for which the plan paid $50,000. This represents unrealized appreciation of $200,000. You would only be taxed on $50,000 at the time of distribution, and when you sell the stock your cost (called your *basis*) would be considered to be $50,000.

When you sell the stock, your gain would be taxable as long-term capital gains, subject to a maximum tax rate of 20%. So not only do you defer the tax, you may be taxed at a lower rate than your ordinary income tax rate. If you contribute the stock to a charity, you would get a deduction for the full value of the stock, without having to recognize any gain.

You can elect to have the unrealized appreciation taxed at the time of distribution. You might do this if the rate you're paying on the distribution is lower than the capital gains rate you'd pay when you sold the stock.

For example, if you are averaging the distribution over 10 years, the rate you pay on the distribution may be lower than 20%. If you make this election, your basis in the stock would be the value of the stock on the date of the distribution.

If you roll the employer stock over into an IRA, you lose the advantage of this lower capital gains rate. When you take money or property out of an IRA, you are subject to the ordinary income tax rate on the entire amount of each withdrawal. If your distribution includes both company stock and other property or cash, you might want to consider rolling over everything except for the stock.

If you die while you're still holding the stock you received on the distribution, your beneficiaries will have to pay income tax when they sell the stock on the unrealized appreciation between the cost to your company's plan and the value at the time it was distributed to you (the gains you deferred when you took the distribution). The appreciation from the date of distribution to the date of death will not be taxed.

MINIMUM DISTRIBUTIONS

Under the tax law, you must begin taking required minimum distributions from your IRA (other than a Roth IRA) or defined-contribution plan no later than April 1 of the year following the year in which you turn 70½ (the "required beginning date"). If you are still working after the time you turn 70½, you may delay taking required minimum distributions from a company-sponsored qualified plan until April 1 of the year following your retirement.

These minimum required distributions are based on both the account balance in the IRA or plan and a life expectancy factor. The account balance is divided by the appropriate factor to determine the amount that must be distributed each year.

If you don't take the required minimum distribution, you will be subject to an excise tax of 50% of the undistributed amount. You can perform the calculation of the required minimum distribution separately for each IRA, but take the sum of these minimum amounts from any one IRA. You must determine and distribute separately the minimum required for each defined-contribution plan in which you participate.

The distribution you take by April 1 is actually for the year you turned 70½ or retired. If you wait until April 1, you have to take a second distribution by December 31, for the current year. (Some people decide to take their first distribution by December 31 of the year in which they turn 70½, because lumping two distributions into the next year will increase their marginal tax rate or the amount of their Social Security benefit subject to taxation.)

Let's look at an example.

E
X
A
M
P
L
E

■ Mike and Courtney are married. Mike was born on February 19, 1930; Courtney was born on November 30, 1935, and is Mike's beneficiary. Mike's IRA balance on January 1, 2000, is $875,000.

Mike turns 70½ on August 19, 2000. He must begin taking distributions by April 1, 2001, but he can take the first minimum distribution by December 31 if he desires.

Since Mike was 70 on his birthday in 2000 and Courtney was 65 on her birthday in 2000, their joint-and-survivor life expectancy in the IRS tables is 23.1. (A copy of the tables for both single life and joint and survivor life expectancy appears in Figure 1.1.)

Mike's minimum required distribution, which must be taken by April 1, 2001, is $37,879 ($875,000 divided by 23.1). By December 31, 2001, Mike must take a second distribution based on his account balance on December 31, 2000.

If Mike waits until April 1, 2001, to take his first distribution, his required distribution for December 31, 2001, is his account balance as of December 31, 2000, minus the April 1, 2001, distribution, divided by 22.2 (the joint life expectancy based on ages 71 and 66).

Each year Mike and Courtney's life expectancy is recalculated and used to determine that year's minimum distribution. If Mike dies, Courtney would be able to take out the balance of Mike's account over her own life expectancy. She could also roll Mike's IRA over into her own IRA.

Another method of calculating life expectancy is the fixed method, where instead of recalculating based on birth dates and ages during the year, the prior year's life expectancy is simply reduced by one. If Mike and Courtney used this method, their life expectancy in 2001 would be 22.1 (23.1 − 1). Using the fixed method allows distributions to continue after both Mike and Courtney die for the balance of the fixed period.

A third method is the hybrid method where one life expectancy is recalculated and the other is fixed. ■

The beneficiary you use to calculate life expectancy must be designated by the required beginning date. Complex rules apply if you name a trust or a nonspousal beneficiary. For example, if you name a nonspousal beneficiary, you must do the calculation as if the beneficiary was not more than 10 years younger than you, and you can't recalculate a nonspousal beneficiary's life expectancy.

If you die after your required beginning date, distributions must continue to your beneficiaries using the method in effect when you died. If you die

FIGURE 1.1 JOINT LIFE AND SURVIVOR EXPECTANCY.

ORDINARY LIFE ANNUITIES—ONE LIFE—EXPECTED RETURN MULTIPLES

Age	Multiple	Age	Multiple	Age	Multiple	Age	Multiple	Age	Multiple
5	76.6	27	55.1	49	34.0	71	15.3	93	4.1
6	75.6	28	54.1	50	33.1	72	14.6	94	3.9
7	74.7	29	53.1	51	32.2	73	13.9	95	3.7
8	73.7	30	52.2	52	31.3	74	13.2	96	3.4
9	72.7	31	51.2	53	30.4	75	12.5	97	3.2
10	71.7	32	50.2	54	29.5	76	11.9	98	3.0
11	70.7	33	49.3	55	28.6	77	11.2	99	2.8
12	69.7	34	48.3	56	27.7	78	10.6	100	2.7
13	68.8	35	47.3	57	26.8	79	10.0	101	2.5
14	67.8	36	46.4	58	25.9	80	9.5	102	2.3
15	66.8	37	45.4	59	25.0	81	8.9	103	2.1
16	65.8	38	44.4	60	24.2	82	8.4	104	1.9
17	64.8	39	43.5	61	23.3	83	7.9	105	1.8
18	63.9	40	42.5	62	22.5	84	7.4	106	1.6
19	62.9	41	41.5	63	21.6	85	6.9	107	1.4
20	61.9	42	40.6	64	20.8	86	6.5	108	1.3
21	60.9	43	39.6	65	20.0	87	6.1	109	1.1
22	59.9	44	38.7	66	19.2	88	5.7	110	1.0
23	59.0	45	37.7	67	18.4	89	5.3	111	.9
24	58.0	46	36.8	68	17.6	90	5.0	112	.8
25	57.0	47	35.9	69	16.8	91	4.7	113	.7
26	56.0	48	34.9	70	16.0	92	4.4	114	.6
								115	.5

FIGURE 1.1 JOINT LIFE AND SURVIVOR EXPECTANCY. (continued)

ORDINARY JOINT LIFE AND LAST SURVIVOR ANNUITIES—TWO LIVES—EXPECTED RETURN MULTIPLES

AGES	35	36	37	38	39	40	41	42	43	44	45	46	47	48	49	50
35	54.0	—	—	—	—	—	—	—	—	—	—	—	—	—	—	—
36	53.5	53.0	—	—	—	—	—	—	—	—	—	—	—	—	—	—
37	53.0	52.5	52.0	—	—	—	—	—	—	—	—	—	—	—	—	—
38	52.6	52.0	51.5	51.0	—	—	—	—	—	—	—	—	—	—	—	—
39	52.2	51.6	51.0	50.5	50.0	—	—	—	—	—	—	—	—	—	—	—
40	51.8	51.2	50.6	50.0	49.5	49.0	—	—	—	—	—	—	—	—	—	—
41	51.4	50.8	50.2	49.6	49.1	48.5	48.0	—	—	—	—	—	—	—	—	—
42	51.1	50.4	49.8	49.2	48.6	48.1	47.5	47.0	—	—	—	—	—	—	—	—
43	50.8	50.1	49.5	48.8	48.2	47.6	47.1	46.6	46.0	—	—	—	—	—	—	—
44	50.5	49.8	49.1	48.5	47.8	47.2	46.7	46.1	45.6	45.1	—	—	—	—	—	—
45	50.2	49.5	48.8	48.1	47.5	46.9	46.3	45.7	45.1	44.6	44.1	—	—	—	—	—
46	50.0	49.2	48.5	47.8	47.2	46.5	45.9	45.3	44.7	44.1	43.6	43.1	—	—	—	—
47	49.7	49.0	48.3	47.5	46.8	46.2	45.5	44.9	44.3	43.7	43.2	42.6	42.1	—	—	—
48	49.5	48.8	48.0	47.3	46.6	45.9	45.2	44.5	43.9	43.3	42.7	42.2	41.7	41.2	—	—
49	49.3	48.5	47.8	47.0	46.3	45.6	44.9	44.2	43.6	42.9	42.3	41.8	41.2	40.7	40.2	—
50	49.2	48.4	47.6	46.8	46.0	45.3	44.6	43.9	43.2	42.6	42.0	41.4	40.8	40.2	39.7	39.2
51	49.0	48.2	47.4	46.6	45.8	45.1	44.3	43.6	42.9	42.2	41.6	41.0	40.4	39.8	39.3	38.7
52	48.8	48.0	47.2	46.4	45.6	44.8	44.1	43.3	42.6	41.9	41.3	40.6	40.0	39.4	38.8	38.3
53	48.7	47.9	47.0	46.2	45.4	44.6	43.9	43.1	42.4	41.7	41.0	40.3	39.7	39.0	38.4	37.9
54	48.6	47.7	46.9	46.0	45.2	44.4	43.6	42.9	42.1	41.4	40.7	40.0	39.3	38.7	38.1	37.5
55	48.5	47.6	46.7	45.9	45.1	44.2	43.4	42.7	41.9	41.2	40.4	39.7	39.0	38.4	37.7	37.1
56	48.3	47.5	46.6	45.8	44.9	44.1	43.3	42.5	41.7	40.9	40.2	39.5	38.7	38.1	37.4	36.8
57	48.3	47.4	46.5	45.6	44.8	43.9	43.1	42.3	41.5	40.7	40.0	39.2	38.5	37.8	37.1	36.4
58	48.2	47.3	46.4	45.5	44.7	43.8	43.0	42.1	41.3	40.5	39.7	39.0	38.2	37.5	36.8	36.1
59	48.1	47.2	46.3	45.4	44.5	43.7	42.8	42.0	41.2	40.4	39.6	38.8	38.0	37.3	36.6	35.9
60	48.0	47.1	46.2	45.3	44.4	43.6	42.7	41.9	41.0	40.2	39.4	38.6	37.8	37.1	36.3	35.6

Figure 1.1 Joint Life and Survivor Expectancy. (continued)

Ordinary Joint Life and Last Survivor Annuities—Two Lives—Expected Return Multiples

AGES	35	36	37	38	39	40	41	42	43	44	45	46	47	48	49	50
61	47.9	47.0	46.1	45.2	44.3	43.5	42.6	41.7	40.9	40.0	39.2	38.4	37.6	36.9	36.1	35.4
62	47.9	47.0	46.0	45.1	44.2	43.4	42.5	41.6	40.8	39.9	39.1	38.3	37.5	36.7	35.9	35.1
63	47.8	46.9	46.0	45.1	44.2	43.3	42.4	41.5	40.6	39.8	38.9	38.1	37.3	36.5	35.7	34.9
64	47.8	46.8	45.9	45.0	44.1	43.2	42.3	41.4	40.5	39.7	38.8	38.0	37.2	36.3	35.5	34.8
65	47.7	46.8	45.9	44.9	44.0	43.1	42.2	41.3	40.4	39.6	38.7	37.9	37.0	36.2	35.4	34.6
66	47.7	46.7	45.8	44.9	44.0	43.1	42.2	41.3	40.4	39.5	38.6	37.8	36.9	36.1	35.2	34.4
67	47.6	46.7	45.8	44.8	43.9	43.0	42.1	41.2	40.3	39.4	38.5	37.7	36.8	36.0	35.1	34.3
68	47.6	46.7	45.7	44.8	43.9	42.9	42.0	41.1	40.2	39.3	38.4	37.6	36.7	35.8	35.0	34.2
69	47.6	46.6	45.7	44.8	43.8	42.9	42.0	41.1	40.2	39.3	38.4	37.5	36.6	35.7	34.9	34.1
70	47.5	46.6	45.7	44.7	43.8	42.9	41.9	41.0	40.1	39.2	38.3	37.4	36.5	35.7	34.8	34.0
71	47.5	46.6	45.6	44.7	43.8	42.8	41.9	41.0	40.1	39.1	38.2	37.3	36.5	35.6	34.7	33.9
72	47.5	46.6	45.6	44.7	43.7	42.8	41.9	40.9	40.0	39.1	38.2	37.3	36.4	35.5	34.6	33.8
73	47.5	46.5	45.6	44.7	43.7	42.8	41.8	40.9	40.0	39.0	38.1	37.2	36.3	35.4	34.6	33.7
74	47.5	46.5	45.6	44.7	43.7	42.7	41.8	40.9	39.9	39.0	38.1	37.2	36.3	35.4	34.5	33.6
75	47.4	46.5	45.5	44.7	43.6	42.7	41.8	40.8	39.9	39.0	38.1	37.1	36.2	35.3	34.5	33.6
76	47.4	46.5	45.5	44.7	43.6	42.7	41.7	40.8	39.9	38.9	38.0	37.1	36.2	35.3	34.4	33.5
77	47.4	46.5	45.5	44.7	43.6	42.7	41.7	40.8	39.8	38.9	38.0	37.1	36.2	35.3	34.4	33.5
78	47.4	46.4	45.5	44.5	43.6	42.6	41.7	40.7	39.8	38.9	38.0	37.0	36.1	35.2	34.3	33.4
79	47.4	46.4	45.5	44.5	43.6	42.6	41.7	40.7	39.8	38.9	37.9	37.0	36.1	35.2	34.3	33.4
80	47.4	46.4	45.5	44.5	43.6	42.6	41.7	40.7	39.8	38.8	37.9	37.0	36.1	35.2	34.2	33.4
81	47.4	46.4	45.5	44.5	43.5	42.6	41.6	40.7	39.8	38.8	37.9	37.0	36.0	35.1	34.2	33.3
82	47.4	46.4	45.4	44.5	43.5	42.6	41.6	40.7	39.7	38.8	37.9	36.9	36.0	35.1	34.2	33.3
83	47.4	46.4	45.4	44.5	43.5	42.6	41.6	40.7	39.7	38.8	37.9	36.9	36.0	35.1	34.2	33.3
84	47.4	46.4	45.4	44.5	43.5	42.6	41.6	40.7	39.7	38.8	37.8	36.9	36.0	35.0	34.1	33.2
85	47.4	46.4	45.4	44.5	43.5	42.6	41.6	40.7	39.7	38.8	37.8	36.9	36.0	35.0	34.1	33.2
86	47.3	46.4	45.4	44.5	43.5	42.5	41.6	40.6	39.7	38.8	37.8	36.9	36.0	35.0	34.1	33.2

Figure 1.1 Joint Life and Survivor Expectancy. (continued)

Ordinary Joint Life and Last Survivor Annuities—Two Lives—Expected Return Multiples

AGES	35	36	37	38	39	40	41	42	43	44	45	46	47	48	49	50
87	47.3	46.4	45.4	44.5	43.5	42.5	41.6	40.6	39.7	38.7	37.8	36.9	35.9	35.0	34.1	33.2
88	47.3	46.4	45.4	44.5	43.5	42.5	41.6	40.6	39.7	38.7	37.8	36.9	35.9	35.0	34.1	33.2
89	47.3	46.4	45.4	44.4	43.5	42.5	41.6	40.6	39.7	38.7	37.8	36.9	35.9	35.0	34.1	33.2
90	47.3	46.4	45.4	44.4	43.5	42.5	41.6	40.6	39.7	38.7	37.8	36.9	35.9	35.0	34.1	33.2

AGES	51	52	53	54	55	56	57	58	59	60	61	62	63	64	65	66
51	38.2	—	—	—	—	—	—	—	—	—	—	—	—	—	—	—
52	37.8	37.3	—	—	—	—	—	—	—	—	—	—	—	—	—	—
53	37.3	36.8	36.3	—	—	—	—	—	—	—	—	—	—	—	—	—
54	36.9	36.4	35.8	35.3	—	—	—	—	—	—	—	—	—	—	—	—
55	36.5	35.9	35.4	34.9	34.4	—	—	—	—	—	—	—	—	—	—	—
56	36.1	35.6	35.0	34.4	33.9	33.4	—	—	—	—	—	—	—	—	—	—
57	35.8	35.2	34.6	34.0	33.5	33.0	32.5	—	—	—	—	—	—	—	—	—
58	35.5	34.8	34.2	33.6	33.1	32.5	32.0	31.5	—	—	—	—	—	—	—	—
59	35.2	34.5	33.9	33.3	32.7	32.1	31.6	31.1	30.6	—	—	—	—	—	—	—
60	34.9	34.2	33.6	32.9	32.3	31.7	31.2	30.6	30.1	29.7	—	—	—	—	—	—
61	34.6	33.9	33.3	32.6	32.0	31.4	30.8	30.2	29.7	29.2	28.7	—	—	—	—	—
62	34.4	33.7	33.0	32.3	31.7	31.0	30.4	29.9	29.3	28.8	28.3	27.8	—	—	—	—
63	34.2	33.5	32.7	32.0	31.4	30.7	30.1	29.5	28.9	28.4	27.8	27.3	26.9	—	—	—
64	34.0	33.2	32.5	31.8	31.1	30.4	29.8	29.2	28.6	28.0	27.4	26.9	26.4	25.9	—	—
65	33.8	33.0	32.3	31.6	30.9	30.2	29.5	28.9	28.2	27.6	27.1	26.5	26.0	25.5	25.0	—
66	33.6	32.9	32.1	31.4	30.6	29.9	29.2	28.6	27.9	27.3	26.7	26.1	25.6	25.1	24.6	24.1
67	33.5	32.7	31.9	31.2	30.4	29.7	29.0	28.3	27.6	27.0	26.4	25.8	25.2	24.7	24.2	23.7
68	33.4	32.5	31.8	31.0	30.2	29.5	28.8	28.1	27.4	26.7	26.1	25.5	24.9	24.3	23.8	23.3
69	33.2	32.4	31.6	30.8	30.1	29.3	28.6	27.8	27.1	26.5	25.8	25.2	24.6	24.0	23.4	22.9

FIGURE I.I JOINT LIFE AND SURVIVOR EXPECTANCY. (continued)

TABLE VI—ORDINARY JOINT LIFE AND LAST SURVIVOR ANNUITIES—TWO LIVES—EXPECTED RETURN MULTIPLES

AGES	51	52	53	54	55	56	57	58	59	60	61	62	63	64	65	66
70	33.1	32.3	31.5	30.7	29.9	29.1	28.4	27.6	26.9	26.2	25.6	24.9	24.3	23.7	23.1	22.5
71	33.0	32.2	31.4	30.5	29.7	29.0	28.2	27.5	26.7	26.0	25.3	24.7	24.0	23.4	22.8	22.2
72	32.9	32.1	31.2	30.4	29.6	28.8	28.1	27.3	26.5	25.8	25.1	24.4	23.8	23.1	22.5	21.9
73	32.8	32.0	31.1	30.3	29.5	28.7	27.9	27.1	26.4	25.6	24.9	24.2	23.5	22.9	22.2	21.6
74	32.8	31.9	31.1	30.2	29.4	28.6	27.8	27.0	26.2	25.5	24.7	24.0	23.3	22.7	22.0	21.4
75	32.7	31.8	31.0	30.1	29.3	28.5	27.7	26.9	26.1	25.3	24.6	23.8	23.1	22.4	21.8	21.1
76	32.6	31.8	30.9	30.1	29.2	28.4	27.6	26.8	26.0	25.2	24.4	23.7	23.0	22.3	21.6	20.9
77	32.6	31.7	30.8	30.0	29.1	28.3	27.5	26.7	25.9	25.1	24.3	23.6	22.8	22.1	21.4	20.7
78	32.5	31.7	30.8	29.9	29.1	28.2	27.4	26.6	25.8	25.0	24.2	23.4	22.7	21.9	21.2	20.5
79	32.5	31.6	30.7	29.9	29.0	28.2	27.3	26.5	25.7	24.9	24.1	23.3	22.6	21.8	21.1	20.4
80	32.5	31.6	30.7	29.8	29.0	28.1	27.3	26.4	25.6	24.8	24.0	23.2	22.4	21.7	21.0	20.2
81	32.4	31.5	30.7	29.8	28.9	28.1	27.2	26.4	25.5	24.7	23.9	23.1	22.3	21.6	20.8	20.1
82	32.4	31.5	30.6	29.7	28.9	28.0	27.2	26.3	25.5	24.6	23.8	23.0	22.3	21.5	20.7	20.0
83	32.4	31.5	30.6	29.7	28.8	28.0	27.1	26.3	25.4	24.6	23.8	23.0	22.2	21.4	20.6	19.9
84	32.3	31.4	30.6	29.7	28.8	27.9	27.1	26.2	25.4	24.5	23.7	22.9	22.1	21.3	20.5	19.8
85	32.3	31.4	30.5	29.6	28.8	27.9	27.0	26.2	25.3	24.5	23.7	22.8	22.0	21.3	20.5	19.7
86	32.3	31.4	30.5	29.6	28.7	27.9	27.0	26.1	25.3	24.5	23.6	22.8	22.0	21.2	20.4	19.6
87	32.3	31.4	30.5	29.6	28.7	27.8	27.0	26.1	25.3	24.4	23.6	22.8	21.9	21.1	20.4	19.6
88	32.3	31.4	30.5	29.6	28.7	27.8	27.0	26.1	25.2	24.4	23.5	22.7	21.9	21.1	20.3	19.5
89	32.3	31.4	30.5	29.6	28.7	27.8	26.9	26.1	25.2	24.4	23.5	22.7	21.9	21.1	20.3	19.5
90	32.3	31.3	30.5	29.5	28.7	27.8	26.9	26.1	25.2	24.3	23.5	22.7	21.8	21.0	20.2	19.4

AGES	67	68	69	70	71	72	73	74	75	76	77	78	79	80	81	82
67	23.2	22.8	—	—	—	—	—	—	—	—	—	—	—	—	—	—
68		22.3	—	—	—	—	—	—	—	—	—	—	—	—	—	—

FIGURE I.I   JOINT LIFE AND SURVIVOR EXPECTANCY. (continued)

TABLE VI—ORDINARY JOINT LIFE AND LAST SURVIVOR ANNUITIES—TWO LIVES—EXPECTED RETURN MULTIPLES

AGES	67	68	69	70	71	72	73	74	75	76	77	78	79	80	81	82
69	22.4	21.9	21.5	—	—	—	—	—	—	—	—	—	—	—	—	—
70	22.0	21.5	21.1	20.6	—	—	—	—	—	—	—	—	—	—	—	—
71	21.7	21.2	20.7	20.2	19.8	—	—	—	—	—	—	—	—	—	—	—
72	21.3	20.8	20.3	19.8	19.4	18.9	—	—	—	—	—	—	—	—	—	—
73	21.0	20.5	20.0	19.4	19.0	18.5	18.1	—	—	—	—	—	—	—	—	—
74	20.8	20.2	19.6	19.1	18.6	18.2	17.7	17.3	—	—	—	—	—	—	—	—
75	20.5	19.9	19.3	18.8	18.3	17.8	17.3	16.9	16.5	—	—	—	—	—	—	—
76	20.3	19.7	19.1	18.5	18.0	17.5	17.0	16.5	16.1	15.7	—	—	—	—	—	—
77	20.1	19.4	18.8	18.3	17.7	17.2	16.7	16.2	15.8	15.4	15.0	—	—	—	—	—
78	19.9	19.2	18.6	18.0	17.5	16.9	16.4	15.9	15.4	15.0	14.6	14.2	—	—	—	—
79	19.7	19.0	18.4	17.8	17.2	16.7	16.1	15.6	15.1	14.7	14.3	13.9	13.5	—	—	—
80	19.5	18.9	18.2	17.6	17.0	16.4	15.9	15.4	14.9	14.4	14.0	13.5	13.2	12.8	—	—
81	19.4	18.7	18.1	17.4	16.8	16.2	15.7	15.1	14.6	14.1	13.7	13.2	12.8	12.5	12.1	—
82	19.3	18.6	17.9	17.3	16.6	16.0	15.5	14.9	14.4	13.9	13.4	13.0	12.5	12.2	11.8	11.5
83	19.2	18.5	17.8	17.1	16.5	15.9	15.3	14.7	14.2	13.7	13.2	12.7	12.3	11.9	11.5	11.1
84	19.1	18.4	17.7	17.0	16.3	15.7	15.1	14.5	14.0	13.5	13.0	12.5	12.0	11.6	11.2	10.9
85	19.0	18.3	17.6	16.9	16.2	15.6	15.0	14.4	13.8	13.3	12.8	12.3	11.8	11.4	11.0	10.6
86	18.9	18.2	17.5	16.8	16.1	15.5	14.8	14.2	13.7	13.1	12.6	12.1	11.6	11.2	10.8	10.4
87	18.8	18.1	17.4	16.7	16.0	15.4	14.7	14.1	13.5	13.0	12.4	11.9	11.4	11.0	10.6	10.1
88	18.8	18.0	17.3	16.6	15.9	15.3	14.6	14.0	13.4	12.8	12.3	11.8	11.3	10.8	10.4	10.0
89	18.7	18.0	17.2	16.5	15.8	15.2	14.5	13.9	13.3	12.7	12.2	11.6	11.1	10.7	10.2	9.8
90	18.7	17.9	17.2	16.5	15.8	15.1	14.5	13.8	13.2	12.6	12.1	11.5	11.0	10.5	10.1	9.6

AGES	83	84	85	86	87	88	89	90
83	10.8	—	—	—	—	—	—	—
84	10.5	10.2	—	—	—	—	—	—
85	10.2	9.9	9.6	—	—	—	—	—
86	10.0	9.7	9.3	9.1	—	—	—	—
87	9.8	9.4	9.1	8.8	8.5	—	—	—
88	9.6	9.2	8.9	8.6	8.3	8.0	—	—
89	9.4	9.0	8.7	8.3	8.1	7.8	7.5	—
90	9.2	8.8	8.5	8.2	7.9	7.6	7.3	7.1

before your required beginning date, the balance of your IRA or plan has to be paid to your beneficiary under special rules that depend on whether your beneficiary is your spouse or not.

If your beneficiary is your spouse, and you die before your required beginning date, he or she has the following choices:

1. Roll the balance over into his or her own IRA.
2. Wait until you would have reached 70½ to begin taking distributions.
3. Begin distributions by the end of the year following your death, and take distributions over his or her own life expectancy.
4. Take out the entire account within five years after the year of your death.

A nonspousal beneficiary can use only options 3 or 4.

SUBSTANTIALLY EQUAL PERIODIC PAYMENTS

With many people accepting inducements to take "early retirement," there is an increasing need for people under 59½ to find penalty-free ways to take retirement money for living expenses during periods of job hunting, starting a new business, or providing income supplemental to savings until they become eligible for Social Security benefits.

If you are between 55 and 59½ when you leave your job, you may take your defined-contribution plan balance as a lump-sum payout without the 10% penalty tax for early distributions.

Of course, you can always roll your distribution over into an IRA and continue its tax-deferred status until you begin taking withdrawals.

But there's a way to get the best of both worlds. It's called *substantially equal periodic payments* (SEPPs). The rules for SEPPs are found in section 72(t) of the Internal Revenue Code. Essentially, they work like this:

Suppose you are 50 and leave your job with $200,000 in your 401(k). If you took the $200,000 in a lump sum, you would pay $56,000 in federal income taxes, if you are in the 28% bracket, and an additional $20,000 penalty tax. If you had a 4% state tax rate, you would pay another $8,000. This would leave you with $116,000 that could be invested or used to support you. The income from these investments would be subject to income taxes each year since they are not in a tax-deferred account.

But if you roll the $200,000 over into an IRA and take distributions from that IRA in SEPPs, you will pay less in taxes and what you have not distributed will continue to grow tax-deferred until you do withdraw it.

You have a choice of three methods to use in determining your distribution: life expectancy, amortization, or annuitization.

For a 50-year-old, the life expectancy is 33.1 years, according to the IRS tables. This gives you a first-year payout of $6,042 on a $200,000 IRA—$\frac{1}{33.1}$ of the total. You don't have to use the IRS tables; you can use a mortality table from a "reputable" company. If you choose the life expectancy method, you must recalculate each year based on the amount in the account as of December 31 and your new life expectancy.

If you choose the amortization method, you determine your life expectancy when you begin taking disbursements, factor in a "reasonable rate of return," and receive equal distributions. For an 8% rate of return, you would receive annual distributions of $17,359 for a $200,000 IRA.

The annuitization method derives a similar amount, $18,003 a year for a $200,000 IRA. To calculate your payments under this method, you divide your account balance by a monthly or annual annuity factor (the present value of $1 per year beginning at the age when distributions begin and continuing for your life).

To some degree, the methodology you choose will depend on your goal. If you need as much income as possible now without incurring penalty, you should choose the amortization or annuitization method. If you want to preserve as much principal as possible, while still deriving some income in order to supplement other income sources, you should select the life expectancy method.

In all cases, your choice of methodology cannot be changed. But you are not required to continue taking withdrawals based on these calculations for your entire life. You can apply the SEPP method to separate IRAs; you are not required to combine your balances.

If you choose SEPPs, you must take withdrawals for at least five years or until you become 59½, whichever comes later. In our example, you would have to take these distributions for 10 years from the time you are 50. Once you reach 59½, you can modify your distributions or stop them altogether. Code Section 72(t) no longer applies. Also, if you die or become disabled, section 72(t) no longer applies. However, if you impermissibly stop or alter your payout, you will have to pay all of the penalty taxes you would have been subject to, plus interest.

You don't need to begin taking withdrawals when the rollover IRA is established, but once you start, you must continue. So, you can roll over a retirement plan distribution into an IRA and go out job hunting. If you are unable to find work and need to begin dipping into your retirement accounts, you can begin taking SEPPs at any time.

You don't need to tell the IRS why you are taking SEPPs, and there is no age requirement to do so. You can take them at any point, but you must continue to take them until 59½.

A "reasonable rate of return" has generally been held by the IRS in private letter rulings to be no more than 2% above the 30-year U.S. Treasury bond.

EXCEPTIONS TO THE 10% PREMATURE DISTRIBUTION PENALTY

Although you are usually subjected to a 10% excise tax for taking money out of an IRA or defined-contribution plan before you turn 59½ (in addition to income taxes), there are some important exceptions. These include:

1. Taking the distribution in the form of substantially equal periodic payments
2. Separation from service when or after you reach age 55
3. Distributions to you from an IRA if you are unemployed, to pay health insurance premiums
4. Distributions from an IRA to pay higher education expenses
5. Distributions up to $10,000 from an IRA for first-time home-buyer expenses. A first-time home-buyer is anyone who did not own a home for at least two years at the time of distribution.

Substantially equal periodic payments are described earlier, so we'll focus on the other exceptions.

Age 55 and Separation-from-Service Distributions

Distributions to you, after separation from service at or after age 55, are not subject to the excise tax. The separation must have happened no sooner than the year in which you turned 55. This exception does not apply to IRAs.

You do not have to be "retired" to use this exception. As long as you left the employer who sponsored the plan, the exception is available. But if you left the employer before you turned 55 and received the distributions after you turned 55, the exception does not apply and you will be subject to the penalty.

Distributions to Pay Health Insurance

If you take distributions from an IRA and use them to pay for health insurance while you're unemployed, the distributions will not be subject to the excise tax. You're unemployed if you have received unemployment compensation for 12 consecutive weeks. Self-employed persons are eligible for this exception if they would have received unemployment benefits had they been employed.

Distributions for Education and First-time Home Buyers

Distributions from IRAs to pay for qualified higher education expenses for yourself or your dependents will not be subject to penalty taxes. Also, you can take out up to $10,000 for first-time home-buyer expenses. A first-time home buyer is anyone who did not own a home for at least two years at the time of distribution. These distributions will be subject to income tax, however (except for Roth IRAs where certain requirements are met).

EXCESS DISTRIBUTIONS AND EXCESS ACCUMULATIONS

The tax law had penalty taxes that applied if you were successful in accumulating assets in employer plans and IRAs. These taxes were imposed on excess distributions in any one year and excess accumulations at your death. The taxes were imposed at a 15% rate. These taxes were repealed as of January 1, 1997.

APPENDIX ▌▌

LONG-TERM CARE INSURANCE

HOW YOU PAY FOR LTC

Medicare LTC benefits are highly restricted and not particularly substantial. For example, Medicare Part A covers only skilled nursing and rehabilitative care in a Medicare-approved facility. The care must be needed on a daily basis. The care must be preceded by at least three days of hospitalization and must commence within 30 days of the patient's discharge from the hospital.

Even then, Medicare pays benefits for only 100 days in a Medicare-approved facility. During the first 20 days, Medicare pays 100% of the cost of care. For days 21 to 100, Medicare pays for costs in excess of $95 per day.

Medicare Part A provides home health benefits for people who are confined to their home and need intermittent skilled nursing care (or therapy) under a physician's supervision. The key criterion here is that the need must be for skilled nursing care. However, there's no requirement of prior hospitalization, and Medicare pays the full cost without a deductible.

In short, Medicare isn't a reliable form of insurance for your overall LTC planning needs. In fact, Medicare pays only about 2% of the costs of LTC. In any event, Medicare doesn't pay for prolonged nursing home stays, meaning a stay of more than 100 days. Medicare covers skilled care, not intermediate or custodial care, which are the levels of care typically needed. Home health benefits under Medicare are also restrictive.

Given this situation, what are your options? You can self-insure, transfer the risk to an LTC insurer, or do both.

An LTC policy will help you pay the costs of one or more levels of LTC. The better policies available today typically cover all levels of LTC described here, although the terms of coverage and the benefits payable vary widely among these policies. Let's look now at these policies' more important features and points of comparison.

Coverage. At least at the start, you should look for a policy offering the most expansive coverage. That is, you should find a policy that covers all levels of care: skilled, intermediate, custodial, and home health care. The better policies today offer such expansive coverage. However, you want to look at some of the definitions of the care provided at each level. Here are some questions you should ask:

• What level of care will you receive in particular types of facilities?
• Is custodial care (the type of care actually required by most people) provided by licensed or certified professionals?
• Is home care (the type desired by many people) provided by licensed or certified people?
• Does the policy offer the benefits mandated by your state of residence?

It's fair to say that the more expansive the coverage and the more flexible the provisions, the more expensive the policy will be.

Benefit Period. You're able to select the duration of benefits under the policy. Choices typically include periods of two to six years or a lifetime benefit for nursing home care. The home health care benefit period can either be integrated with the nursing home benefit or stated (and determined) separately. Some policies set the maximum limits in terms of days of care, some in years, and some in dollars. The way the benefit period is measured (or "capped") can be meaningful. For instance, you might pay for a benefit of $150 per day but actually incur lower costs of care. A policy maximum measured in dollars would extend the benefit period. A policy may also provide that if the benefits available for one type of coverage—for example, home health care—are exhausted, remaining nursing home benefits will be available.

Here again, the longer the benefit period, the more expensive the policy. The duration of the healthcare benefit is likely to be commensurate with the nursing home benefit.

Benefits. Most LTC policies are indemnity policies; that is, they pay a certain fixed dollar amount for each day (or month) of care. You can select from a range of benefit amounts between perhaps $30 and $250 for nursing home care. The home health care benefit can be equal to the nursing home benefit or, quite commonly, about one-half the nursing home benefit. For each benefit, you can determine whether the policy pays the full benefit amount, 100% of the actual expenses up to the benefit amount, or a lesser percentage of the expenses, up to the benefit amount.

One way to select a benefit amount is to find out the cost of care in your geographical area. From there you can determine how much of that cost you could reasonably afford.

Elimination Period.   The elimination period refers to the deductible—meaning the number of days of care in a facility (or visits at home) you must receive before the policy pays its benefits. The longer the elimination period, the lower the cost of the policy. Of course, there's more to selecting the elimination period than meets the eye. You need to know if the elimination period is the same for all levels of care. You should also know if the policy counts calendar days or days when you actually receive care, for instance, a home visit.

Selection of an elimination period is, in part, a function of the premium and, once again, the extent to which you wish to retain the LTC risk or transfer it to the insurer. Bear in mind that you may require several short-term stays in a nursing home, for example, for postoperative care, so a policy with an extended elimination period may not prove to be particularly worthwhile.

Benefit Eligibility.   A key provision in any LTC policy is the set of conditions under which you'll be eligible for benefits.

Gatekeepers.   Unlike policies of several years ago, competitive policies today require no hospitalization before you enter a nursing home. (Such prior hospitalization was called a gatekeeper.) Typically, you don't need prior hospitalization for home health care benefits either. In fact, the better policy won't impose a requirement of receiving a higher level of care before receiving the care for which the benefits are sought.

Benefit Triggers.   Lacking these sorts of gatekeepers, what condition or conditions will trigger payment of benefits? It's now common for an LTC policy to condition eligibility for benefits on such criteria as the following:

- Your doctor (or other healthcare professional) certifies that care is medically necessary.
- Your doctor certifies that care is necessary due to cognitive impairment.

• Your doctor certifies the need for assistance with a certain number of activities of daily living, such as bathing, dressing, using the toilet, transferring from bed to chair, taking medication, and so on. Policies typically require that you need assistance with at least two out of five or six such activities.

A policy that follows the disability model of design will pay benefits once you've met the applicable conditions. You don't actually have to receive LTC services as a condition for benefits. A policy that follows the reimbursement model will not only require you to meet the applicable conditions but also incur expense for the applicable care.

Nonforfeiture Benefits. Much like a term life or disability policy, most LTC policies provide no residual value. Once the policy lapses, the coverage ceases. Some policies now offer some form of nonforfeiture benefit. Under certain conditions, there will be some residual benefit when the LTC policy lapses or you die. The nonforfeiture benefit can take at least two forms:

1. The insurer will return a certain percentage of the premiums you've paid (minus the benefits you've received) when you either terminate the policy or die.
2. You may be entitled to a smaller benefit amount if the policy lapses after being in force for a minimum number of years.

Guaranteed Renewable. This provision is extremely important. It guarantees you that the policy can't be canceled as long as you pay the premium.

Premium Increases. Even though the LTC policy may be guaranteed renewable, the insurer has the right to increase the premium for that class of policies. This provision clearly brings all elements of uncertainty (and risk) into the acquisition, particularly because insurers simply don't have the indemnity experience in LTC that they have in more traditional forms of insurance.

Waiver of Premiums. Policies generally provide that premiums are waived (excused) during periods when LTC benefits are being paid. Waiver provisions vary significantly among LTC policies.

Inflation Riders. You should be concerned about the impact of inflation on your benefits' purchasing power. Policies generally offer two or three options (riders) that address the inflation concern. Typical options include:

- *Simple increases.* The policy's benefit amounts will automatically increase each year by 5% of the original benefit amount.
- *Compound increases.* The policy's benefit amounts will automatically increase each year by 5% of the previous year's benefit amounts. These riders call for additional premiums, but the premiums are level.
- *Future purchase options.* You'll be offered the option to buy more benefits at certain intervals, such as every three years, based on the increase in the Consumer Price Index. Premiums under this option increase whenever the benefit increases.

Many insurance professionals tend to recommend the compound option over the simple option. However, the inflation rider is expensive, so you should be young enough to have a significant probability of getting your money's worth out of the rider.

The Ten Standard Medigap Plans

Medigap Plan A consists of these five core benefits:

1. Coverage for the Medicare Part A coinsurance amount ($191 per day in 2000) for days 61 through 90 of hospitalization in each Medicare benefit period.
2. Coverage for the Part A coinsurance amount ($388 per day in 2000) for each of Medicare's nonrenewable lifetime hospitalization inpatient reserve days used.
3. Coverage for 100% of the Medicare Part A eligible hospital expenses after all Medicare hospital benefits are exhausted. Coverage is limited to a maximum of 365 days of additional inpatient hospital care during the policyholder's lifetime.
4. Coverage under Medicare Parts A and B for the reasonable cost of the first three pints of blood or equivalent quantities of packed red blood cells per calendar year unless replaced in accordance with federal regulations.
5. Coverage for the 20% coinsurance amount for Part B services after the $100 annual deductible is met.

Medigap Plan B includes the basic coverage plus:

6. The Medicare Part A inpatient hospital deductible ($776 per benefit period in 2000).

Medigap Plan C includes the core coverage in plan A and Part A deductible in plan B plus:

7. The skilled nursing facility care coinsurance amount ($97 per day for days 21 through 100 per benefit period in 2000).
8. The Medicare Part B deductible ($100 per calendar year in 2000).
9. Medically necessary emergency care in a foreign country. This benefit is subject to a $250 deductible, but then pays 80% of emergency care in another country up to a lifetime maximum of $50,000.

Medigap Plan D includes the core coverage in plan A, the Part A deductible in plan B, plus items 7 and 9, plus:

10. At-home recovery. The at-home recovery period pays up to $1,600 per year for short-term, at-home assistance with activities of daily living (bathing, dressing, personal hygiene, etc.) for those recovering from an illness, injury, or surgery. There are various benefit requirements and limitations, but essentially this benefit covers the personal services needed for someone receiving skilled home health care under Medicare.

Medigap Plan E includes the core coverage in plan A, the Part A deductible in plan B, plus items 7 and 9, plus:

11. Preventive medical care. The preventive medical care benefit pays up to $120 per year for such things as a physical examination, flu shot, serum cholesterol screening, hearing test, diabetes screening, and thyroid function test.

Medigap Plan F includes the core coverage in plan A, the Part A deductible in plan B, plus items 7, 8, and 9, plus:

12. 100% of Medicare Part B excess charges. This benefit covers the entire difference between the physician's charge and the Medicare-approved amount for a Medicare-approved service.

Medigap Plan G includes the core coverage in plan A, the Part A deductible in plan B, items 7, 9, and 10, plus 80% benefit for item 12.

Medigap Plan H includes the core benefits from plan A, the Part A deductible in plan B, items 7 and 9, plus:

13. 50% of the cost of prescription drugs up to a maximum annual benefit of $1,250 after the policyholder meets a $250-per-year deductible. This is called the "basic" prescription drug benefit.

Medigap Plan I includes the core benefits from plan A, the Part A deductible in plan B, and items 7, 9, 10, 12, and 13.

Medigap Plan J includes the core benefits from plan A, the Part A deductible in plan B, items 7, 8, 9, 10, 11, and 12, plus:

14. 50% of the cost of prescription drugs up to a maximum annual benefit of $3,000 after the policyholder meets a $250-per-year deductible. This is called the "extended" drug benefit.

Figure III.1 shows how these plans build on one another.

FIGURE III.1 TEN STANDARD MEDIGAP PLANS.

CORE BENEFITS	PLAN A	PLAN B	PLAN C	PLAN D	PLAN E	PLAN F	PLAN G	PLAN H	PLAN I	PLAN J
Part A hospital (days 61–90)	X	X	X	X	X	X	X	X	X	X
Lifetime reserve days (91–150)	X	X	X	X	X	X	X	X	X	X
365 Life hospital days, 100%	X	X	X	X	X	X	X	X	X	X
Parts A and B blood	X	X	X	X	X	X	X	X	X	X
Part B coinsurance, 20%	X	X	X	X	X	X	X	X	X	X
ADDITIONAL BENEFITS	**A**	**B**	**C**	**D**	**E**	**F**	**G**	**H**	**I**	**J**
Skilled nursing facility coinsurance (days 21–100)			X	X	X	X	X	X	X	X
Part A deductible		X	X	X	X	X	X	X	X	X
Part B deductible			X			X				X
Part B excess charges						100%	80%		100%	100%
Foreign travel emergency			X	X	X	X	X	X	X	X
At-home recovery				X			X		X	X
Prescription drugs								1	1	2
Preventive medical care					X					X

Core benefits pay the patient's share of Medicare's approved amount for physician services (generally 20%) after $100 annual deductible, the patient's cost of a long hospital stay ($194 a day for days 61–90, $388 a day for days 91–150, approved costs not paid by Medicare after day 150 to a total of 365 days lifetime), and charges for the first 3 pints of blood not covered by Medicare.

Two prescription drug benefits are offered:

1. A "basic" benefit with $250 annual deductible, 50% coinsurance, and a $1,250 maximum annual benefit (plans H and I above)
2. An "extended" benefit (plan J above) containing a $250 annual deductible, 50% coinsurance, and a $3,000 maximum annual benefit

Each of the 10 plans has a letter designation ranging from A through J. Insurance companies are not permitted to change these designations or to substitute other names or titles. They may, however, add names or titles to these letter designations. While companies are not required to offer all the plans, they all must make plan A available if they sell any of the other nine in a state. Numbers are for 2000.

INDEX